MW00813496

First published by Busybird Publishing 2024

Copyright © 2024 Errol Amerasekera

ISBN:
Paperback: 978-1-923216-05-1
Ebook: 978-1-923216-06-8

This work is copyright. Apart from any use permitted under the *Copyright Act 1968*, no part of this publication may be reproduced, stored in a retrieval system or transmitted in any form or by any means, electronic, mechanical, photocopying, recording or otherwise, without the prior written permission of Errol Amerasekera.

The information in this book is based on the author's experiences and opinions. The author and publisher disclaim responsibility for any adverse consequences, which may result from use of the information contained herein. Permission to use any external content has been sought by the author. Any breaches will be rectified in further editions of the book.

Cover Image: Melitas

Cover design: Busybird Publishing

Layout and typesetting: Busybird Publishing

Illustrations: Amara Devereux

busybird
publishing

Busybird Publishing
2/118 Para Road
Montmorency, Victoria
Australia 3094
www.busybird.com.au

This book is dedicated to my parents, who showed me the importance of making a difference in the world.

And to my beloved pets, Matao, Solomon, and Saphira, who through their non-judgemental and unconditional love, were always impeccable models of antiracism.

Contents

Not everything that is faced can be changed,
but nothing can be changed until it is faced.

— James Baldwin —

Introduction

The tyranny of hope

Wednesday 21st April, 2021. It's just past 9 a.m. on the east coast of Australia. I had an abnormally late start to my working day, which means I have been able to complete my gym workout at a slightly more civilised hour of the morning than usual. As such, I am just about to step into the shower before I ease into my day. I have the television news going on in the background. Through the haziness of my post-workout endorphins (or perhaps fatigue), the news announcer says something that catches my attention and sharpens my focus:

The verdict on the George Floyd murder trial is in.

I stop in my tracks, grateful that, on this morning, despite having things to do, nothing is particularly urgent or time sensitive. The spaciousness I have in my agenda affords me the rare luxury of being able to listen to and absorb the verdict with the least possible distractions.

When the verdict is handed down by the judge amidst a flurry of captions and juror numbers – none of which mean a lot to me – all I hear to the respective charges is, 'Guilty. Guilty. Guilty.'

I have an ever-so-fleeting moment of joy, so fleeting it's like a gentle mist being evaporated as soon as it is exposed to the intensity of the sun's rays. The joy is replaced by waves of relief that roll up my body. Once those waves reach my face, tears stream down my cheeks. My reaction surprises me. Somehow, I thought I would be happier, more celebratory perhaps. But the overwhelming feeling is simply *relief*.

When I refocus on the television footage of the crowds gathered in various locations waiting for the verdict, the feeling of those crowds seems to very much mirror my own reaction – a transient and minimal expression of joy, seen in people cheering and celebrating, but beyond that, a sense of deep relief. I was struck by the woman who, when interviewed, spoke about it being 'poetic', in that George Floyd could not breathe, and after the verdict, for the first time in ages, she felt like she could take a breath. Others spoke about it as a moment of reprieve, and the relief which comes from finally being able to breathe life in – both metaphorically and literally.

Deeply embedded in the relief, to the point where it is almost unrecognisable, is *hope*. Hope that this will somehow be a moment in time that changes everything. Hope that this will now enable discourse at a deeper level, beyond the polarities of right and wrong, of black and white. Hope that complex and entrenched challenges, such as racism, can be addressed in a manner which captures and values *all* our individual and shared experiences. And hope that this moment of justice will be extrapolated into the future, where it can provide some kind of juxtaposition to the way that many Black and Brown folk have been treated by the justice system until now.

But hope alone is not a strategy.

For hope to be translated into something more tangible, more pragmatic, something which transforms the divisiveness and complexity entrenched in issues around race, and diversity in general, is not an easy or straightforward process. And while hope is an essential ingredient for any transformative process, many other elements are also required to transform these dynamics, regardless of whether that transformation is intended to address racial inequity across society, within an organisation, or even as part of an inter-personal setting.

I know that somewhere, deeply embedded within the relief, lies the hope that the verdict of the Derek Chauvin trial will initiate some kind of paradigm shift in how we move towards a society where inclusion, equity, and justice are part of its fundamental tenets. I know this because it represents the myriad of times that I, and others, have oscillated between hope and hopelessness, between rage and exhaustion. And so, if people really thought and accepted that this guilty verdict was simply a 'one-off', and it would not lead to any longer-term change by addressing those systemic elements which gave rise to this event in the first place, then the relief would most likely not even be present. In its place would be something very different …

In its place would be the rage, the anger, the fatigue, the grief, and the despair that are all too commonplace in the lives of people who, historically and currently, have less privilege within the rarely spoken racial hierarchy of our culture. We have seen these reactions before in the form of riots and protests when people believed that justice was not served; where they felt they did not have a seat at the table of inclusion and equity and are therefore being pushed even further towards the fringes of society. When Dr Martin Luther King Jr. famously said, 'riots are the voice of the unheard,' he was suggesting that riots and protests are a symptom of something far deeper, and something much more ingrained, than the murder of George Floyd

For many people, though, relief is very much needed. In some cases, relief from the outer hostility, which almost invariably becomes internal turmoil, is literally a matter of life and death. But relief can also be dangerous. Relief can make us complacent. Relief can make us underestimate, even temporarily forget, the very thing that we are requiring relief from. So, in our quest to build an antiracist organisation, we cannot forget what Black, Indigenous, and People of Colour (BIPOC)[1] are requiring relief from. Ta-Nehisi Coates, in *Between the World and Me*,[2] pulls no punches when he frames racism the following way:

> *'But all our phrasing – race relations, racial chasm, racial justice, racial profiling, white privilege, even white supremacy – serves to obscure that racism is a visceral experience, that it dislodges brains, blocks airways, rips muscle, extracts organs, cracks bones, breaks teeth. You must never look away from this. You must always remember that the sociology, the history, the economics, the graphs, the charts, the regressions all land, with great violence, upon the body.'*

And while the graphic and confronting nature of the way he describes racism may not be applicable to organisations in a literal way, unless we move vigilantly towards an antiracist culture, subtle aspects of this description and its dynamics will still echo through the boardrooms, hallways, and workspaces of our organisations.

Michael's [pseudonym] story

Michael had done all the right things in order to work his way up to middle management within an Australian mining company. After completing his degree in engineering, he entered a graduate program within the company and, over several years, worked his way up from

---

1 I fully appreciate that BIPOC is far from an ideal acronym. By its very nature, the acronym conflates, and therefore 'makes same', the experiences of groups of people that have great diversity of experiences relative to racism, both between and within these groups. But to be honest, I could not find a better term, even though other terms such as People of Colour (POC); ethnic minority; Black, Asian, and Minority Ethnic (BAME); and People of the Global Majority (PGM) exist. Many of these terms are region-specific, hence why despite it being far from ideal, I felt that BIPOC was the most generic, as well as the most inclusive.

2 Ta-Nehisa Coates, *Between the World and Me* (New York, NY: Spiegel & Grau, 2015), 10

there. Michael is hard-working, intelligent, and ambitious, and also happens to be an Indigenous Australian man.

When he was offered the opportunity to work remotely in a fly-in fly-out capacity, and in a more senior role he saw it as a good opportunity for career progression. Whilst the idea of being away from his young family was a concern, he felt the additional income would be a good investment in the financial future of his family.

Once on-site, he found the culture of his new team, in particular his peers, was very different to what he experienced in his previous role as part of the city-based office. From the start he had a sense that he was not welcome, like for some reason there was an invisible yet distinctive barrier which kept him distanced from his colleagues. This barrier made him feel like an outsider, even though he had been with the organisation longer than most of his colleagues on-site. However, he minimised his reaction and attributed his insecurities to the fact that he was the 'new person', and he had joined a team where there were already established relationships. He believed that, over time, as he became more embedded within the team, he would no longer be perceived as the new person, and would therefore feel more welcome and included as part of the team.

But as the weeks and months passed by, his sense of being an outsider did not diminish; in fact, it only grew stronger. After he had been in this new role for about six weeks, his colleagues started joking with him. For example, they joked about him not needing sunscreen because of his 'suntan'. Initially, he went along with the jokes, laughing with his colleagues, because he wanted to believe that the jokes were a sign of his acceptance; after all, part of the 'bonding' process of Australian males has a certain irreverence and mocking aspect to it. But there was a particular subtle tone to these jokes that made Michael feel they were something different to simply good-natured humour.

After these kinds of jokes persisted for a while, and showed no signs of abating, Michael eventually confronted his peers about these jokes. In a calm and deliberate tone, he told his peers that he actually found these jokes, offensive. He did not specifically speak about the racist connotations for fear of further exacerbating these behaviours; rather, he spoke more from his own personal experience of these so-called 'jokes' being hurtful. At which point he was told he was being 'too sensitive' and was accused of 'not being able to take a joke'. Despite their denial of anything more malicious being behind these jokes, his peers took offence at their behaviour being challenged, and as a result, their behaviour escalated. The tone of the jokes increased in their sharpness, and at the same time he was regularly excluded from discussions and information that directly related to the requirements of his role.

For a period of time, Michael had to endure bananas being 'randomly' left in his workstation and within his locker. For many weeks he considered escalating the complaint by going to HR, but his fear was that, by formalising the complaint, things would only intensify. [One of the ways that people deal with the trauma of racism is to go into an 'appeasement' mode as a way of maintaining their safety]

After these episodes had persisted for several months, Michael noticed that he started dreading having to fly back to the mine site. Not only that, these experiences were affecting his mental health, his self-confidence, and also the quality of his work. When things finally became unbearable, he decided that nothing could be worse than the current situation and he lodged a formal complaint with the HR department. After a lengthy investigation process, the conclusion of the HR department was that none of the behaviours he experienced, including bananas being left at his workstation, were in breach of any policy, because there was no specific evidence of racial vilification. Part of the findings of the investigation were that *leaving bananas in someone's workstation could not be construed as bullying or racial vilification, because, after all, bananas are 'just fruit'.*

Michael subsequently left the organisation. He took several months off work in order to address and get support around his mental health. And after some time, he accepted a lesser role with a different organisation.

Racism through the lens of organisational culture

In an organisational context, this, or some version of this, is what people experience where there is not an antiracist culture, or, at least, a movement towards one. This is what BIPOC are requiring relief from. And this is part of what should also fortify our resolve to transform the fertile ground that gives rise to such occurrences. I say, 'part of what should fortify our resolve', because as we shall discuss, antiracist initiatives that are not also aligned with, and supportive of, a thriving organisation and a high-performance culture, are not sustainable for the enterprise itself or for its team members, irrespective of their race. Thus, the decision for an organisation to cultivate an antiracist culture should be evaluated on the basis of humanitarian as well as commercial rationales.

Given the current cultural backdrop, and the associated tensions and challenges around diversity, the organisations that continue to thrive into the future will be able to seamlessly weave together the principles of humanitarianism, in the form of connection, belonging, and inclusion, with those commercial imperatives that optimise performance.

Therefore, prior to embarking on a journey towards antiracism, leadership needs to ascertain if there is sufficient case for change; are the reasons for antiracism sufficiently compelling to undertake such an initiative? Narratives will abound, which favourably compare the prevalence of racism in 'our organisation', to what occurs throughout society at large. And these narratives might, with good justification, challenge the need for any strategic focus, and an investment of resources, on diversity, equity, and inclusion. However, the critical question that leadership needs to respond to is:

If just one person in your team is experiencing racism, or any other form of discrimination, does this matter to you? Is that one person's experience significant enough, meaningful enough, for you to take some form of action to address the cultural underpinnings which gave rise to their experience?

How leadership responds to this question will inform how, or even if, they engage with the challenges of creating inclusive and culturally safe organisations. However, other factors also need to be taken into consideration as these questions are pondered. The nature of the 'social license' that organisations have is in flux, as society's expectations of businesses have changed to include a 'purpose beyond profit' motive. This is critical as businesses have employees, customers, and other stakeholders who increasingly share those same expectations. This is still an evolving perspective, as there are many who believe organisations will ultimately suffer if they lose the primacy of profit motive. For many, including myself, there is the viewpoint that the corporate landscape has evolved too far for a complete reversion to a single bottom-line perspective.[3] This requires leadership to meet and address these increasingly competing expectations, where the idea of purpose beyond profit

---

3 This is in reference to the concept of a 'triple bottom line' which suggests that organisations should measure their social and environmental impact, as well as their financial performance. The idea of a triple bottom line is frequently captured in the three Ps: profit, people, and the planet.

has been pitted against a single bottom-line approach to how we measure success.

Not all examples of racism will be as obvious (to most) as Micheal's experience. Some will be more subtle, where the indignation and inequity is delivered through the lens of unconscious bias or even a 'good-natured' joke (as occurred in the initial stages of Michael's experience). Our collective enculturation in race-related biases and attitudes and their subsequent normalisation means that many of the more subtle versions of these dynamics occur at levels beyond our conscious recognition.

And believe it or not, in comparison to Michael's experience, other examples will be even more explicit and overt in the way racism is dispensed through the insinuation of a racist trope, the perpetuation of a racist stereotype, or outright bullying, vilification, and harassment. Again, we see this in Michael's experience with the bananas playing on a racist trope implying that BIPOC are ape-like, and therefore less evolved, less intelligent, and less human. These more explicit examples occur because, to those propagating the harm, their behaviour makes sense to them, given the cultural context in which they are operating (as we will discuss further in chapter twelve).

These kinds of behaviours become normalised because the cultural context reinforces their acceptability. This same cultural context affirms, even subtly, the sense of superiority of those who exhibit such behaviours, as well as grants them a degree of immunity from the consequences of their actions. After all, given that bananas are 'just fruit', how can leaving them in the locker belonging to an Indigenous man be construed as racism?

Therefore, even within an organisational context, there is no one way that racism and racial inequity get expressed. To try to narrow these down to a concise picture vastly oversimplifies the complexity of these dynamics and the almost infinite number of ways that racism reveals itself in a particular setting. But make no mistake: no matter how racism is configured or expressed, when it lands, its impact is visceral.

In how we start to explore and think about racism and the creation of an antiracist organisation, the challenge therefore is to be mindful of our own tendencies to get too matter-of-fact, too rational, and perhaps even too solution-focused in the way we discuss something that impacts people so viscerally, so personally. The fact that Michael's experience, or some version thereof, is perhaps more commonplace than we would like to admit, should in no way diminish or dilute the internal distress that may get constellated within us as a result of hearing his story. We should not dilute our reactions, because for Michael the way this experience impacted his well-being, his sense of worth, and indeed his career, was anything but 'dilute'.

These are organisational equivalents of the ripped muscles, cracked bones, and broken teeth that Ta-Nehisi Coates refers to when he reminds us that, amongst everything else, racism is also a visceral experience. The system of racism (which we will discuss further in chapter three) that normalises, perhaps even condones, the behaviours and attitudes of Michael's peers, does not necessarily intend these transgressions upon his humanity to be experienced so personally. Yet, the impact of these behaviours and attitudes is experienced by Michael as a personal assault on every fibre of his being.

At the same time, it is physically and emotionally exhausting to continually be cognisant of the ongoing impacts of racism within an organisational context; this is not sustainable for organisational leaders, team members (of any race), or for the organisation itself. Being overly consumed by, or hyper-aware of, racism within an organisation diverts the focus and the application of energy and intent away from its core business – most likely to that organisation's detriment. And so, one of the fundamental challenges of building an antiracist organisation is:

> *How do we not minimise or become desensitised to the impact that racism and racial inequity has on ourselves and our colleagues, and at the same time, approach the task of building an antiracist organisation in a manner that is emotionally, energetically, and financially sustainable for the individual as well as the organisation?*

This is a critical dilemma that we must find our way through if we are going to be successful. This 'way' will be informed by the responsibilities of our respective role within our organisation; the need to be sufficiently openhearted and supportive of our own vulnerability so we don't become desensitised to the emotional and visceral impact of racism; and, finally, to do all of this in a way which is aligned with the commercial imperative of the organisation and is sustainable in terms of our personal well-being.

So, as we step onto, or continue along the pathway, of building an antiracist organisation, this is something that we need to keep front of mind. This needs to be a driving force and therefore inform the process of how we build an antiracist organisation, as well as the desired end point.

The myth of binary thinking

The intention of this book is to provide your organisation, and those people who work within it, with a guiding hand as you continue, perhaps even start, to take steps towards the creation of a more diverse, inclusive, and equitable organisation; one that is high performing *as well as* antiracist. If, from reading these pages, you arrive at the conclusion that, through the process of building an antiracist organisation, there is also a performance and a commercial advantage, then my deepest wish has been fulfilled.

However, to balance out any delusions that this process is going to be uncomplicated or effortless, I want to state clearly at the outset that the journey of building an antiracist organisation is neither simple nor straightforward. This work is demanding; this work is arduous; this work is challenging. Therefore, this work may not be suitable for all leaders, or for all organisations.

The suitability of this work for your organisation is contingent on a mysterious combination of your appetite for the work; your capacity to lean into the places where it becomes challenging; where your organisation is positioned along its maturation or developmental pathway; and, finally, its ability to align the purpose, the vision, and the commercial imperative of the organisation to antiracist initiatives.

My own sense of ethics and duty of care precludes me from suggesting an organisational development initiative that might be more detrimental to an organisation and its outcomes than it is beneficial. As such, there are a couple of checkpoints along the way, specifically in chapters seven and nine, which, in the absence of being able to confirm this alignment, I respectfully suggest that this might not be the place and time to embark on building an antiracist organisation. I am flagging this now so you do not get to those points in the process and feel let down or as though your time has been wasted.

Throughout the following pages, I see part of my role is to contextualise, and therefore normalise, the thoughts, feelings, reactions, and challenges we experience as we step into an area that is relatively unknown, treading along a path which, for the most part, is yet to be cleared. The controversy, animosity, and fractious nature of the discourse around this topic, and many other topics related to diversity, equity, and inclusion (DEI), are not helpful in achieving the outcomes we all want. In my experience of facilitating and coaching athletes, executives, and leaders to assist them in their performance, I have never found belittling and shaming to be effective vehicles for transformation. So, I fail to see why these strategies would be any more effective in fostering collective change at either an organisational or societal level.

With that said, does this book reflect the times in which we live, where we are grappling with the challenges of diversity, inclusion, and justice? Absolutely! Is it also born out of my own desire to see a world where there is more equity and acceptance, and, to put it simply, where we are just kinder to each other? Definitely. But to see this book through these intentions alone would not do justice to the potential of this work.

This work is absolutely grounded in principles of organisational performance. We have been brainwashed to believe that an organisation can either be purpose-driven and values-based *or* it can be performance-focused; that it can value and place a premium on people and their experience *or* it can be competitive; that we can be relationship-focused and work to deepen and build more connection *or* we can focus on outcomes, getting stuff done, and not fluffing around with the frivolities of feelings, fears, and insecurities. This is an absolute myth.

Being purpose-driven, values-based, vision-led, and relationship-focused unequivocally drives performance. And, in turn, not much lubricates the cogs of relationship and connection like success. To see this as a binary decision is a vast and dangerous oversimplification. It is a narrative dreamed up and then purported by those who perhaps need more imagination and creativity in order to simultaneously hold these seemingly mutually exclusive perspectives. And by leaders whose inability to transform complexity forces them to view organisations through one lens or the other, but never both. As we shall see, the cultural foundations that enable organisations and teams to perform optimally and drive commercial outcomes are very similar to those that are essential in the creation of an antiracist organisation.

These apparent contradictions are the dilemmas we are required to unravel, and the capacities that we must develop to assist us in building an antiracist organisation. When I frame it like that, it sounds relatively simple. But when what is actually required of us is to dismantle the systems that are no longer serving us, it is no mean feat. Systems have a way of perpetuating their own survival, and they therefore tend to push back against even the best thought out change initiatives (we shall discuss this further in chapter three). This applies as much to organisational systems as it does to systems of oppression and systems of thinking. But, like anything in life worth doing, it takes determination, persistence, and an effective plan.

As much as I would like to, I am unable to provide you with the determination and persistence; it is contingent on you to find those within yourself. However, what I hope the following chapters will provide is a clear strategy with practical steps which, if followed, will not only build an antiracist organisation, but will also foster those elements that enable the creation of a high-performance culture.

Until we are all free …

This book explicitly focuses on providing a practical set of steps to assist you in the creation of an antiracist organisation. And yet, there are so many other challenges that organisations, and also society in general, are grappling with when it comes to social justice, inclusion, and equity. The focus that this book places on racism in no way diminishes, or intends to compete with, the need and importance to address other aspects of structural discrimination, such as sexism, homophobia, gender diversity, anti-Semitism, Islamophobia, transphobia, ableism, and classism, just to name a few. I wholeheartedly agree with the sentiment expressed by American author Emma Lazarus, who said:

'Until we are all free, we are none of us free.'

I believe that the practical guide described here can be extrapolated, to some extent, in how organisations talk about and address these other forms of discrimination. However, where the relevance may not be as transferable, it is my fervent hope that people take the steps required to build an antiracist organisation, and improve them, refine them, and adapt them where necessary, in order to build organisations that are also anti-sexist, anti-homophobic, anti-anti-Semitic, anti-Islamophobic, anti-transphobic, etc.

A blurring of the boundaries

No matter how firmly I am wearing my consultant or coach hat, my compartmentalisation skills are not so advanced as to be able to explore and discuss a topic such as racism in a purely objective manner. It is inevitable that my personal experience and feelings about the subject matter will infiltrate their way into the conversation. So, rather than set myself an unattainable goal, I am allowing myself, where necessary, to momentarily let go of my need to be objective, thereby enabling me to speak about and from my personal experience of racism. As a result, you will notice that I appear to randomly go back and forth from speaking about racism in the first person to the third person. What appears random is actually quite intentional. This is because it distinguishes between me sharing a personal experience (where I write in the first person), and me writing about a more generic experience, which may be similar to my own lived experience, but also more than likely reflects the experience of many (when I write in the third person).

I have lived my life as a brown-skinned man in predominantly White societies. This experience has shaped me in ways that I will never fully understand, and if I am being perfectly honest, in ways I am still coming to terms with. Therefore, I cannot help but view culture in general, and, more specifically, organisational culture, at least in part, through the lens of my own experiences and those aspects of my learning that have shaped who I am. So, yes, this topic, this work, is very personal to me. I will write more about this in chapter two.

And then in my professional life, I am owner and director of Bluestone Edge Pty Ltd, a consulting business that works with organisations, primarily within the sporting industry, around leadership, sound cultures, high-performance, and the challenges of diversity. As an organisational consultant, I deeply understand the commercial imperatives that drive the need to succeed and thrive in highly competitive and changeable business ecosystems. This is perhaps even more germane working with elite sports, where the performance cycles are sometimes a week, or even less, and the 6- or 12-month performance cycles that corporates have feels like an unrealistic luxury (this is not to say that there is not immense pressure on corporate organisations and they do not experience pressure to deliver on their respective performance metrics, it's just that the nature of the pressure is perhaps different).

Being a consultant, facilitator, and performance coach, I view the world, and my own experience within that world, very much through those psychotherapeutic and coaching frameworks. This means an approach that is primarily human-centric because it places a value on the experience of people and their feelings. This also means I am interested in what impacts the quality of people's life and work experience, as well as their ability to perform at sustainably high levels. What is irrefutable is that the quality of our relationships, a sense of belonging, and whether we feel as though we are contributing to something greater than ourselves, are all inextricably connected to the levels of fulfilment and meaning we experience in life. It is these aspects of who I am, and what I believe is important, that inform and influence how I see organisational culture, performance, and leadership.

This book brings together my two worlds – personal and professional – which to me is both frightening and exciting in equal measures. And in doing so, my hope is to blur the boundaries between these two worlds of mine. This book is written in two parts, and these parts reflect these two worlds. In part one, I will discuss the underlying principles, dynamics, and impacts of structural racism; in particular, how these manifest in an organisational context.

If we are going to be successful in our task of building an antiracist organisation, it is undeniable that we need to understand the complexities and nuances of how racism impacts the sense of belonging and overall wellbeing of the people in our organisation, but also their ability to perform optimally. In part two, I will apply the concepts from part one in discussing practical steps and processes which enable us to build an antiracist organisation and then (hopefully) make the case that this supports the creation of a high-performance culture, rather than detracts from it.

I have also included the stories of people I have interviewed, from a range of roles within organisations, who have shared their experiences of racism. Accounts of this nature are rarely heard; there is usually neither the space nor the prioritisation within organisations for people to feel safe enough to share in this way. As such, I appreciate their honesty, their vulnerability, and the courage it most likely took to share what are sometimes quite harrowing recollections. I suspect that what enabled their courage is the hope that, in sharing their stories, they will make a difference to the way that racism is talked about and addressed within organisations, but also across society more broadly. Therefore, it is the stories of these people that have coalesced to form the 'spirit' of this book. If these stories do nothing else, they provide a reminder to us all about the importance of building antiracist organisations.

The foundations of the following pages are part autobiographical, part organisational development principles, part performance psychology, and part DEI frameworks. My most ardent hope is that I have been able to weave together these areas which, on the surface, at least, appear to be disparate, in a way which makes sense and is useful to organisational leaders. As a result, you will notice throughout this book, I go back and forth, revisiting various concepts, each time from a slightly different perspective. While at times this may feel repetitive, my intention is to create linkages and synergies between these concepts, so rather than a collection of discrete ideas, we can start to create an integrated and holistic approach to building inclusive and high-performance cultures.

I wish you well as you embark on your own journey of building an antiracist organisation, or, at least, as you start to think about the process. While I can't predict how the following pages will land upon you, based on your own lived experience and objectives for reading them, my hope is that you find them as comforting as they are confronting; as expansive as they are precise; and as hopeful as they are challenging.

Part One:

Unpacking the dynamics and impacts of structural racism

Chapter One:

Laying the foundations – framing a shared understanding

Building an organisation that is not only antiracist but also high performing is an undoubtedly complex undertaking. This chapter discusses the relevant terminology and concepts which will be beneficial as we embark on this process. I have decided to frame them here because, in order to fulfil our stated objective, relative to the 'how to' (referencing the subtitle) aspect of this venture, a shared understanding of these concepts will support a more effective implementation of the various insights, strategies, and transformative actions that emerge.

Unpacking antiracism

I acknowledge that the term 'antiracist' is controversial. There is a range of opinions relative to its validity and usefulness. As such, I thought it might be useful spending some time unpacking the concept of antiracism, and to also be transparent about why I chose to use this term as the focal point for our work.

'Antiracism encompasses a range of ideas and political actions which are intended to address racial prejudice, systemic racism, and the oppression of specific racial groups.'[4] Therefore:

---

4 'What Is Anti-Racism?', Diverse Educators, accessed August 23 2021, https://www.diverseeducators.co.uk/anti-racism-toolkit/

*Antiracism actively works to address the systems,
policies, culture, and beliefs that create and perpetuate
racial inequity. Its goal is to create equitable outcomes for
all people, irrespective of their race.*

The origins of antiracism as a principle can be traced back to the 16th and 17th century. For example, in 1511, a Dominican friar named Antonio de Montesinos became the first European to challenge Spanish authorities for their treatment of Native Americans, identifying it as 'cruelty and tyranny'.[5] Similarly, in 1688 German immigrants created the first American document of its kind, advocating for equal human rights for everyone, when they constructed the Germantown Petition Against Slavery. Over subsequent centuries, there have been numerous initiatives and movements with the intention of creating equal rights for all people, irrespective of their race. For example, the abolitionist movement in the late 19th century, the civil rights movement of the 1960s, and, in more recent times, the #BlackLivesMatter movement. These social movements were born out of the ideals and the spirit of antiracism. It is this same spirit which, when infused into the purpose, vision, and strategy of an organisation, informs the philosophical framework of how we build an enterprise that is antiracist.

In contrast to the principles of antiracism which go back centuries, the term 'antiracism', shot to prominence within popular culture in more recent times, when Ibram X Kendi's *How to Be an Antiracist* became a New York Times bestseller. In his book, Kendi defines an antiracist as:

---

5 'Antonio de Montesinos (1511)', Digital History, accessed November 15, 2022, https://www.digitalhistory. uh.edu/active_learning/explorations/spain/spain_montesinos

'One who is supporting an antiracist policy through their actions or expressing an antiracist idea.'[6]

Despite the controversy surrounding the term, I chose to use 'antiracist' to define the desired outcome of a cultural transformation process, for a couple of reasons. Firstly, 'antiracist' challenges organisational members to be active in how they think about and address the dynamics and impacts of racism. This is in comparison to a term like 'nonracist' which, while suggesting people are not in favour of racism, also has an intonation of passivity about it. We need to continually remind ourselves that racism, and racial inequity, are the direct consequences of a long-standing, well entrenched, and robust system of oppression. Therefore, any kind of passivity in our approach to building an antiracist organisation will not yield the outcomes we seek.

Secondly, 'antiracism' focuses on a set of behaviours, policies, belief systems, and social constructs, as opposed to an individual person or people. This frames antiracism, and therefore racism, as something where there is a choice involved, and an option whether we behave in a racist, or an antiracist manner. Maintaining the focus of our work on behaviours, policies, and belief systems means that racism and antiracism can be viewed and explored through these lenses. This is in comparison to a narrative which suggests that there is something inherently wrong with a person's character, or their sense of morality. Questioning people's character when it comes to such complex challenges as dismantling racism becomes a slippery slope into the identity politics that, up till now, has been so divisive and unproductive when it comes to transforming and shifting the way we think about, and talk about, racism.

---

6   Ibram X. Kendi, *How to be an Antiracist* (London, England: Bodley Head, 2019) 13

So, what is an antiracist organisation?

An antiracist organisation is one that through its culture, systems, policies, and processes works to actively dismantle racism and therefore create racial equity within the workplace.

This definition in turn, requires us to define racism:

> *Racism is a combination of actions, beliefs, and policies*
> *which perpetuate and normalise the discrimination*
> *and therefore the disadvantaging of one race, and the*
> *simultaneous advantaging of another race.*

Equity strives to allocate the resources and opportunities required so that, as much as possible, individuals and groups are able to reach an equal outcome. This contrasts with equality, which means that individuals or groups of people are granted the same resources and opportunities. We will discuss this further in chapter four.

Racism gets manifested primarily through inequity.

The inequity between races can be seen in all facets of society and life. For example, in many countries there are substantial differences in longevity; health outcomes; employment rates; wealth and income; rates of mental health challenges; and rates of incarceration, home ownership, and education levels, based on race. These inequities demonstrate that racism is embedded and normalised throughout the structures of society, and within our institutions, such as education, law, media, and sport. Therefore, it is often referred to as 'structural racism'. We will unpack this concept further in chapter three.

Within an organisational context, dynamics of racism manifesting primarily through inequity are equally applicable. For example, the consequences of racial inequity are revealed when, based on race, there are differences in income levels, rates of promotion, and the number of people in senior positions, within an organisation. As well as these more objective measures of inequity, there may also be subjective differences in people's experience based on their race. For example, BIPOC will often feel less safe; they may also feel less understood, and like no one 'gets them'; BIPOC might believe that they do not belong; or like they are less able to reveal, let alone celebrate, various aspects of their personality, beliefs, and culture. Inequity based on race within the context of an organisation is sometimes referred to as 'institutional racism'. The process of building an antiracist organisation, therefore involves utilising the culture, systems, and policies of the organisation to create equity across these metrics, and others, for all its members, regardless of their race.

You will notice the above definition of racism is race neutral, in that it doesn't state which one race is advantaged and which one is disadvantaged. This is because of the many ways that racism gets expressed. When we think of racism, we almost invariably associate it with the dynamics and levels of inequity, between White people and Black people, or between White people and BIPOC. But there is also racism in the way that some Chinese owned companies operate in African countries, that creates advantage for Chinese people, and simultaneously disadvantages the local people. And in contrast, the significant increase of non-BIPOC people violently attacking Chinese people during the COVID-19 pandemic, was also racially motivated. Then there is the racism in the way the Burmese military perpetrated a series of persecutions and killings of the Muslim Rohingya people.

While it is likely that the most common form of racism – what we most readily associate it to – occurs when White people are advantaged, and BIPOC are disadvantaged, the complexity of racism is that it can be based on many attributes, apart from race and skin colour. For example, and to further complicate matters, there is yet to be universal agreement on whether discrimination based on caste or on someone's religion, such as anti-Semitism or Islamophobia, can also be considered as racism.

These dilemmas highlight how in even deconstructing what is racism, there is so much yet to be agreed upon. This begins to explain why we are so challenged in our ability to have constructive conversations about race and racism – because before these discussions even commence, we are operating from such divergent systems of reality.

The normalisation of discrimination (and our defensiveness when confronted with it)

In the above definition of racism, a key aspect which gets frequently overlooked is how racism normalises discrimination, and therefore normalises one race having advantage at the disadvantage of another. Because racism is so embedded in the broader culture, over time, all of us, irrespective of our race, tend to internalise society's attitudes, belief systems, and biases, both conscious and unconscious, pertaining to the hierarchical value that individuals are assigned based on their race. This 'hierarchy of advantage' has been normalised and is subliminally reinforced to the point that most of us tend not to question, or even notice, how these inequities manifest in our perceptions, behaviours, and day-to-day interactions.

For some of us, the previous paragraph may already elicit certain reactions. I mean, suggesting there is some invisible hierarchy which deliberately advantages certain races seems preposterous, particularly if we are already diligently working to create racial equity in our own workplace. These reactions, including our own defensiveness, are natural and to be expected, for they have been hardwired into our psychology and physiology as essential survival mechanisms since the time we first walked out of caves.

Humans have evolved so when we feel under threat, real or perceived, we utilise certain mechanisms which, over time, have proven to be useful in enhancing our personal survival. These survival mechanisms are commonly referred to as the 'fight or flight' response, although nowadays neuroscience and trauma research also includes two more responses – freeze and appease – to the list of possible responses. These same responses also get elicited when our sense of identity feels threatened, or our perceived reality feels like it is being challenged.

When we read something that suggests we may be unaware of, or inadvertently complicit with, racial inequity, we naturally get defensive, particularly if we identify as someone who is more aware of such dynamics. Alternatively, we might go into denial at the suggestion that racism is thoroughly embedded in the broader culture, because, in our corner of the world, we believe racism does not exist.

It is important that we start by seeing these responses as normal, perhaps even predictable. To not get defensive because a 'fight' response has been elicited, or go into denial because a 'flight' or 'freeze' response gets provoked, would be to go against the process of evolution itself, not to mention our own hard-wired and innate survival instincts. Perpetuating the expectation that we will somehow not react in these ways, particularly when our sense of identity or reality gets challenged, or feels threatened, is only setting ourselves up for failure.

What we can do, however, is to notice our own defensiveness and/or our tendency to go into denial, and then, with compassion and a non-judgemental attitude, support ourselves to move through these experiences. This is important because, while being defensive and going into denial are natural reactions, they also result in us stepping away from a more critical and thorough analysis of how our collective conditioning and subsequent biases result in racial inequity being perpetuated within our organisation. Left unexplored and unchallenged, dynamics of racial inequity become further normalised and, therefore, more deeply entrenched. This is one of the subtle yet powerful ways that systems of oppression such as racism perpetuate themselves. We will talk more about this in chapter three.

As such, this book could not achieve its intended outcome – to provide a practical guide to building an antiracist organisation that also has a high-performance culture – if there were moments when the content was not challenging and caused certain uncomfortable reactions within us. I expect that the contents of the following pages will stir a variety of reactions and emotions within many of us. Whilst waking up to what we have inadvertently normalised can be unnerving for some, my aim is to guide us through this process as gently as possible.

I expect there will be people who disagree when I speak about racism being 'embedded' in the broader culture, and therefore also in our collective psyche. This difference in people's reality is partly based on how we define, and therefore perceive, racism. For some of us, our association to the term 'racism' conjures up perceptions of overt bullying, name-calling, and people in white sheets carrying tiki torches and burning crosses. While these kinds of behaviour unfortunately do exist, especially with the recent rise of right-wing, White supremacist groups across many parts of the world, these behaviours are not usually normalised by most of the population. If this is what we believe racism is, we could very reasonably make the case that it is far from embedded and normalised within the broader culture. Although it is important to note that, as extreme and unacceptable as these behaviours are now considered, at one point in time they were normalised to the point where lynchings were advertised in the newspaper, and people would arrive in their Sunday best to witness the spectacle.

However, if we define racism as an issue of equity, where one race is advantaged whilst another is disadvantaged, then the lens through which we perceive racism and explore the extent to which it is present is very different. When viewed through the lens of inequity, the kind of racism that gets normalised is much more subtle, in part, because it is also a subjective experience. It is the kind of racism that, even when we are confronted by it, we are left wondering whether it was even racism. This was one of the challenges highlighted in Michael's story (page 4), where the HR department did not perceive that what he was experiencing could be classified as racial vilification or bullying.

At one stage in my life, I owned a fancy convertible sports car. Almost invariably, when I got pulled over by the police, the first question I would get asked is, 'Whose car is this?' Was this question racist? I don't know. One way to answer this is to hypothesise that if I was a White person driving the same car, would that have still been the first line of questioning? I am not suggesting that the policeperson was being intentionally racist. But what I am suggesting is that the belief that a BIPOC would not, or could not, legitimately own a fancy convertible sports car has been normalised in their thinking, and this is what informed their first line of enquiry.

If there was an element of racism in the way I was questioned by the police, it was in how those exchanges reinforced inequity and my position within the unspoken racial hierarchy. This was the inequity in my subjective experience, in comparison to what a non-BIPOC person may have experienced in a similar situation. It was how I had less access to the safety and freedom that goes along with the presumption of innocence and having to endure the indignity of being unfairly questioned by the police because of the colour of my skin and the car I was driving.

The inequity of racism, as well as other forms of structural discrimination, does not always have to manifest as something objective and measurable, such as levels of income, health outcomes, or rates of incarceration. It can also manifest as a subjective experience, such as someone's access to safety in a particular context; or the freedom to be who they are without fear of ridicule, persecution, or 'othering'; or the extent to which they experience a sense of belonging in workplace; or something as commonplace as when the stranger you say: 'good morning' to ignores your pleasantries, whether you believe it's about them having a bad day or about the colour of your skin.

These are all subtle manifestations of racism because they all result in an inequity of some aspect of a BIPOC's subjective experience in comparison to that of a non-BIPOC person. Many of these occurrences, which manifest as differences in safety, access, belonging, and well-being, can be explored through a framework of privilege, which we will discuss further in chapter four.

Grappling with the zeitgeist of diversity

The term 'zeitgeist' refers to a mood or spirit which defines a certain period in history. The zeitgeist is embodied by the most entrenched challenges, the conflicting ideologies, and the highest ideals, hopes, and beliefs that are characteristic of a particular period. As such, a zeitgeist can also be viewed as a 'meta-frame' for where our society and culture have reached certain developmental sticking points. The zeitgeist also encapsulates where the homeostasis of entrenched cultural norms is being disrupted. This is happening because society itself is being challenged to transform and advance beyond its current conventions, so it can establish a more contemporary set of norms, that hopefully indicate forward progress in society's evolution.

It is at these developmental sticking points that conflicting ideologies come to the fore and can become even more polarised, which can lead to the divisiveness we see in many parts of society today. From one perspective, this polarisation serves a purpose. By having various perspectives, each of which are resolute in their position, it provides the collective psyche with an opportunity to understand itself better. This is because when viewpoints get so polarised, there are distinct boundaries between them; there is no blurring the lines, no merging of beliefs and approaches, no middle ground.

In the absence of an amorphous middle ground, we are required to explore and evaluate which aspects of these polarities most resonate with our own beliefs, values, and ideologies. Therefore, what was once left unexplored and unchallenged now requires us to qualify our allegiance, or at least resonance, to a particular viewpoint of how the culture should look, feel, and function. This allows the collective psyche to get to know itself better by becoming aware of the diverse perspectives within it. This is one way that a culture advances, as it shifts and evolves in distinct directions.

On the other hand, polarisation can be painful and damaging; we see this not only within politics and business, but also within friendship groups and relationships. It is not uncommon, in recent times, to see long-standing friendships and relationships placed under duress, sometimes to the point of rupture, because someone else has a contradictory viewpoint on which they are uncompromising, as uncompromising as we about our own viewpoint. In theory, having different or diverse perspectives can be seen as something to be celebrated, perhaps even a competitive advantage. But it is the uncompromising quality of these perspectives that gives rise to the ideological impasses that appear to be so emblematic of the current times.

As part of this zeitgeist, we are being challenged to evolve in the way we relate to and include those who we perceive to be different than us. And I am not only talking about diversity in our respective social identities such as race, religion, gender, and sexuality. In these polarised times, maintaining a functional relationship with colleagues who have a diversity of thinking or a different communication style can feel like a monumental task. We appear to be more divided than ever, and while this divisiveness is arguably most obvious in the political arena, we are also divided by our community groups, socio-economic status, and international relationships.

When an organisation is less able to grapple with, and then reconcile, the diversity within itself, there is the tendency for it to also become divided. Clearly, this jeopardises fostering a culture of inclusion, connection, and collaboration, and, therefore, the organisation's ability to perform optimally.

Another manifestation of the current zeitgeist is that, in recent years, many countries, particularly those in the Western Hemisphere, have experienced politico-social movements founded on principles of social justice and equality. Here in Australia, in late 2017, we voted in support of marriage equality for all couples, regardless of their gender. This was also voted into law in the United Kingdom in 2013, and in the United States in 2015. In all these countries, the discourse in the lead up to the laws changing was particularly fractious, painful for many, and at times led to personal attacks.

The phrase 'me too' had been around on social media for about 10 years before it became prominent in late 2017 because of sexual abuse allegations made against Harvey Weinstein. At this point in time, the #MeToo hashtag and movement went viral as it bought awareness to sexual assaults, misogyny, and rape culture. As our attitudes have started to (slowly) shift, and what was once normalised has now become unacceptable, we have witnessed a multitude of men fall from grace. Many of these men were powerful, successful, and influential in the worlds of business, sport, and popular culture.

Even though these underlying dynamics have been present for centuries, there is something about the current period that is forcing us to confront and change these deeply held and discriminatory narratives. And while there have been substantial shifts in society's attitudes and tolerance to sexual violence and misogyny, many would agree we still have a long way to go.

The #BlackLivesMatter movement started in 2013 after the acquittal of George Zimmerman for the shooting death of an African American teenager, Trayvon Martin, and for many years the movement remained mostly based in the United States. However, #BlackLivesMatter rose to international prominence in 2020 when a video of Minneapolis police officer Derek Chauvin murdering George Floyd was seen around the world. Yes, the graphic nature of the video was part of what solidified the movement around the unfortunate death of George Floyd. But also, the zeitgeist of the times propelled the issue of police violence against Black people, and racism in general, into the collective consciousness to such an extent that marches and protests happened in cities all around the world.

Each of these movements was born out of a particular system of oppression; in this case, homophobia, patriarchy, and racism, respectively. The underlying reason for the very existence of these important movements is our shared inability to resolve or reconcile the tension between diverse perspectives or systems of reality.

At the same time, these movements have played pivotal roles in challenging long-held views and cultural norms, to the point where there is more awareness than ever of LGBTQIA+ issues, gender equity, and racism.

These various manifestations of the zeitgeist are challenging each of us to develop our thinking about, and our capability in, how we approach the task of relating to those with different lived experiences from our own. This same capability is critical in how we go about the process of building an antiracist organisation, so in this way, the task we are embarking on throughout this book very much belongs to the current zeitgeist.

Racism is not only a problem within the United States

I have used the term 'zeitgeist' very intentionally. One of the reasons for this is that the term has connotations of a spirit or mood of a particular time in history that is more global, rather than regional. Because of the prominence and centrality of the United States throughout the world, especially within the Western Hemisphere, those of us who live outside the United States tend to develop the perception that racism predominantly resides in the United States. After all, some of the best-known events and iconic people who represent our collective battle with racism have emerged out of the United States: the Emancipation Proclamation, James Baldwin, Martin Luther King Jr., Rosa Parks, Malcolm X, the civil rights movement in the 1960s, and in more recent times the emergence of the #BlackLivesMatter movement and the murder of George Floyd. Yes, when we see racism through this lens, we could make a rather compelling case that racism is primarily based in the United States.

But for all those of us who live outside the United States, making that case would be to our detriment. Racism is every bit as problematic in Australia, in the United Kingdom, in parts of Asia and Africa, and in the European Union, as it is in the United States. There are examples of this rooted in European and British histories of slavery and colonisation; the centuries-old caste system in India, which continues to this day; how in Australia, our First Nations people are yet to be recognised in our country's constitution; and how, in the Arab world, there are many forms of intolerance against non-Arab people, in particular those from India, Pakistan, Bangladesh, and Sri Lanka.

Our perception that racism is primarily a United States problem is more a function of how our media ecosystem (both traditional and social) is structured in who feeds us the stories we are consuming, rather than reality. Therefore, at the outset, I want to challenge those of us who reside outside the United States to be mindful of how we think about whose challenge racism is. As soon as our thinking starts to creep in the direction of projecting the challenges of racism as emanating primarily out of the United States, we need to foster sobriety in our thought process. We need to cultivate a genuine curiosity, and an openness to the possibility that racism is also prevalent in our country, in our organisation, and perhaps also within ourselves, irrespective of our race.

Baby steps

As we have already discussed, the polarisations and tensions we encounter when dealing with diverse perspectives and experiences contain within them the opportunity for the broader culture to get to know itself better. Ideally, this supports the advancement and evolution of our culture.

To realise this latent potential, these positions cannot remain only polarised; there needs to be a shift or a deepening in our understanding. This does not necessarily require a relinquishing of one's own position, but, rather, simply being open to hearing the perspective and lived experience of the other. Therefore, facilitating and leaning into deeper conversations that are somewhat more personal, more transparent, perhaps even more vulnerable, is what is required here. But, as we shall see, this is a cultural muscle that, as a collective, we are still in the process of developing.

When we are learning to walk, trips, falls, and bruises are an inherent, potentially unavoidable, part of the process. In fact, falling over can be seen as a sign that the toddler is working at their limits, challenging themselves, and thus continually increasing their capability, until at some point, they take their first steps unassisted. Therefore, trips and falls are not only unavoidable, they are also an essential part of the maturation process. Our struggles with diversity and inclusion are similar. The confusion and inadequacy many of us experience in this area is perhaps more a function of the fact that we are still in the early stages of the maturation process, rather than a deficit in our commitment to build capability around these developmental challenges.

This particular set of developmental sticking points are a relatively new occurrence in the long history of humanity. The zeitgeist infusing current culture means that never in our history has there been such a strong and intense focus on themes such as diversity, inclusion, equity, social justice, and racism. This also means that embedded in these developmental sticking points are questions and challenges that we are collectively required to address, perhaps for the first time in our history. Our approach to these complex and unfamiliar challenges requires the attitude that they are the steps yet to be taken as part of our ongoing maturation process. Therefore, the same encouragement, empathy, and generosity of spirit that we would extend to one of our beloved children as they learn to walk needs to be central in our attitudinal approach to building an antiracist organisation.

If our goal is to build an antiracist organisation, then at some point this requires us to have a conversation about race and racism; this comment is as complex as it is obvious. These days, in parts of society, including many organisations, simply starting a conversation about race or racism has become a precarious act of great courage, some would even say stupidity. This thinking is reinforced by a narrative that suggests even starting a conversation about something as complex as racism has the potential to be hurtful or offensive and should therefore be avoided. This results in a tiptoeing around, even avoidance of, such conversations.

So, on one hand, as a collective, we are becoming more aware of the historical and present inequities based on the constructs of our social identities. And yet, for the most part, we seem unable to develop a way of having a conversation about these themes in a way that is not instantly polarising and ends up with people agreeing to disagree as the best-case scenario, or the disagreement escalating to the point where people get hurt, angry, and disillusioned as the more likely outcome.

One contributing factor for this is the rise in prominence of political correctness. I understand and really appreciate the care and sensitivity that politically correct thinking stands for; care and sensitivity are necessary ingredients in building an antiracist organisation. However, if political correctness advocates for the shutting down or avoidance of essential conversations, where, in effect, we are not getting off the floor as we precariously attempt our first steps, then we will stagnate at this critical juncture in our development.

Organisational life cannot be separated from society in general

The dynamics of how we meet and grapple with the challenges related to our collective maturation process clearly abound in broader society, but we sometimes forget that organisations are also a reflection of society. This is because organisations are comprised of people, and people make up society. Therefore, no matter the organisation, the sector it belongs to, or the type of organisation it is, it will, to some extent, emulate the same attitudes, perspectives, and developmental sticking points that we see in society at large.

Any group or organisation, even one which considers itself to be more evolved or adept at attending to the challenges of diversity and inclusion, is simply just like any other group or organisation. I have worked with numerous not-for-profits whose purpose, values, and the services they provide are deeply grounded in principles of social justice and equity. Yet, when push comes to shove, they experience similar developmental sticking points, and feel as challenged as any other organisation, when it comes to addressing racial justice within their own organisation.

This is because organisational life and our broader culture are inextricably connected. There is a pervasive influence that each exerts over the other. This connection means that the dynamics which confront our society also appear, perhaps in a more overt way, in the challenges that organisations are required to wrestle with. At first glance, the challenges that organisations and societies face may appear dissimilar and unrelated; however, this perceived difference is more a function of the context they are occurring in, rather than the inherent nature of the challenges themselves.

For example, society currently faces significant challenges around public engagement, and a prevailing attitude of apathy in relation to key issues. This is seen in the disengagement around politics; the lack of engagement and action around climate change; and the escapism that social media, video games, and reality TV provides. At the same time, for many organisations, a central challenge is how they generate greater engagement from team members, as well as other key stakeholders. Is it possible that both these respective challenges arise out of the same fertile ground? And if so, could the strategies and breakthrough thinking that organisations discover to better address something like team member engagement also be useful in how we, as a society, engage people in those issues that impact our quality of life and collective future?

Organisations are uniquely positioned to find creative and innovative solutions to many of the disturbing dynamics that society currently faces, and, therefore, to be thought leaders in this space. By finding better ways to create inclusive, connected, and more equitable cultures in their own backyard, they are able to actively contribute to a broader societal shift in these same areas. This is a little like how the technology developed in Formula One racing cars eventually filters down and gets utilised to make everyday cars more efficient and safer to drive. So, in this way, we all benefit from those technological advances.

Just to be clear, I am definitely not saying that for an organisation to be successful it is required to address these large-scale societal issues. An organisation should categorically focus its resources and intentions on building the capability it needs to perform effectively and be a flourishing enterprise. But one potential measure of how well an organisation is grappling with these complicated themes internally is the degree of positive impact it is having on society at large, as a side-effect of it striving towards its own vision and commercial imperative. This requires organisations to engage with the following question:

From a commercial perspective, it is critical that we
focus our resources on those elements that enable our
organisation to thrive and perform optimally. However,
from an ethical, and perhaps even a moral, perspective,
how much responsibility do we have for the community
in which our organisation is embedded,
and also for society in general?

There is no right or wrong response to this question. But the answer, one way or the other, does inform the way in which an organisation will go about, or even *if* they go about, building an antiracist organisation. This is also linked to the purpose and vision of the organisation, which we will discuss further in part two.

Your reflections and insights are an essential part of your development in how you apply this work

At the end of every chapter there will be a reflection to assist you in starting to think about the practicalities of building an antiracist organisation. While it may be tempting to skip over these, each of these reflections represents a vital piece of the puzzle; they will start to form a more coherent and useful picture in chapter fourteen.

Cultivating a more inclusive and high-performance culture will most likely require you to think and work in slightly different ways. These reflections are specifically designed to assist you in exploring your organisation and its culture from different perspectives; perspectives that up till now may not have been considered. The intent of these reflections is to support you in developing an approach to building an antiracist organisation that is most applicable to you and your leadership role (formal or informal), as well as the distinctive context and cultural positioning of your organisation.

Being accountable to yourself and your intellectual rigour by challenging your thinking and comfort zones in how you approach these reflections will be the determining factor in their benefit. Essential to building a high-performance culture and an antiracist organisation is developing the capability to have uncomfortable conversations. The benefits of these reflections, therefore, are not only in the strategies and insights you will encounter by exploring your organisation and its culture from a different perspective, but also in your increased capability to sit with discomfort as part of the transformation process.

Reflection #1:

Reviewing key concepts and addressing defensiveness

1. Review your understanding of key terms and concepts such as antiracism, an antiracist organisation, racism, and how racism gets manifested primarily through inequity.

2. What were your three main insights or learnings from this chapter?

3. When you explore your organisation through the definition of an antiracist organisation, are there areas where the organisation is already behaving in an antiracist manner? If so, what are the examples?

4. When you explore your organisation through the definition of an antiracist organisation, are there areas where there needs to be greater focus on building an antiracist organisation? If so, what are the examples?

5. When you think about a hierarchy of advantage based on race that has been normalised, do you notice yourself getting even slightly defensive and/or going into a bit of denial?

6. If so, what might be the origins of these reactions? (hint: if you are going into 'fight' mode, it might be because you are experiencing or fearing an attack or a criticism. If you are going into 'flight' or 'freeze' mode, are you experiencing or fearful of experiencing something that

is uncomfortable or overwhelming?) Be as specific as possible. For example, is the fear of an attack perceived or real; based on a previous experience or a present situation; an attack from an external source or emanating from a critical voice that is part of your internal dialogue?

7. Whatever your reactions are to the notion of a hierarchy of advantage, how are they normal and reasonable given your role; given the current cultural context you are operating in; and given your own history and experience of discrimination?

8. Assuming your responses to the above questions are not only personal but also representative of your organisation, what are your thoughts and feelings about the need for a greater focus on building a culture that is antiracist and more inclusive?

9. Have these thoughts and feelings changed since reading this chapter? If so, what has changed? If not, can you identify any barriers to change?

Chapter Two:

Full disclosure – for me this is personal

Being professional

As a consultant, coach, and facilitator, it is a faux pas to make things about oneself. The intent of our actions has always to be in service of our client, and the purpose of our work with them. So it is with some trepidation that I reveal something about my own history. I have decided to do this is because I feel it would be useful for you to understand some of the context and experiences which have informed and motivated the discussion that will follow. My hope is that, by better understanding this context, it might be helpful in facilitating a process whereby you find greater relevance, usefulness, and meaning within the subsequent pages.

In addition, imperative on our journey towards building an antiracist organisation, is the need to understand the complexity of the dynamics of racism. And even framing it as the 'dynamics of racism' as I just did, implying that racism can be reduced to a set of 'dynamics', is in itself a vast oversimplification. One reason that racism, like every other system of oppression, is complex and nuanced is because there is no one version, no standard experience, or no generic response to racism and the ways it impacts and plays out in someone's life. Every individual will have their own distinctive experience. This is because the way racism is experienced by each person is deeply personal. So, while it is impossible not to make comparisons between individual experiences, we need to be aware that we are rarely ever comparing apples to apples.

When it comes to building an antiracist organisation, like any organisational initiative, it has to start with a conversation. And yet, as we discussed in the previous chapter, there is something about the culture of the times or zeitgeist which makes initiating a conversation about racism complicated, perhaps even controversial. Furthermore, the lived culture within many organisations can make it taboo to speak too personally, to be overly revealing of one's experiences, especially about something as delicate and painful as racism. This is often the norm despite an espoused culture of openness, nonjudgement, and authenticity. But this is where we need to start if we are going to build an antiracist organisation; these are the cultural foundations we must lay, which not only provide the sturdiness and stability required for what we are about to build, but also inform how an antiracist culture will look and feel.

In corporate life, there is an expectation that we be professional. If 'professional' means we should be respectful, ethical, obey the laws, and act in the best interest of our organisation, then we should absolutely be professional. However, in appealing for us to be professional, there is also the implication that we should not be too personal. In other words, we should not permit our personal experiences of life to permeate, to any significant extent, into how we take up our organisational roles. These aspects include, but are not limited to, our hopes, our dreams, our fears, our insecurities, where we have been hurt and traumatised, where we feel lonely and yearn for more belonging, and how we wish to contribute to our community, both locally and globally.

I don't know about you, but the expectation that we can effectively compartmentalise these deeply held elements, elements that are intrinsic to who we are, and then hold them at arm's length in how we take up our organisational roles seems unrealistic. For many of us, our work *is* personal; the way our organisation's culture impacts us, for the better or for the worse, *is* personal; and leadership is categorically personal.

These personal attributes represent the richness of our humanity and life experience. Embracing what is personal can leverage these experiences, which, in turn, unleashes potent drivers of performance. In contrast, when we are expected to deny or marginalise their existence, we are depriving our organisation of these enablers of greater performance. Just to be clear at this juncture, I am not suggesting that our personal experiences are embraced in a way which is self-indulgent or a distraction from core business; rather, finding approaches to welcome the complexity and totality of who we are, in ways that are humanistic at their roots, but that also cultivate an inclusive and high-performance culture.

The challenge of encouraging a more personal dialogue is that while sometimes these experiences are uplifting and inspirational, at other times there is pain and discomfort from those occasions when our lives have been particularly challenging, and not at all pretty. However, if we are going to drive performance by embracing these more personal aspects, we cannot be selective about which experiences we allow. We cannot selectively welcome those aspects which indulge our own comfort – for example, people's vision, motivation, and their desire to make a difference – but at the same time deny those aspects of people's experience which may result in us feeling less comfortable – like their pain, fears, and insecurities. To drive organisational performance, we need to permit, even welcome, the entirety of people's humanity.

Therefore, to support organisational outcomes, we are required to build our collective capability to not only speak more personally about our own experiences, but to also intently listen to the stories and perspectives of others as they do the same. This is how we prepare the fertile ground where the seeds of an antiracist culture can be planted and subsequently flourish.

Me starting this conversation and doing it in a way which is quite personal is intentionally challenging those cultural norms, and hopefully modelling an alternative way of initiating dialogue. This is because, no matter how much we talk about structural or institutional racism, or no matter the extent to which we examine policies, systems, and processes for racial biases, racism remains an intensely personal experience. So, this is where I need to start ...

When the unconscious becomes conscious, and the pain once buried becomes unearthed

As you have probably guessed, for me this is deeply personal. The dynamics and impacts of race and racism, much like a lifelong friend, have been with me and around me for as long as I can remember. That is not to say they have always been front and centre in my consciousness, yet, somehow, the flavours of racism have infused themselves into almost every aspect of my life. My self-esteem challenges; my ambition; my perfectionism; my challenges in relationships; my need for independence; my sense of deep and chronic loneliness; my love of food; my moods; my resilience; and my perception of myself, have all at one point in time been influenced, as well as scrutinised, through the lens of my brown skin.

The paradox of my life to date is that the very thing that has resulted in my self-doubt, my pain, and at times even my self-loathing, has also ignited the fire that has forged my resilience, my compassion, and my ability to hold and be with tension and turmoil, both within myself and in the people and organisations that I work with. And, somehow, I know that this experience, as personal as it may be, is not mine alone. While individual contexts and circumstances will vary, this experience of our most ongoing and painful challenges, also being the vehicle through which we deepen our awareness and understanding of ourselves, is shared by many others, perhaps even yourself.

I participated in a #BlackLivesMatter march in Brisbane, Australia, in June 2020 which was attended by more than 30,000 people. Once we found our place amidst the masses, I took the opportunity to look around me and really take in the moment, the people, the feeling of the crowd. The surprising thing to me was that there were so many White people, especially young White people. But even more surprising was that they were effectively saying that the lives of people who look like me, matter. It was a feeling I could barely take in; a message I could hardly believe to be true.

For much of that afternoon I managed to keep that message at bay, to distance myself emotionally from letting the impact of it wash over me. But in moments, I could hold it out no longer; and my heart was flooded with the feeling that all these people, total strangers, mostly White people, were there giving their time, their spirit, holding up placards, and chanting slogans saying that my life mattered. In those moments tears would stream down my cheeks.

They were tears of relief; tears of appreciation; tears of healing. My surprising realisation was that this feeling that I somehow mattered, was totally foreign to me; it went against so much of what I had been told and taught, through the words and actions I experienced, especially in the early part of my life. Subsequently, what was once buried somewhere in my subconscious, unexpectedly bubbled to the surface, and coalesced into the realisation that I have a deeply held belief that I do not matter, that what I felt, and my experience was not important. Contained within my tears was not only the recognition of this subconscious narrative, but also the relief that comes from acknowledging the pain associated with these experiences, so it could finally start to be alleviated and healed.

But where did this belief come from? Who or what authored this story that formed such a strong and deeply held narrative, but also one that I was barely conscious of?

My parents are from Sri Lanka. I was born in England, and we migrated to Melbourne, Australia, in the early 1970s. Not coincidentally, that was not long after the abolishment of the White Australia policy.[7] As a result, we were amongst the first waves of non-White migrants to land on the shores of Australia.

When we moved to Melbourne, I was the only brown-skinned kid at my primary school, and one of only a handful of non-White kids at my secondary school. So from the start I was seen as someone different, as someone who did not belong, someone who was 'less than'. As a result, I was picked on, beaten up, called names, spat on, and would have 'Go home (n-word)' graffitied on my textbooks. These were regular experiences for me through the latter part of primary school and in those first few years of high school. Being shy, introverted, and a bit of a nerd didn't help, either, as it only made me more of a target. Unfortunately, back in those days, there was not the awareness of mental health there is today. Looking back now, for many of those years I was probably experiencing some form of mental health challenge.

The messages I received, via people's words, as well as their actions, was that I did not belong and that I was not welcome. For much of that time, I felt that there was no place for me. So, fast

---

7 The White Australia policy was enacted by the Australian Government in 1901 and effectively restricted people of non-European descent migrating to Australia. The policy was progressively dismantled between 1949 and 1973.

forward the best part of four decades, it is perhaps unsurprising that so much of my work involves supporting organisations and teams to create cultures where people feel welcomed, included, and like they belong. This goes to the heart of our purpose in life, and the deepest 'why' of our existence. We will discuss purpose further in chapter six.

It wasn't until I finally hit puberty (I was a late bloomer) and the results from my gym workouts started to pay off, and I developed enough of a physical presence and threat that, over time, the bullying began to abate. But by then it was too late, the damage had already been done.

I had received those messages – that I did not belong, and that what I was feeling, my experience, and perhaps even my life did not matter – so many times, that I now believed those messages … (To be continued on page 131)

The experience of racism is in itself diverse

When it comes to race and racism, there is a great diversity in people's experience. The assumption that people from the same race, a similar background, or even with a comparable skin tone, have any degree of consistency when it comes to their experience of racism, is fraught with danger. This is because, for any individual, there are numerous 'layers' which simultaneously influence and shape their understanding of race and racism. Appreciating this is critical as we go about the process of building an antiracist organisation, as it highlights the need to familiarise ourselves with people's lived experience by speaking to them, connecting with them, and getting to know their stories.

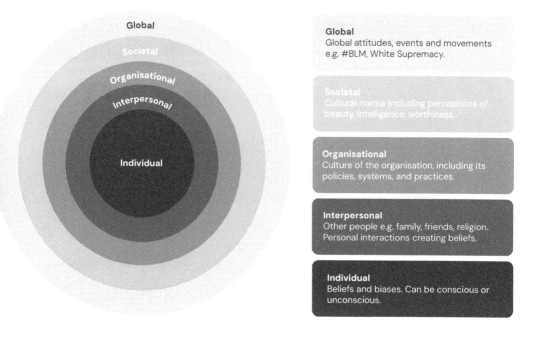

Figure 1: The layers of influence that shape our understanding of race and racism.

The innermost of these layers focuses on the individual, so it is the most personal. This is how a person's history and experience of racism, irrespective of their race, informs their beliefs, biases, and attitudes relative to their own race and the race of others. These beliefs and biases are shaped, as well as created, by each of the outer layers. Through the influence of these outer layers, people also internalise beliefs about their own inferiority (known as 'internalised oppression'), or superiority (known as 'internalised superiority'). We will discuss these concepts further in chapter four. For any individual, these beliefs and attitudes can be conscious or unconscious, most commonly a combination of both. Thus, most people have elements of their conditioning and belief systems which they are aware of, but also areas where there are blind spots they are less identified with or less conscious of.

The next layer is interpersonal. This is how an individual experiences racism through interpersonal interactions, both historically and in the present. It is also how people in their life, most often those closest to them such as family and friends, have created and reinforced certain narratives which inform how that person sees themselves relative to their race and in comparison to other races.

The organisational layer is how the culture of the organisation and its policies, systems, and practices perpetuate racist attitudes resulting in inequity. This layer is the primary focus of this book, so I will elaborate more on this in part two. However, it is useful to deepen our understanding of the bigger picture, and how there is a causal relationship between this layer and other layers of influence.

The fourth layer is societal. This is how society, as well as the community, influences thinking, cultural norms, and perpetuates a racial hierarchy. Racial hierarchy is where some races, ethnicities, or even skin tones are viewed as more desirable, intelligent, worthy, or beautiful. This is also known as structural racism.

Finally, the outer layer refers to global attitudes, events, and movements. The hashtag #BlackLivesMatter is an example of a global movement, as is the rise of right-wing White supremacist groups. Although these groups are usually situated within particular regions, because the rise in these groups is happening all over the world, they represent a large-scale trend embodied within the current zeitgeist, and therefore indicative of global influences.

These layers simultaneously exert an accumulative influence on individual behaviours. It does this by orienting how people think about and experience the concept of race, even if this happens at levels below our conscious recognition. This is one reason why there is such a diversity of thinking, attitudes, and experiences when it comes to race and racism – for each of us there will be a difference in how each layer impacts us and works in concert with other layers to establish and reinforce certain beliefs and biases.

Therefore, I can only speak from my experience in the same way another person can only speak from theirs. And while there may well be people from all races who see elements of commonality in my story, there is a greater probability that someone reading this, even someone who looks a little like me, will have a very different experience of racism.

Sometimes history reverberates into the present

When my parents left Sri Lanka and migrated to Australia (via England) they came willingly, embodying that common, almost to the point of clichéd, hope of wanting a better life for their children. They were not fleeing persecution; in fact, being Sinhalese made them part of the dominant class in Sri Lanka – Christian, middle-class, and educated in English-speaking schools. They were not escaping a war – the civil war in Sri Lanka started in 1983, some 17 years after they left. They were leaving a relatively good life in comparison to the reasons many migrants leave their country of origin – to escape violence, tyranny, persecution, and war. The fact that my parents came to Australia willingly means that they were not taken against their will as slaves or transported to a different country for a life of indentured servitude to a dominant class.

Even just this aspect of my own history shapes and influences my relationship to race and racism. My parents' decision to migrate to Australia was founded upon their free will and their personal intention. It was also fuelled by hope that, in this new land of opportunity, anything was possible. That sense of hope was subsequently infused into the deepest recesses of my psyche, where I had an intrinsic belief, perhaps naïvely, that I could accomplish great feats. So, it was not until much later into my formative years that I slowly started to realise how having brown skin in a predominantly White society would impact not only my sense of hope and hopelessness, but also my ability to keep believing in the expansive and limitless nature of my ambition.

And that makes me wonder about those people whose parents and/or ancestors arrived in a country different from their land of origin, where they did not have a choice, and how this experience differs from my own. How does one's sense of hope and then the idea of limitless possibilities get passed onto future generations if there is no choice or intention to leave one's country of origin in the first place?

And then what about those races and peoples who have been colonised? What is it like to feel unwelcome on your own land, land whose sovereignty was never ceded to those who colonised it? What does it do to a person's relationship to hope when there have been ongoing and systematic attempts to erase your people, your culture, and your connection with that land?

Sri Lanka was initially colonised by the Portuguese in the 16th century, and then again by the Dutch in the 17th century. By the time the British took control in the early 19th century, Sri Lanka (or Ceylon as it was known then) had currency, commerce, and infrastructure. Perhaps it was for these reasons that the British decided that those Sri Lankans they colonised were somehow more human? And they were therefore more worthy of value and respect than those they encountered who they considered to be more primitive, when they, and others, landed on the shores of, and colonised, North America, South America, Australia, and New Zealand. [Even as I write this, I can feel the anguish in my body in referencing an entire race as 'less human' in comparison to another.]

As a result, the process of the British colonising Sri Lanka did not include the widespread murder, rape, and genocide of my ancestors. In fact, when the British left Sri Lanka in 1948, they conferred social, political, and financial power onto the Sinhalese – my ancestors. So, while my ancestors were colonised, which creates complexity we will discuss shortly, it is a very different history to the nature of colonisation that occurred in South America, North America, Australia, and New Zealand, in how the indigenous peoples of those lands were seen, valued, and treated by their respective colonisers.

From one perspective, this makes my experience of racism more personal in nature. Of course, all racism is experienced as personal, primarily because it is an attack on our very person. But my experience, for the most part, does not include strong historical elements where my ancestors experienced unspeakable atrocities and where the agony and trauma of those transgressions have been passed from one generation to the next.

And yet, even this does not fully capture the complexity.

Even though the British might have thought those Sri Lankans were more deserving of value and respect (in comparison to the indigenous peoples from other lands that they colonised), it did not diminish the belief that their (the British) way was better, and therefore British customs and thinking should be adopted by the Sri Lankans for their own benefit. So, at some point in time, my ancestors started to favour English as their language of choice as opposed to Sinhala; they chose to eat with a knife and fork as opposed to their fingers, as their forebears did; they adopted the British version of currency and measurement; and Christianity became a more prominent choice of worship.

These changes in culture, the gradual degradation of what was once our way in favour of the way of the colonisers, is underpinned by a narrative that the White (in this case, British) way is better than the Black or Brown (in this case, Sri Lankan) way. The process of colonisation is when, over time, a race repeatedly receives the message that the way they think, the way they feel, the gods they worship, their culture, customs, and language, and their relationship with land and country are all inferior to 'our' way, the way of the coloniser. And while, in the case of Sri Lanka, this external colonisation did not happen with the level of violence and atrocity that happened in many colonised countries, there is an internal colonisation that is perhaps more subtle but still perpetrates its own version of violence.

Throughout the process of growing up, I was never taught our language (Sinhala) or exposed to our customs, never taught to make traditional Sri Lankan food, which, as a foodie, now absolutely breaks my heart. So, while, as a country, the process of colonisation in Sri Lanka did not include the levels of violence that other countries experienced, there was, in some respects, a violent internal colonisation. By this I mean there was an abrupt and deliberate cutting off, and separation from my Sri Lankan heritage and the very things which inform who I am and where I have come from. This 'colonisation' served a purpose: it allowed my family and me to fit into Australian culture more, or at least stand out a little less. It was done from the point of view of survival, with the underlying rationale being 'the more you can act like an Australian, talk like an Australian, eat like an Australian, be interested in what Australians are interested in, the less you will be seen as different and, therefore, the less you will be targeted'.

The irony, of course, is that, no matter how I talked, what I ate, or what my interests were, having brown skin in a largely White society, I was always going to be 'the other'. Therefore, one of the complexities for those of us who have been colonised externally and/or internally is the constant tension between fitting in by appeasing the coloniser as a mechanism of survival, and a deep yearning to feel a connection with and represent our own culture, traditions, and ancestors.

In contrast, I have Indigenous friends and colleagues who, despite Australia's violent history and the way Indigenous people were treated by the colonising British and subsequent Australian governments, have been able maintain a connection with their language, their tradition, their spirituality, and their sense of community. They have managed to do this despite centuries of systemic discrimination, to the point where First Nations people are yet to be recognised in the Australian Constitution. This demonstrates that, even though a race and culture can be colonised in the external (literal) sense, it does not necessarily mean there is a simultaneous process of internal colonisation where the values, ways, and culture of the coloniser are seen as better than our own.

We cannot decouple racism from history. This is because racism has shaped and influenced so many aspects of history; after all, one of the underpinning rationales of racism is 'our way is better than your way'. When it comes to racism, history shows up trans-generationally in the way that the experiences of our ancestors are transferred through the generations, not only through their stories but also through the pain and trauma they endured.

History also shows up in how our past experiences continue to reverberate through our being by influencing how we see ourselves and the worth we attach to our emotions, our experience, and perhaps even our life itself. In this way, history plays out in the present when the narratives about the worth of our ancestors, purported by those who oppressed or colonised them, eventually become internalised, and these same beliefs subsequently echo through our own lives. This is demonstrated in the way that, while I never personally experienced actual colonisation, there has been a process where my internal colonisation means I favour a more western approach to life and marginalise those elements which connect me back to my Sri Lankan heritage.

And just to be clear, in saying this, I am in no way justifying and definitely not minimising the impact of the history in countries and continents like Australia, South America, New Zealand, and North America, where there have been painful and dehumanising atrocities committed in the name of colonisation. I am not making an equivalency between these kinds of traumatic histories and my own personal history.

But what I am saying is that the experience of racism is complex; there is an outer experience of racism and also an internal experience of racism. Both send us messages about our worth, and our place in the world, the only difference is where that message emanates from.

This is my story. This is why this work is so personal to me.

But what's your story? Are there places in your history, both your personal as well as your family history, where there have been dynamics of racism and/or colonisation? Where and how have your ancestors been the colonised, or where and how have they been the colonisers? And what about people you work alongside in your organisation, what is their story? How does your story and your history intersect with their story and their history, and then play out, usually unconsciously, in the way you take up your respective roles within the organisation? And how might this impact the team or organisation in its culture, effectiveness, and performance?

This is where we need to start the conversation, this is the process of breaking ground on building an antiracist organisation.

Reflection #2:

Lived culture and organisational outcomes

1. Irrespective of your race, what are your personal experiences of racism? (hint: your experience of racism will largely depend on your perspective – whether you are advantaged by racial inequity, disadvantaged by racial inequity, or have been a witness to racial inequity.)

2. Based on the diagram on page 51, what are the layers of influence that have informed and contributed to your own racial identity and concept of race?

3. Based on the lived culture of your organisation, how much permission and how free do you feel to speak about and share more personal experiences? How could doing this a little more (but without being self-indulgent or a distraction from core business) make you more effective in your role?

4. In your organisation, what are the cultural enablers that give people permission to speak more personally?

5. In your organisation, what are the cultural barriers that make people hesitant to speak more personally?

6. How might dynamics of race and racism, of the colonised and the coloniser, be playing out unconsciously and unintentionally between individuals or groups within your organisation? And what is the impact of this on the culture, on team dynamics, and on performance? (hint:

it might be useful to also think metaphorically here; for example, is there a culture of colonising other people's thoughts and ideas? Are there examples of people's attitude being 'my way is better than your way'?)

Chapter Three:

Systems of oppression – the invisible enemy

I would like to say at the outset that there are parts of this chapter which for some of us will be confronting to read and challenging to hear. This is because they have been difficult to write. So, I want to support and encourage you to take care of yourself throughout this chapter – take a break, walk on the grass, do yoga, get support from a friend; do whatever you need to do to look after your whole being as we wade into some pretty murky and painful waters.

Bad apples or rotten trees?

In the aftermath of the George Floyd murder trial verdict, one of the discussions which strongly arose was around the question, 'is the Minneapolis Police Department, perhaps policing more generally in the United States, inherently racist?' Or, to reframe the question within the context of this book: Is the Minneapolis Police Department a racist organisation?

Trevor Noah is my favourite comedian. I am in awe of the way he questions and challenges the status quo by seamlessly weaving political commentary and astute observations into his humour. He sums up the George Floyd murder trial verdict with an eloquence that I do not possess:

'If we're meant to believe that the police system in America, the system of policing itself, is not fundamentally broken, then we would need to see good apples. And what I mean by that is, where are the cops who are stopping the cop from putting their knee on George Floyd's neck?

'We don't see them [the good apples] because they themselves know if they do something, they are going against the system. The system is more powerful than any individual. The system in policing is doing exactly what it's meant to do in America, and that is to keep poor people in their place. Who happens to be the most poor in America – Black People. It is a system, it's not broken, it is working the way it's designed to work. We are not dealing with bad apples; we are dealing with a rotten tree.'[8]

In determining the extent to which any particular organisation exhibits tendencies which create and perpetuate racial inequity, we must obviously take into account the behaviour and attitudes of the individuals within that organisation. However, what Trevor Noah articulates so elegantly is the power of the system to impact and influence the beliefs, attitudes, and behaviours of an individual within that system. Therefore, and perhaps more importantly, there needs to be an evaluation of the organisational system itself. The 'system' refers to the ways racism and racial inequity are embedded, even very subtly, within the policies, processes, and culture of an organisation, to the point where they are normalised in people's attitudes and behaviours.

The other point that Trevor Noah makes is that, when it comes to policing in the United States, 'It's a system, it's not broken, it is working the way it's designed to work'. What he is alluding to is that, when it comes to racism, the system is doing exactly what it was

---

8   A Few Bad Apples, 'Trevor Noah's Take On "Bad Apples"' YouTube Video, 4.22, 2022, https://www.youtube.com/watch?v=gDW-haLL8YU

designed to do, which is to perpetuate dynamics of racial inequity so that some races are advantaged and others are disadvantaged. Seeing racism as a system and understanding the strategies that this system utilises to sustain and reinforce itself is what we shall discuss throughout this chapter.

Christina's [pseudonym] story

'Racism is just always there. It is like a blanket that never moves. It doesn't seem to turn off, there is no alleviation of it, it is always in the background,' responded Christina when I asked her about her experiences of racism in her workplace. Christina is a highly accomplished professional and has a doctorate in her respective field. She also happens to be Black woman living on the east coast of the United States and working for a pharmaceutical company.

Christina spoke about the comments she receives such as, 'You speak so well, for a Black woman,' or being questioned, 'Is that your real hair?'. Christina also contrasted her experiences with her various managers. She said that with most of her [White] managers, she did not feel supported or as though advocating for her was a priority for them. On the other hand, she always felt supported and as though her career has advanced when she has had a Black manager. 'They [her Black managers] increased my visibility and they said my name in rooms where I needed them to say it. So, I felt very supported. I don't know if it's racism [the reason why my career did not advance with White managers], but it definitely didn't come across as something that had to do with my skill set. But I still have to constantly grapple with the question, is my lack of career advancement [with White managers] due to racism, or something to do with my skills?'

Now that she is in a leadership role, Christina said that her skills are not necessarily questioned; now it is more a case of her delivery, or how she is saying something, versus what she is actually saying. 'So, the racism shows up slightly differently when you are a leader. When you are a junior employee there is just so much more to grapple with. You are just grappling with imposter syndrome, especially when you are a minoritised group, because you don't know if you are In thut position because of your race or because of your skills.'

Christina also alluded to how the dynamics of racism are constantly shifting and adapting. 'Racism is an evolving phenomenon. It just evolves from generation to generation. It is always one step ahead. By the time we try to solve one thing, it has already evolved into something else and showing up in a different way. And the laws, policies, and attitudes of the times just shift right along with it. By the time we are approaching a potential solution, it just shifts into something else, it morphs and then everyone pivots right along with it. It is like a monster.'

Christina discussed how Black people, and Black women in particular, need to have all these accolades and qualifications just to get somewhere. 'It feels like we have to do extra just to get to the same place as a White person. We [Black people] cannot do the bare minimum at all, there is no bare minimum for us. Racism is something I have come to expect now. I just have to manoeuvre around those experiences and still be very focused on what my end goal is.'

When asked about the narratives and attitudes that she has internalised from having to work and function in an environment where there is structural racism, Christina responded, 'I am dealing with internalised racism much better the older I get. When I was younger, I think it really affected my self-esteem. It affected my confidence levels. I had to constantly ask myself, "Do you belong here? Do you deserve this? Did they make the right choice when *they hired me?" There was an overarching feeling, all the time, of not deserving something.'*

The cultural soup in which we all swim

The system of racism is like the cultural soup in which all of us, irrespective of our race, swim. There is no escaping it; it has become normalised in our life. It has become so normalised, in fact, that for many of us it has become almost impossible to discern where the boundary of our own autonomy and ability to think as an individual stops, and where this cultural conditioning starts.

This conditioning infiltrates our attitudes and beliefs, which in turn inform how we construct the racial hierarchy; it's like that thin layer of dirt or oil on our sunglasses that distorts how we see the world, sometimes without us even realising. This is the 'blanket that never moves' which Christina describes in her story. But most importantly, it is how we have accepted and then normalised a particular set of beliefs and biases, which results in us being barely aware of their presence, how they influence our thinking, or even how they took residence within our consciousness in the first place.

Two young fish are swimming in their pond, chatting about everyday stuff. An older, wiser fish approaches them and enquires, 'How is the water today, friends?' With a quizzical look on their face, one of the young fish looks at the other young fish and asks, 'Water? What's water?'

I love the simplicity of this analogy in demonstrating something that can be hard to grasp. We live in a culture that is all around us. When that culture is everything that we have ever known, it makes it difficult to see what that culture is, let alone the extent to which its pervasive nature influences and impacts what we feel about ourselves and the world around us.

So, let's go back to our two friendly fish. Their whole life all they have known is the water in their pond; they don't know any other way of being in the world. This is the cultural soup that they have come to accept as their version of normal. But what if the water in their pond has an unusual set of currents? What if the current provides assistance to one fish by flowing in the same direction in which they are swimming, whilst at the same time creating a resistance for the other fish by flowing in the opposite direction to which they are swimming (and I appreciate this is an analogy, so please afford me some poetic license here, as opposed to a literal evaluation of the fluid dynamics within ponds 😊). Even though these two fish have more or less the same swimming ability, it soon becomes apparent to the other fish in the pond that one of those two fishes is a much better, a much more capable swimmer than the other.

Given this observation, the other fish in the pond will react in various ways. Some of them might develop programs to support that 'less capable' fish. The 'more capable' fish, if they are good-natured, might help the other fish and find food for them, seeing as they are too slow to catch their own food. Other fish will assume the 'less capable' one is lazy, unintelligent, or lacks the ambition required to get fitter so they can swim as well as the 'more capable' fish. Others will say to the 'less capable' fish, 'If the more capable fish can swim really well, surely you can too?' And when that 'less capable' fish gets tired and frustrated from their continued efforts to keep up with the 'more capable' fish, some other fish can't help but think it is because of a lack resilience, that fish being weak, or having a victim mentality, or perhaps even being melodramatic.

And while this is going on amongst the other fish in the pond, at some point that 'less capable' fish starts to actually believe they are less capable, and that this is somehow their fault. They start to believe and internalise what the other fish are thinking and saying about them. This, of course, creates insecurity, self-doubt, perhaps even self-loathing within that 'less capable' fish, which, when seen by the other fish, only serves to reinforce the narrative that this fish is somehow inferior and therefore is unable to be helped. Both the fish are swimming in the same water, so the underlying assumption is that the water influences each fish's ability to swim equally. But what is less obvious is how the currents within the water itself benefit how well one fish can swim whilst, at the same time, establishes barriers for the other fish.

In this scenario, blaming the 'more capable' fish for their superior swimming ability is not helpful, nor is it even justified. They are just going through life, swimming around in their pond and doing what they need to do to survive. The real source of the disparity in their swimming ability and the resulting inequity is the nature of the water itself. While it is the favourable current which benefits the swimming ability of that one fish, it is also the current that leads that 'more capable' fish to believe they should be credited, and therefore rewarded, for their superior swimming ability. In contrast, the discrepancy in swimming ability created by the water fosters the narrative within the 'less capable' fish that their inferior swimming ability reflects some intrinsic deficit in themselves, which is their fault. And so, they believe that they are not worthy of enjoying the benefits and advantages that come from being a good swimmer.

When people deny the existence of structural racism or claim that it was something that happened in the past, I believe they are telling their truth. This difference in perspective is based on two things. Firstly, as we discussed on page 28, it is how we define racism – whether we see racism as only overt bullying, physical violence, and vilification, versus seeing racism also as a system which creates and perpetuates inequity between racial groups. For example, if we recall in Michael's story (page 4), even the HR department did not deem leaving bananas in his locker to be racial vilification. In this case, there might not have been overt bullying, name-calling, physical violence, or something tangible and objective. However, what the HR department failed to take into consideration was Michael's subjective experience of feeling ostracised and devalued as a result of the racial stereotyping (being compared to apes or monkeys) that he experienced.

Secondly, it is a matter of someone's day-to-day experience and the advantages they are or are not granted based on their race. Unless you have a lived experience of racial inequity, you may not be aware that such discrimination even exists. So, the 'more capable' fish swims around believing this is just how life is meant to be. In contrast, the 'less capable' fish, over time, will become increasingly aware of the ways the currents are not as supportive of their swimming ability and that they are less able to reap some of the benefits that are granted naturally to the 'more capable' fish.

It is a matter of the 'less capable' fish's personal growth and journey through life as to whether they keep believing that their 'inferior' ability to swim reflects a personal deficit that is somehow their fault, or they progressively become aware that it is primarily their environment which creates the discrepancy in their swimming ability. This characterises the process of coming to terms with our experiences of internalised oppression or, in the case of the 'more capable' fish, our internalised superiority, both of which we will discuss further in chapter four.

The benefits which are naturally granted because of our social identity is based on the idea of privilege. The key point here is that, for many of us, especially those with more privilege when it comes to race, how we perceive and experience systemic racism, perhaps even the extent to which we believe in its existence, is much like how those fish perceive the water in their pond:

Systemic racism? What's systemic racism?

The powerful and poignant reminder in this analogy is that, when it comes to organisational life and how we support achievement and deliver performance, we tend to overestimate the importance of talent, work ethic, and personal capability. At the same time, we underestimate how those barely perceptible cultural currents influence not only achievement and performance but also people's sense of belonging and the informal hierarchies that get created based on race, gender, sexuality, religion, class, education levels, and able-bodiedness, just to name a few.

Structural racism enforces systemic racism

This book has an explicit focus on dismantling structural racism, but given it embodies one of many systems of oppression, we have to be mindful to not underestimate the cumulative impact on an individual when they are faced with multiple systems of oppression. *Intersectionality* is a framework that acknowledges how multiple social identities intersect and interact to shape an individual's experiences and outcomes. It recognises that people's lives are influenced not by a single dimension of identity, such as gender, sexuality, race, or class, but by the interplay of these various aspects. For example, a Black woman's experiences are shaped not only by her gender but also by her race. She may face structural discrimination and challenges that are unique to the intersection of being both Black and a woman, which are distinct from the experiences of Black men or White women. Intersectionality highlights that systems of oppression, privilege, trauma, and structural discrimination are all interdependent. It emphasises the importance of considering the cumulative impact of these intersecting identities when addressing issues related to social justice, equity, and inclusion.

The 'system' in systemic racism refers to a system that was founded on racist principles and ideals and uses these principles to perpetuate racial discrimination and inequity. Systemic racism utilises structural racism as a way of increasing its effectiveness by ingraining those racist principles into day-to-day life, so they are seen as normal and as 'the way we do things'. The terminology is a little confusing, so here is one way to think about it. If systemic racism was an organised crime syndicate, then structural racism would be its hit-person or enforcer. In a criminal organisation, the enforcer's role is to ensure that its members fulfil their expectations and comply with the unwritten code of the organisation. Structural racism urges people to comply with the unwritten principles of systemic racism, thereby upholding and enforcing its fundamental tenets.

This tendency to go along with the unwritten rules of the system is what Trevor Noah was alluding to by the fact that none of the other police present stopped Derek Chauvin from putting his knee on the neck of George Floyd. This is an example of how structural racism upholds the tenets and furthers the agenda of systemic racism.

Structural racism has to do with how racism is embedded throughout society, throughout our institutions (education, media, law, sport, etc) and normalised in our attitudes, policies, systems, and practices. The racism is determined by who is advantaged and who is disadvantaged by these elements.

It is structural racism which reinforces our beliefs, attitudes, perceptions, and biases – both conscious and unconscious – when it comes to race. We need to realise that structural racism is part of a system, and an effective system at that. This is what Trevor Noah was referring to in this metaphor of a rotten tree in comparison to bad apples.

Any kind of discussion on racism, especially one whose goal it is to build an antiracist organisation, has to include an understanding of structural racism. For when there is insufficient awareness of this overarching and pervasive dynamic, the best-intentioned antiracist initiatives, even when executed with precision, will not deliver the outcomes desired. This is because these initiatives will come up against an invisible yet powerful resistance embedded within the system of oppression – the system's inbuilt capacity to shore up its own survival, particularly when it is challenged. This is what Christina was alluding to:

> *'Racism is an evolving phenomenon. It just evolves from generation to generation. It is always one step ahead; by the time we try to solve one thing, it has already evolved into something else and showing up in a different way.'*

While we are not required to completely dismantle structural racism in order to build an antiracist organisation, we do need to be aware of the strategies that structural racism utilises in order to ensure its survival. This is so that, when they occur, there is less chance that we will be blindsided or surprised by them. When we know or are even expecting the system to deploy certain survival mechanisms when its effectiveness is threatened, we are better equipped to disarm the system when these mechanisms arise. Using our understanding of these dynamics to create practical and actionable strategies which can start to dismantle structural racism is one of the essential aspects of building an antiracist organisation.

This capacity to protect and perpetuate itself is why racism, as a system of oppression, is centuries old and has withstood not only the test of time but has also thrived despite the many attempts to dismantle it by passionate, knowledgeable, and well-equipped individuals and groups.

Assigning responsibility for racist behaviours and attitudes only to the individual is over-simplistic as well as problematic

Systemic racism has a pervasive influence over organisational cultures. Much like our two friendly fish, this is the cultural soup in which we are all swimming. This is because when systemic racism deploys its enforcer – structural racism – it embeds and then normalises racial inequity within organisational cultures. If culture is most simply defined as 'how we do things around here', then those behaviours, attitudes, and practices that the culture both rewards and resists combine to determine the cultural norms within an organisation. In evaluating organisational cultures through the lens of race and racism, it is these cultural norms which determine the extent to which, but also how, racial inequity gets expressed and perpetuated.

But here is the complexity …

Within an organisational context, when it comes to expressions of racist behaviours and attitudes (keep in mind our definition of racism and how it gets manifested primarily through inequity, which can be objective measures or subjective experiences) we tend, most commonly, to ascribe responsibility for these expressions entirely to the individual. In doing so, we underestimate, or perhaps do not even consider, the complex and insidious ways the system of racism runs in the background of organisational cultures and thus exerts its ubiquitous influence on individual behaviours and attitudes in ways which are almost imperceptible. This requires us to unpack the extent to which an individual within that system is wholly and solely responsible for their behaviour.

How do we reconcile the need for individual responsibility with the fact that an individual's environment plays a significant role in shaping their behaviour?

This philosophical dilemma is one of the complexities that underpins many discussions about structural racism, but one that is rarely talked about explicitly. At the crossroads of this dilemma, however, we tend to default to the path that sees those behaviours which perpetuate racial inequity primarily through the lens of individual responsibility. After all, it is far less convoluted and not as dilemma-inducing to see an individual such as Derek Chauvin and condemn them by ascribing the totality of their behaviour to a function of their own choices and personal agency.

However, if we don't see how Derek Chauvin's behaviour is also influenced by the structural racism embedded at every level of society, including the culture of the Minneapolis Police Department, then we are not doing justice to the complexity of an individual's actions. Subsequently, we discontinue our analysis of racist behaviours at the limits of individual responsibility and, as a result, suspend our exploration of those more systemic or cultural origins of people's behaviour. This is not intended to endorse an abdication of personal responsibility for individual behaviour, but unless we also take into consideration the effect the system has on that person's behaviour, we are underestimating the complexity of the challenge that lays before us.

At first glance, the concept of personal responsibility appears to be mutually exclusive with a viewpoint which takes into consideration the environmental and systemic influences on individual behaviours. Yet, it is our ability to simultaneously hold both these viewpoints – the personal and the systemic – that will ultimately be one of the fundamental determinants of our success in building an antiracist organisation and a high-performance culture.

This complexity extends well beyond dynamics of structural racism and is pertinent for all behaviours exhibited by individuals, including those that determine an organisation's or team's performance. Organisations and their leaders must therefore ongoingly meet the challenge of untangling how to uphold a culture of personal accountability for unwanted behaviours, and at the same time not underestimate the influence the culture has in founding and then rewarding those behaviours.

By framing this dilemma and understanding the inherent complications around it, we are able to better recognise why discussions around racism are so often fraught with tension and divisiveness. Whether we deem a particular individual or organisation to be exhibiting racist behaviours will be determined by the perspective we are utilising to explore those behaviours – a different perspective may well yield a different conclusion. Therefore, as soon as we align too strongly with only one of these perspectives, we alienate the other perspective, along with the people who are viewing their own experience of organisational life through a similar framework. There is an ironic elegance that, even in our philosophical approach to building an antiracist organisation, it requires us to be more inclusive of a diversity of perspectives and approaches.

Apart from being oversimplistic, assigning responsibility for racist behaviours and attitudes only to the individual is also problematic. This is because when we hold the individual wholly and solely responsible for unintentionally exhibiting racist behaviours, there is a greater tendency to construct the narrative that they have some inherent defect or malicious intent as part of their character, and they are therefore intrinsically flawed.

Calling into question someone's intrinsic nature and their character starts to create a justification for using shame and belittling as means of holding them accountable. Yes, people need to be held accountable for their behaviours, but to foster the psychological safety needed to create an inclusive and high-performance culture, accountability needs to be viewed as a developmental process rather than a punitive one. This is because, while being shamed and reprimanded may produce a short-term behaviour change, they will do little to support the cohesion and overall sense of safety within the culture, and over time this will invariably undermine sustained performance.

By the way, I said 'unintentionally racist' two paragraphs ago because in my experience of working with organisations, the vast majority of people within them are kind, considerate, and well-intentioned. Therefore, attitudes and behaviours that have a racist element to them usually arise out of (i) the need for more awareness of their own unconscious biases and beliefs; (ii) the need for more education in the history of racism, particularly in their own context, and its associated dynamics and impacts; (iii) an individual's own fears and insecurities, which get externalised and/or projected as unintentional or unconscious racism; (iv) some combination of the previous three elements. Given the underlying assumption that most people are not being intentionally hurtful or malicious, these reasons highlight the need for support, education, and development. In chapter eleven we will discuss further how a developmental approach is needed in how individuals take up their respective roles to support the creation of an antiracist culture.

To build an antiracist organisation, we therefore need to understand the ways that racism gets perpetuated and entrenched, even in subtle and unintentional ways, in both individual behaviours as well as in the culture of the organisation. We cannot proactively address something that we do not understand, let alone a dynamic that plays out in barely perceptible ways. To better address the system of racism, we first need to understand how systems function in general.

In order to survive, systems (including systems of oppression) must counteract entropy

Systems can be seen and studied in every aspect of life. A system is a group of interdependent and interrelated components that integrate and function together to achieve a specific goal. Therefore, the human body is a system. An organisation is also a system. A pond with its various frogs, fishes, insects, bacteria, and other related flora and fauna is a system – more specifically, an ecosystem. This ecosystem then sits within layers of other ecosystems. For example, the pond sits within a particular area of marshland, which in turn sits within a forest.

One of the challenges that all systems face is entropy. According to Katz and Kahn, '[The] entropic process is a universal law of nature in which all forms of organisation move toward disorganization or death … [but] by importing more energy from its environment than it expends, the open system can store energy and acquire negative entropy.'[9]

Simply put, systems have a natural tendency to, over time, move towards disorganisation, death, and, in the case of systems of oppression, perhaps irrelevance. According to Burke, 'The point is that organisational systems are not self-sufficient; they are unstable and will not survive or grow unless active and deliberate effort is expended.'[10]

Systems are not self-sufficient because they are not able to sustain themselves using only their internal resources; they are therefore required to import energy from sources outside the system. This is the main way that a system counteracts the entropic process, and so becomes one of the key functions a system is

---

9 Daniel Katz and Robert L. Kahn, The Social Psychology of Organisations (New York, NY: John Wiley and Sons, Inc., 1978)

10 Wyatt Burke, Organisation Change: Theory and Practice (Thousand Oaks, CA: Sage, 2002)

required to perform to keep perpetuating itself, thereby ensuring its own survival.

For example, the system of the human body needs to import energy in the form of air (oxygen), food, water, and nutrition in order to counteract the effects of entropy (the power of the entropic process is demonstrated by the fact that, no matter how much energy we import from the outside, at some stage we all cease to exist. While importing energy might slow this process down, at some stage entropy gets the better of us all). Similarly, an organisational system imports energy in the form of revenue, team members, expertise, and innovative ideas.

A system or ecosystem such as a pond imports energy via the sunshine needed for photosynthesis, and the rainwater required to sustain and preserve the lives within it. In each of these cases, if we restrict or discontinue the system's ability to import energy so it can no longer counteract entropy, that system will start to decline and will eventually cease to exist. How long this process takes depends on how much energy is stored within the system. But if the energy a system is able to import is less than the entropic forces, then, whether it's six weeks, six months, or sixty years, at some stage that system will no longer exist – it's a case of when, not if.

The system of oppression known as 'racism' gets perpetuated by structural racism

In order to counteract entropy, a system of oppression, like all other systems, needs to import energy from its external environment. It does this by normalising beliefs, policies, and practices that reinforce the dynamics of advantage and disadvantage, which in turn perpetuate inequity. The main function of structural racism, therefore, is to support and perpetuate systemic racism by importing energy through the dynamics of inequity relative to race; in fact, one could argue that this is its *only* function.

Structural racism utilises three main strategies so it can fulfil this objective. These represent the 'active and deliberate effort' alluded to by Burke that all systems must deploy In order to counteract the effects of entropy. These three strategies, or some version thereof, are the ones that all systems of oppression utilise, but for obvious reasons I will explore them within the context of race.

You will see that, on the surface, the strategies themself are relatively simple. But it is the depth to which they are entrenched in the broader culture which contribute to their effectiveness and intractable nature. Furthermore, these three strategies do not operate in unison, separate from each other; there is a synergistic relationship between them, where the deployment of one strategy provides a beneficial effect to the others.

In discussing these three strategies, I will provide examples of how they get manifested. These are simple examples that many people will be familiar with. The purpose of describing them here is less about giving a detailed account of the example itself, but, rather, demonstrating how these examples are ways that structural racism gets operationalised in our lives, sometimes without us even realising.

Strategy #1:
Structural racism uses policies, systems, and practices to keep certain races oppressed, marginalised, and disenfranchised

In Australia, in the period between approximately 1905 and 1967, children of Aboriginal and Torres Strait Islander descent were forcibly removed from their homes and placed in the care of Christian missionaries. This program was carried out by Australian federal and state government agencies based on laws passed by successive Australian governments. Mixed race children with First Nations and White (European) heritage were particularly susceptible to removal based on the belief held by the authorities that, because of their lighter skin, these children could be assimilated more easily into the White community.

Once within the missions, these children, who have now become known as the Stolen Generations, suffered unspeakable trauma and abuse, including emotional, physical, and sexual abuse. Additionally, there was no contact with their parents, siblings, or community. Their names were effectively declared void, only to be replaced by a number. They were encouraged to reject their own culture, heritage, and language, and therefore to become more 'White'. One of the stated goals of this program was that 'everything necessary (must be done) to convert the half-caste into a White citizen'. The Stolen Generations have had devastating impacts for the people who were forcibly removed as children, their parents, families, and their descendants. All these groups of people experience high rates of depression, anxiety, post-traumatic stress, and suicide, as well as poor health and socioeconomic outcomes.[11]

As I write this, lawmakers in Georgia, United States, are attempting to change the laws so that people cannot cast an early vote in elections on Sundays. On the surface, this looks like a relatively innocuous change in the voting process. However, local lawmakers are well aware of a program called Souls to the Polls. This is an initiative whereby Black folk go to church on Sunday, and then get in church buses, get in cars, and, as a group, go to vote. Therefore, restricting early voting on Sundays undermines the ability of Black folks to vote via this initiative. This is one example among many of laws currently being changed in numerous states and districts

---

11 Leilani Darwin, Stacey Vervoort, Emma Vollert and Shol Blustein, Intergenerational trauma and mental health. Australian Government Catalogue, number IMH 18, Australian Institute of Health and Welfare, 2003)

across the United States to restrict the ability of BIPOC to exercise their democratic right and cast their vote in future elections. If, in a democracy, one of our inalienable rights is to partake in the democratic process and choose our elected leaders, then these laws have the effect of taking away people's rights and therefore their say in how the future of their country is determined.

Despite the Stolen Generations in Australia and the current attempts at voter suppression going on in the United States being decades apart and on different continents, there are some striking similarities. Both cases are initiated by the government enacting a set of policies. Laws and policies that create inequity are one of the main tools used by structural racism. This is why it is so essential that we have greater diversity in our law-making bodies and at senior levels of organisations; representation at these levels of institutions can influence policy creation. But, as we shall soon see, representation alone is not always enough.

Another similarity is that both governments present what on the surface, at least, looks like a reasonable case to legitimise the policy, because it is made to appear as though it is solving a particular problem. In the case of the Stolen Generations, the policy was underpinned by the concept of assimilation, based on the assumption that the lives of these children will be better if they were raised in White culture. Similarly, voter suppression laws are being legitimised because they will address so-called issues with election security. Finally, both examples disadvantage one group of people politically, financially, emotionally, or in their health outcomes. It is this disadvantage which creates a flow of energy away from the disadvantaged group towards the advantaged.

Strategy #2:
Structural racism uses policies, systems, and practices to create advantage for certain races

Obviously, strategy #1 and strategy #2 are inextricably connected. In some ways these strategies operate under the principles of a zero-sum game. The term zero-sum game originates in game theory and economic theory and suggests that, in a situation where there are two sides, the advantage or benefit that is won by one side means that the other side loses by a proportional amount. Structural racism loosely adheres to the principles of a zero-sum game by transferring energy in the form of benefits, advantages, and privileges from one racial group to another.

In the United States, Australia, and the United Kingdom, the demographics of our respective governments do not reflect the diversity of the populations they represent; White people are significantly overrepresented in these countries. In Australia, those who have non-European and Indigenous backgrounds make up approximately 24% of the population, yet 94% of the parliament is comprised of those with Anglo-Celtic or European heritage.

The current 118th United States Congress is the most racially diverse in American history. However, of the 535 voting House and Senate members, 133 (25%) identify as belonging to minority racial groups, primarily Black, Hispanic, Asian, Pacific Islander, or Native American. This is in comparison to approximately 41% of the population in the United States identifying as non-Hispanic White. Given it is the politicians that are responsible for creating the laws which govern us, why would they make a conscious decision to create different laws and, in the process, potentially relinquish some of the advantages the majority of them enjoy?

This is one of the many ways that the system has been cleverly constructed so it is self-perpetuating. If the policies, systems, and practices related to structural racism did not also provide a benefit to an alternative group of people (as per strategy #2), there would possibly be more incentive and impetus for those people to modify those policies and practices. After all, they would have nothing to lose by making those changes. But when the system operates according to the principles of a zero-sum game, where one group's disadvantage becomes another group's advantage, the advantage itself undermines the incentive to change.

The ways that the dominant race benefits from structural racism can be seen across a wide range of elements, which are broadly reflected in the opportunity we each have to live a life of freedom, prosperity, health, and happiness. Data collected in the United Kingdom by the Cabinet office in 2017[12] found that 75% of working-aged people who identify as White British were employed, in comparison to 50% of working-aged people who identified as Pakistani or Bangladeshi being employed. The same research found that people living in households headed by someone Asian, Black, or in the 'other ethnic' group, were more likely to be on a low income. These groups were also more likely to live in persistent poverty (defined as having less than 60% of median outcome before housing costs in three out of the last four years) with 20%, 18%, and 16% of 'other ethnic', Asian, and Black households respectively, satisfying the criteria for living in persistent poverty. This is in comparison to 9% of people living in households headed by someone identified as White British satisfying the criteria for living in persistent poverty.

---

12 'Race Disparity Audit Summary Findings from the Ethnicity Facts and Figures' www.ethnicity-facts-figures. service.gov.uk, accessed February 21, 2022, www.ethnicity-facts-figures.service.gov.uk/static/race-disparity-audit-summary-findings.pdf

In the United States, in 2014, 73% of White families lived in owner-occupied homes, in comparison to 41% of Black families.[13] Furthermore, according to the US Federal Reserve,[14] the average Black and Hispanic or Latino households earn about half as much as the average White household and own only about 15 to 20% as much net wealth. And this wealth gap has only widened in recent decades!

It might come across as being emotionally detached to reduce structural racism down to a series of facts, figures, and statistics, because for many people it is such a painful and personal experience. But sometimes we have to explore the objectivity of the statistics to see the impact structural racism has on different demographics within our society. If the purpose of structural racism is to use dynamics of advantage and disadvantage to create and perpetuate inequity between racial groups, then these statistics are a verification of the capacity of structural racism to fulfil this intended purpose.

Some of us, even as we see these statistics with the significant disparities based on race, will rationalise that the reason for these disparities is something different to structural racism. And, yes, these are all complex social and political dynamics, and to reduce everything down to a single cause is likely an oversimplification. However, I would urge us all to remember our two friendly fish. We will recall a tendency to think that the reason for that fish being a less capable swimmer is primarily about the fish, as opposed to how the water benefits the 'more capable' fish and creates barriers for the 'less capable' one.

---

13 'Quarterly Residential Vacancies And Homeownership, First Quarter 2019', U.S. Census Bureau, accessed March 13, 2022, https://www.census.gov/housing/hvs/files/currenthvspress.pdf.

14 'Wealth Inequality and the Racial Wealth Gap', Board of Governors of the Federal Reserve System, October 22, 2021, accessed March 5, 2022, https://www.federalreserve.gov/econres/notes/feds-notes/wealth-inequality-and-the-racial-wealth-gap-20211022

Our collective tendency to view these statistics through the lens of personal responsibility underestimates or perhaps even ignores the extent to which the system we are swimming in influences outcomes. From this perspective, the outcomes reflected in these statistics have very little, if anything, to do with personal responsibility, individual capability, motivation, or work ethic, and much more to do with a system that advantages one group of people, at the expense of another. One example of such a system is the South African apartheid regime.

Apartheid was a system of institutionalised segregation, based on race, that existed in South Africa between 1948 and the early 1990s. Successive South African governments endorsed apartheid policies, which ensured that the country's minority White population controlled the political, social, and economic power. The policy itself created a caste system or racial hierarchy where individuals were classified into one of four categories based on ancestry, appearance, socio-economic status, and cultural lifestyle. These classifications were 'Black', 'White', 'Coloured', and 'Indian'. Access to housing and employment opportunities were dictated by these racial classifications. In addition, apartheid law made it illegal for most South African citizens to marry or pursue sexual relationships across racial lines.

Between 1960 and 1983, as a result of apartheid legislation, 3.5 million Black Africans were removed from their homes and forced into segregated neighbourhoods; this remains one of the largest mass evictions in modern history.[15] One aspect of the government's rationale for the apartheid system was to support South Africa's burgeoning economy and process of industrialisation by segregating and creating a class of people that could be used as cheap labour in industries such as mining. In this way, apartheid provided benefits

---

15 Martin Abel, 'Long-Run Effects of Forced Resettlement: Evidence from Apartheid South Africa.' *The Journal of Economic History.* 79(4): (2019) 915-953. doi:10.1017/S0022050719000512

to a particular class of people by using segregation as a vehicle by which to garner cheap labour. Obviously, it is no coincidence that this class of people happened to be predominantly White.

During the 1970s and 1980s, some reforms were made to the apartheid system which allowed for 'Indian' and 'Coloured' representation in the South African Parliament. These changes, however, did not have any kind of significant bearing on the overarching impacts and outcomes of the apartheid system.

When it comes to building an antiracist organisation, representation of all races throughout the organisation, but especially at senior levels, is an important milestone. However, while an important step and certainly a significant marker as part of a longer journey, representation should be seen as part of a process, rather than the outcome itself. Representation of BIPOC in governments, executive leadership teams, boards, and committees, does not change structural racism. This is because representation alone is not sufficient to change the systems, structures, and policies that perpetuate racial inequity. In the absence of understanding how structural racism manifests itself within organisations, and an accompanying commitment to dismantle it, representation might be viewed as tokenistic rather than a genuine move towards equity.

In South Africa, non-Whites make up the majority of the population, and even when people from these racial groups were permitted to enter government, they were still not able to deconstruct the overall apartheid (racist) political structures. This is because the apartheid system leveraged structural racism in order to ensure that the White minority are the beneficiaries of advantage because of having control of the political, social, and economic power. Even after Nelson Mandela was elected as president and there were more non-White people in senior positions within the government, it was the White minority that still controlled the power and, therefore, the advantages and benefits that were gained because of that power.

One of the reasons that strategy #2 is so effective at perpetuating structural racism is that it invariably provides a multitude of benefits and a degree of relative comfort to the privileged. Comfort is the companion of complacency; comfort is also the nemesis of urgency and intention. Luxuriating in this comfort is a powerful de-motivator to do anything to actively address the system which grants us this sanctuary in the first place. This is indicative of the cleverness of structural racism, and why it is such a formidable opponent to conquer. This is also why, throughout these pages, it has been my intention to create a narrative which, in places, makes us uncomfortable. Like anyone, I would like to live a comfortable life; comfort has its place. But if we are serious about building an antiracist organisation, we have to be mindful that the luxurious sense of contentment and satisfaction, that frequently accompanies being comfortable is not always conducive to our intended outcome.

My family migrated from London, England, to Melbourne, Australia, on a ship. During that 31-day voyage, children and adults were allocated into separate mealtimes, and because of the assigned seating arrangement, one had no choice but to always sit with the same people. On the table next to my brother and I at children's mealtimes were two young Australian girls, approximately the same ages as us. They were on the second part of their around-the-world trip and were headed back to their home in Melbourne. After sharing meals in the early days of the voyage, the four of us became friends and spent many hours together engaged with the activities on the ship; the four of us basically became inseparable.

On the voyage from London to Melbourne, one of the ports that the ship stopped at was Cape Town, South Africa. At Cape Town, passengers had the opportunity to leave the ship and spend some time in town. Our respective families, excited at the prospect of getting off the ship and exploring the city, planned a day trip to Cape

Town. As part of that day trip, as kids frequently do, we all needed to go to the toilet. At that point, something changed. That feeling of the four of us being inseparable dissipated very quickly. We went from four kids with the innocence that played with their friends for the pure joy of it to now being forced to see our playmates, who we had shared activities with, shared meals with, and used the same toilet block on the ship, as 'the other'. The two girls went to the 'Whites only' toilet, which even from the outside looked as though it was kept in a much better condition. My brother and I had to go to the 'Coloured' toilet. My overwhelming recollection of that experience was the putrid stench coming out of that toilet, which clearly had not been maintained in the most basic standards of sanitation and hygiene. I remember asking my mother, 'how come we have to go to a different toilet?' but, for some reason, I can't recall her response. I think this is the first experience of racism that I can recall.

While the inequity in this experience is clear, the transfer of energy and advantage is perhaps less so. In that instant, when I asked, 'how come we have to go to a different toilet?' I immediately personalised the experience. In that moment, I started to think there must be something wrong with me; I must be defective in some way because I don't get to use the nice toilet. And yet, even at that age, the advantage of having access to that nice toilet supported the identity of those two young (White) girls in terms of their importance and their place in the world, while at the same time it made me question why I am not worthy of using the nice toilet and, perhaps even less consciously, what do I have to do to become worthy of that nice toilet.

The transfer of energy in the form of advantage comes from having security in one's identity; from having one's self-esteem and intrinsic worth reinforced; and from the benefit of being a six-year-old child and not having to plough through one's internal landscape in an attempt to understand where I am defective. As I write this, almost 50 years after the incident, I can feel the tears, as well as the rage, swirling around inside of me.

Pearl's [pseudonym] story

Pearl had been an Allied Health professional in a hospital on the west coast of the United States for 14 years. She was very accomplished in her respective field and popular with her colleagues. She also happened to be a Black woman who is originally from the East Coast.

Pearl attended a meeting where there were multiple managers from two of the hospital clinics that had some patients in common. At the meeting, a [White] manager, who was not Pearl's direct manager, enquired as to why some patients were being sent to the wrong clinic. Pearl responded by saying, 'Because they [the doctors] are ignorant, meaning they don't know about our clinic or that the treatment we offer exists.'

Pearl said that she was called in almost right away to her supervisors, who were also present at the meeting. The manager who had made the enquiry [about patients being sent to the wrong clinic] had made a complaint about Pearl's 'direct' communication style and did not think she should be using the word 'ignorant'. Pearl had also observed [White] colleagues being direct in various situations, but there were no such consequences for them. Pearl clarified the context of how she used the word and what she meant by it, and said she would not use that word ever again.

Over time, Pearl noticed that she was no longer being asked to attend marketing events with doctors; this was an aspect of her role she had become accustomed to doing on a regular basis. This went on for numerous years, before Pearl finally asked another manager why she was no longer being asked to attend marketing events, to which the manager replied, 'It's because you have a history of negative communication.' Pearl then clarified with the manager if her being seen as having a negative communication style was based on the comments she made in the meeting all those years earlier, to which the manager replied in the affirmative. This series of incidents contributed to Pearl eventually leaving the organisation.

In her reflections, Pearl said that she was aware that people from her part of the East Coast can be more direct in their communication, and on the West Coast that can be perceived as being aggressive or assertive. Pearl also said, 'Even though I didn't mean to challenge the manager, in some ways I did challenge him by being confident and just speaking from my knowledge and expertise, but also being a Black woman. So most likely the White manager took offense to me calling the White doctors ignorant or saying they didn't know anything since I am not a doctor, and so as an Allied Health professional and a Black woman I should be beneath them. But the angry Black woman stereotype was most likely a factor as well.'

Strategy #3:
Structural racism utilises racial stereotypes to perpetuate differing outcomes and inequity

Back to my fancy convertible sports car and getting pulled over by the police (from page 29).

When the first question the police would ask me was, 'whose car is this?' my instant reaction was intense rage. How dare they assume that, just because a Brown person is driving this car, I must've stolen it! How dare they make the immediate association between the colour of my skin and my criminality! And how f**king dare they assume that I did not have the intelligence or the education or the work ethic where I could make enough money to legitimately afford this car!

And yet, in this moment of rage, I also had enough awareness about my place in society relative to my race to know that, if I let too much of that rage seep into how I communicated with those police, my safety and freedom could be significantly compromised. I also knew that, if I expressed that rage in any kind of overt or obvious way, it would only serve to confirm their preconceptions and fears so the next BIPOC they pulled over would have even less room to manoeuvre in how they reacted to a similar line of questioning.

Unfortunately, this experience is far from mine alone. In fact, in many parts of the world, but particularly in the United States, BIPOC parents are required to have 'the talk' with their children. 'The talk' is a colloquial expression for a conversation BIPOC parents are compelled to have with their children and teenagers about the dangers of escalating their behaviour when confronted by (White) authority figures, particularly the police.

When questioned by the police, 'Whose car is this?' my immediate, but still suppressed, rage propels me to a perilous crossroad. One direction would be to express that rage, but doing so may well compromise my safety and freedom. The other direction is to smile, play nice, and appease those in authority. Thankfully, and unlike many people, I always departed those interactions with the police with my physical safety and freedom intact. But when faced with such judgement and derision, and then feeling unable to stand up for my innocence and humanity, I always left feeling like something else deep inside me had been damaged. While a strategy of appeasement might safeguard one's safety and freedom, what gets compromised is one's dignity. And when this happens frequently enough, there is an accumulative impact on one's sense of worth, the consequences of which ripple out much further than an encounter with a couple of police.

One of the main reasons that people get placed in these no-win situations, and that BIPOC parents are required to have 'the talk' with their teenagers, is because of the way stereotypes are formed and then played out, mostly unconsciously, within our interpersonal interactions.

We can see this in Pearl's story, when her direct communication style was labelled as 'negative communication' and likely interpreted as threatening. This is because the way she communicates is perceived, in part, through the lens of the angry or aggressive Black person stereotype. Another analysis of Pearl's story is that, as a Black woman, she dared to challenge the authority of the White, male manager, and was subsequently reprimanded.

In an organisational setting, the most accurate representation of the lived culture is people's behaviours. Culture is created in every moment by those behaviours that we reward and those that we resist. It is the messages that we send or don't send that determine what people feel is acceptable in how they turn up to work and behave. In this way, society is no different. The messages we receive not only from those closest to us – such as family and friends, but also the media (traditional and social), government, aspects of the legal system – such as the police, and advertising combine to create an ongoing and powerful narrative which tells us how we should turn up and play the game of life.

These messages, however, also convey to us where our respective place is within a largely unspoken cultural hierarchy based on our social identities, such as race, gender, sexuality, and socio-economic status (class), just to name a few. In some ways, these societal messages work like a casting director in a movie. They allocate us certain roles and then create the expectation, in ourselves and others, that we behave in accordance with that informal role we are allocated. Structural racism leverages this process very effectively in order to create stereotypes.

Stereotyping is the process whereby we associate certain attributes, characteristics, and behaviours to a group of people, and form the generalisation that all members of that group will demonstrate these same attributes, characteristics, or behaviours. We see this in Christina's story (page 63), when people comment, 'you speak so well … for a Black woman.' People's surprise at Christina's obvious eloquence and intelligence is founded upon a stereotype that Black people, especially Black women, are not as intelligent or as educated in comparison to their White counterparts.

The process of stereotype formation is a complex one; primarily because so many of the mechanics occur subconsciously. Yet, there are two generic steps which are involved in the creation of all stereotypes.

The first step is how our direct experience, influence from other people, as well as influence from larger institutions such as media and advertising all play a significant role in the construction of stereotypes. Our brains are wired to see patterns and make associations, so when we are repeatedly exposed to messages that associate certain groups of people to particular attributes or characteristics, we can't help but create stereotypes based on that association. The messages we receive via traditional media such as television, magazines, billboards, and advertising, as well as the repetitive and subliminal bombardment we are exposed to from social media, means that the way we think about critical aspects of our life and lifestyle, such as our value, beauty, and happiness, is being constantly fashioned and formed by the creators of that content.

The influence of the media therefore plays a substantial, yet also underestimated, role in the creation of stereotypes. However, this influence is further amplified when people have limited opportunities for, or do not actively pursue, meaningful relationships and exchanges with people from outside their own social and/or racial group.

Stereotypes, both positive and negative, abound for most groups of people. However, there is a tendency to have more negative stereotypes associated with groups that have been historically, as well as currently, disenfranchised. Most of us will know the stereotypes associated with women, Asians, gay men, and Jewish people. I am very intentionally not referencing the actual stereotypes here, firstly because I find them offensive, but secondly because I don't want to be part of the process where the association between a particular group of people and certain negative attributes or characteristics is further reinforced.

Numerous stereotypes exist that indirectly or directly perpetuate structural racism. To elaborate on and discuss all of them is probably not relevant or useful within the context of this work. However, I thought it would be interesting to narrow the field of discussion to me getting pulled over by the police in my sports car and my simultaneous reactions of rage and caution.

The dynamics of stereotyping are playing out when the police see a person with my skin colour driving a fancy convertible sports car, pull them over, and the first question they ask is, 'whose car is this?' In this case, the stereotype is associating a man of colour with criminality, violence, and therefore feeling threatened by him. But where does this stereotype come from, how is it formed and then reinforced within both the police and even myself, perhaps without any of us even realising?

Dixon and Linz conducted a content analysis of a random sample of local television news programming in Los Angeles and Orange counties, United States, to assess representations of Blacks, Latinos, and Whites as lawbreakers and law defenders.[16] They found in comparisons of perpetrators (Black and Latino vs. White) that Blacks and Latinos are significantly more likely than Whites to be portrayed as lawbreakers on television news. They also found that Blacks and Latinos are more likely to be portrayed as lawbreakers than as defenders, whereas Whites are significantly more likely to be portrayed as defenders than as lawbreakers. Finally, they found that Blacks are overrepresented as lawbreakers, and Latinos and Whites are underrepresented as lawbreakers on television news compared to their respective rates of crime, obtained from the California Department of Justice for Los Angeles and Orange counties.

Research done in 2016 by the Equality and Human Rights Commission in England found that, relative to the population, the rates of prosecution and sentencing for Black and ethnic minorities in England and Wales were three times higher in comparison to White people.[17] Additionally, the rate of incarceration for ethnic minorities is over five times that of White people.

Wilson found that people have a tendency to perceive Black men as larger and more threatening than similarly sized White men.[18] Research participants judged the Black men to be larger, stronger, and more muscular than the White men, even though they were actually the same size. Interestingly, and perhaps surprisingly, even

16 Travis Dixon and Daniel Linz, 'Overrepresentation and Underrepresentation of African Americans and Latinos as Lawbreakers on Television News', *Journal of Communication*, Volume 50, Issue 2, (June 2000): 131–154

17 'Healing a divided Britain: the need for a comprehensive race equality strategy', Equality and Human Rights Commission, accessed August 15, 2021, https://www.equalityhumanrights.com/our-work/our-research/healing-divided-britain-need-comprehensive-race-equality-strategy

18 John Wilson, Kurt Hugenberg and Nicholas Rule, 'Racial Bias in Judgments of Physical Size and Formidability: From Size to Threat,' *Journal of Personality and Social Psychology* (Published online Mar. 13, 2017)

Black research participants displayed this bias, although not to the same extent as the White participants. The research also found that participants believed that the Black men were more capable of causing harm in a hypothetical altercation and, troublingly, that police would be more justified in using force to subdue them, even if the men were unarmed.

From this research, you can start to see how stereotyped narratives begin to get created about Black men. Our brains make the unconscious associations based on the images, stories, and content that we are exposed to, that Black men are larger, more muscular, more of a threat, and more prone to criminality in comparison to their White counterparts.

Speaking personally, even when I see a mugshot of another BIPOC man on the evening news I can't help my reflex reaction to be, 'Great work, buddy, now you have made us all look bad.' My reaction demonstrates that even BIPOC, to some extent, internalise the stereotypes in the way we see ourselves (this is a consequence of internalised oppression, which we will discuss further in chapter four). This is also why in Wilson's work, discussed above, even Black research participants displayed the bias of perceiving Black man as larger and more threatening than similarly sized White men.

My reaction also reveals the power of association. The public see a mugshot of an accused rapist, who happens to be White, on the evening news, and for the most part their reaction is, 'He must be a bad person.' But when they see a mugshot of an accused rapist who is a BIPOC man, in a split second a pre-existing stereotype in their subconscious gets both activated and confirmed, and this creates the thought that very few people will admit to, let alone say aloud: *That BIPOC man is an accused rapist, therefore all BIPOC men must be rapists.*

Upon seeing this research, my personal reaction is a combination of both sadness and relief. I feel sad because these kinds of dynamics occur and are still so entrenched in our culture. On the other hand, my relief is because when the police pull me over and I am inherently cautious and anxious about letting my rage seep into my communication, my cautiousness is confirmed by the research, and it's not just me being paranoid. As someone who, by most objective measures, is larger than average, the research confirms that I have even less margin for error in expressing my rage because my Brownness amplifies my size, and therefore the threat associated with me, even further.

Although I have used my experience of getting pulled over by the police as a launching point to discuss the stereotypes related to males of colour, it does not mean that similar dynamics do not also play out for women of colour as well. Black British women are four times more likely to be detained under the mental health legislation in comparison to White British women, while mixed ethnicity women are seven times more likely to be detained.[19] Women of colour share the stereotype with their male counterparts of being angry and aggressive. But another stereotype for women of colour, which is not so associated to men of colour, is that they are overly emotional, perhaps even hysterical. This stereotype contributes to the discrepancy between women of colour and White women in terms of being detained under mental health legislation.

The second component of stereotype formation is how the stereotype itself creates the stereotypical behaviour, and in doing so becomes a self-fulfilling prophecy. Word, Zanna, and Cooper demonstrated the effects of stereotypes in the context of a job

---

19 'Healing a divided Britain: the need for a comprehensive race equality strategy', Equality and Human Rights Commission, accessed August 15, 2021, www.equalityhumanrights.com/sites/default/files/healing_a_divided_britain - the_need_for_a_comprehensive_race_equality_strategy_final.pdf

interview.[20] White participants interviewed Black and White subjects who, prior to the experiments, had been trained to act in a standardised manner. Analysis of the videotaped interviews showed that Black job applicants were treated differently. They received shorter amounts of interview time and less eye contact; interviewers made more speech errors (e.g., stutters, sentence incompletions, incoherent sounds) and physically distanced themselves from Black applicants.

In a second experiment, trained interviewers were instructed to treat applicants, all of whom were White, like the Whites or Blacks had been treated in the first experiment. As a result, applicants treated like the Blacks of the first experiment behaved in a more nervous manner and received more negative performance ratings than interviewees receiving the treatment previously afforded to Whites.

The results of the first experiment indicate that Black applicants were treated less well than White applicants. The results from the second experiment then indicate that this treatment can then negatively influence the performance of those candidates who were treated less well (like the Black candidates in the first experiment) and, interestingly, this was irrespective of race. Simply put, if stereotypes result in people of a certain race getting treated differently (less well), then those people may start to behave in a way which confirms those negative stereotypes, which creates a self-fulfilling prophecy and the perpetuation and strengthening of the stereotype itself.

Another example is, when the police pull me over, the way I get treated in terms of my assumed criminality and level of threat directly contributes to me feeling angry. If this happened to occur on a day where my ability to manage my reactions was, for some

---

20 Carl Word, Mark Zanna and Joel Cooper, 'The nonverbal mediation of self-fulfilling prophecies in interracial interaction' *Journal of Experimental Social Psychology* 10 (2): 109–120 (1974)

reason, compromised and I permitted my rage to permeate into the interaction, it would have very quickly confirmed, in their minds, the stereotype of the angry Black or Brown man.

Donald Trump uses these racialised stereotypes to his great advantage. By harnessing the power of stereotypes, in combination with racist dog whistles, he very effectively stokes fear into those people who identify as disenfranchised and marginalised White people.

A 'dog whistle' is a phrase which on the surface appears relatively innocuous, but in its subtext communicates something more insidious to a certain subset of the audience. Racist dog whistles play on racial stereotypes, but they are even more subtle (the term 'dog whistle' itself references a frequency outside normal ranges for humans to hear but only heard by dogs i.e. a certain segment of the population). Even though dog whistles are built on a foundation of racial stereotypes, the subtle and indirect nature affords the one who utters such phrases plausible deniability. In other words, whilst people who understand the subtext will immediately make the association between the dog whistle and the racist stereotype, others will hear the phrase and think it harmless, hence the plausible deniability.

When we hear phrases such as 'bad hombres', 'inner cities', 'America first', 'law and order', and 'coming to take your country' through the lens of the research findings we have just discussed and the formation of stereotypes, we are better able to decouple the subtext from the actual content. We can then see how structural racism is baked into these comments because they are positioned atop of a stereotype which says that BIPOC, especially male BIPOC, are violent, ghetto-dwelling criminals, and they pose a threat not only to your safety but to everything you and your forebears worked so hard to build. From this perspective, it is easy to see why, when the police pull over somebody who looks like me driving a fancy sports car, in a split second a series of stereotypes, associations, and assumptions get activated, resulting in their first line of enquiry being, 'Whose car is this?'

Addressing racial inequity makes it harder for systemic racism to sustain itself

These three strategies utilised by structural racism are synergistic in that they each provide a beneficial effect to their companion strategies. When strategy #1, which uses policies, systems, and practices to keep certain races oppressed, marginalised, and disenfranchised, and strategy #2, which uses policies, systems, and practices to create advantages for other races, are deployed in unison, the inequity they create results in worse outcomes for BIPOC. This inequity is reflected in the numerous objective measures we have already discussed. And it can also be seen in the inequity of people's subjective experience, for example, the inequity of security, the inequity of belonging, the inequity of power and access, and the inequity of safety.

The worse outcomes for BIPOC that these inequities bring about in turn reinforce and perpetuate stereotypes, and thus the unspoken (in most circles) narratives about BIPOC; this is the deployment of strategy #3. Therefore, these three strategies also co-create a vicious cycle, because the more effective they are, the more they reinforce the dynamics of racial inequity. And then these strategies can be deployed with even greater effect because people within the system have less power, safety, and energy to challenge the system and fight back.

What sustains the system of oppression is the continual transfer of energy into the system *from* those people who are disadvantaged by it and *towards* those people who experience benefits and certain privileges as a result of it. This serves to counteract entropy. As a result, racism as a system of oppression is able to ensure its own survival. Therefore, like any other system, without this transfer of energy from outside the system, systemic racism would be less able to sustain and perpetuate itself.

This is exactly the same process that occurred with our two friendly fish. My intention (for those of you who haven't guessed already) was to utilise the neutrality of the fishes as an analogy for structural racism, in the hope there is less emotionality and defensiveness, in comparison to addressing a topic which can be divisive and controversial in a more direct manner. Hopefully this enables us to see with more clarity how these three strategies utilised by structural racism perpetuate inequity in the outcomes that are essential for all of us to live a life of freedom, prosperity, happiness, and health.

In how we go about creating an antiracist organisation, it is essential to keep in mind that it is the system of racism that creates, perpetuates, and then normalises racist attitudes and behaviours. Thus, even if individuals within that system are held accountable for their racist behaviours, there will not be a sustainable shift towards antiracism until we have addressed the system itself. Once again, referencing Trevor Noah's metaphor, this is like pulling the bad apples off the tree, but not addressing the reason why the tree is rotten in the first place.

Reflection #3:

Evaluation of structural racism within your organisation

1. How does your organisation think about behaviour and performance? Does it view them primarily through an individual perspective, or are the influences of culture and the environment also considered? Are there examples of each which come to mind?

2. How do you think about behaviour and performance? Do you view them primarily through an individual perspective, or are the influences of culture and the environment also considered? Are there examples of each which come to mind?

3. Reflect on the policies, practices, and culture that have been normalised in your organisation. How might these create disadvantages for BIPOC? (hint: if you notice yourself getting a bit defensive and/or going into denial, or gripped by shame or guilt, revisit questions 5, 6, and 7 from reflection #1)

4. Reflect on the policies, practices, and culture that have been normalised in your organisation. How might these create advantages for non-BIPOC? (hint: if you notice yourself getting a bit defensive and/or going into denial, or gripped by shame or guilt, revisit questions 5, 6, and 7 from reflection #1)

5. In your organisation, do people overlay stereotypes in the way they refer to or think about people and

situations? If so, think of some examples. Or do people make assumptions based on race or perceived racial identity? If so, think of some examples.

6. Given that responses to the last three questions are representative of some aspect of structural racism, what are three actionable strategies which, based on your role, you can implement to start to dismantle these aspects of structural racism in your organisation?

Chapter Four:

Upgrading operating systems – a developmental focus

Cultural challenges reveal developmental opportunities

In the previous two chapters, we have discussed the dynamics and impacts of racism from a personal perspective, and then from a structural perspective. I appreciate that the content has been quite dense and, at times, rather confronting, so I appreciate you hanging in there with the process thus far.

Ideally, we need to align an initiative to build an antiracist organisation – or any other DEI program for that matter – with those performance elements that support the purpose and vision of the organisation. To build the required capability around these specific performance elements, we need to explore this process through a developmental lens. This is because, as we move towards the creation of an antiracist culture, we will invariably encounter certain developmental sticking points. These are aspects of the organisational system which historically may have proven beneficial but have progressively become less effective in creating the desired culture and driving sustainable performance.

These historical aspects, initially founded on 'tradition' but then reinforced by reflex and habit, have become fortified in the cultural norms of the organisation. As these norms, which represent less evolved or less mature versions of an organisation's operating system, become increasingly entrenched, they exert greater levels of influence over our ways of thinking, our ways of behaving, and our ways of working. Imagine still using Windows 7 when the current version, as I write this, is Windows 11 – some programs will still work, others might be a bit clunky, while others will be totally incompatible. Obviously, what is needed is for the operating system to be upgraded to a version that enables the programs we are utilising to perform optimally. We can think about culture in a very similar manner, where the beliefs, attitudes, and processes which run in the background of an organisation are representative of its operating system.

The cultural challenges and tensions we encounter at these developmental sticking points shine a light, sometimes uncomfortably, on where an organisation's operating system or thinking approach is incompatible with the creation of an inclusive and high-performance culture. While these developmental sticking points frequently manifest as chronic challenges, seemingly intractable polarisations, a dogmatic resistance to adaptation, or perhaps even cultural crises, they also represent immense opportunities. This is because if we are able to cultivate an attitude of genuine curiosity, and then summon the courage to lean into the trepidation of exploring even the most provocative of challenges, they hold within them the potential to transform our organisation in its effectiveness as well as its maturity.[21]

As part of building an antiracist organisation, there are four developmental sticking points that we will almost invariably encounter. In order to build the capability needed, a strategic focus on these sticking points is essential. The purpose of this chapter is primarily to frame and bring our awareness to these four elements

---

21 The maturity of an organisation has nothing to do with its age. It is about the effectiveness of its thinking approach, the degree of sophistication in how it approaches its development, and the strategies it applies to these challenges.

of the organisation's operating system. So, please consider this chapter the linkage between what we have already discussed in the dynamics of structural racism and the way that addressing these dynamics also facilitates the creation of high-performance cultures. These four developmental sticking points are summarised in the table below and integrated as part of the practical approach described in part two.

	Developmental Sticking Point	Developmental Focus Required
1.	Creating connection and cultivating belonging	Increasing psychological safety, so that openness, vulnerability, and the sharing of stories and experiences become the cultural norm.
2.	Unleashing latent energy through racial equity	Develop our 'energy intelligence' so we can start exploring performance through the lens of energy.
3.	Re-visioning our approach to confidence and self–doubt	Understanding and addressing the causal links between structural racism and confidence.
4.	Walking a mile in the shoes of BIPOC	Optimising discretionary effort by welcoming the totality of people's experience and emotions.

Table 1: The four developmental sticking points

Developmental Sticking Point #1:
Creating connection and cultivating belonging

A deep and robust connection between team members is a powerful driver of performance. Working in elite sport, one of the elements that coaches are continually seeking ways to improve is the connection between their players. Greater levels of connection are also beneficial for corporate teams, where it strengthens trust, supports a unified approach to the strategy, and lubricates the cogs of collaboration. There are many ways of strengthening the bonds of connection between teammates, but one of the most functional, most enduring forms of connection between teammates is created upon a lived experience of inclusion and belonging.

It is possible that the acronym DEI, referring to 'Diversity, Equity, and Inclusion', does this work a disservice. DEI programs have become a staple requirement in most corporate environments. This has been driven, especially in recent times, by a combination of social justice movements such as #MeToo and #BlackLivesMatter; the need for increased legal protection in the event of a discrimination lawsuit; and to satisfy the demands of being seen as socially progressive. And as a result, the acronym DEI has made its way into common corporate vernacular. When the acronym just casually rolls off our tongue, however, we might be more inclined to discount or underappreciate the practicality, as well as the complexity, of its component terms, in particular 'inclusion'.

Given that Diversity and DEI programs are often used synonymously, it is worthwhile unpacking the individual components of DEI. This is because a more sophisticated and nuanced appreciation of what these terms mean will help us to clarify what we intend to achieve via these initiatives. This in turn will assist us to formulate the most effective strategies to deliver our intended outcomes.

Diversity: most simply comes down to demographics. It is the breakdown of groups and how they are represented within an organisation's workforce, particularly those groups that have traditionally been underrepresented and/or disenfranchised.

Most people think of diversity as being based on those characteristics that make someone's identity relatively easy to distinguish; for example, race and ethnicity. But diversity also includes a broader range of social identities and experiences, many of which may not always be obvious; these include socio-economic background (class), gender identitiy, sexual orientation, marital status, religion, disability, and neurodiversity.

So, while a diverse workforce is essential, diversity alone says nothing about the extent to which people, especially those from minority or traditionally underrepresented groups, feel included and as though they belong within organisational structures and cultures.

Equity: is often used synonymously with equality, but they actually mean very different things. Equality means that individuals or groups of people are granted the same resources and/or opportunities. Equity, on the other hand, takes into account an individual's or group's different circumstances, including their social identities, life experience, and privileges. Equity, therefore, strives to allocate the resources and opportunities necessary so that, as much as possible, individuals and groups are able to reach an equal outcome.

Figure 2: Equality versus equity.

Inclusion: is very different to diversity. Inclusion refers to the culture, systems, and policies within an organisation that determine the extent to which all people, regardless of their social identities and life experience, feel welcome, valued, and included. It means everyone is seen as a whole and equal human being. And at the same time, there is an awareness of the potential hardships and disadvantages people may endure due to marginalisation and discrimination based on their social identity.

Inclusion is not about overlooking or minimising our differences, but rather about deepening our understanding and appreciation of those differences. Hence, while an organisation can have a diverse workforce based purely on its demographics, it does not necessarily mean there is an inclusive culture if people do not feel welcomed, valued, and included. So, while diversity is 'simply' a matter of recruitment, inclusion is the real driver of connection, belonging, and performance.

Inclusion is both an internal and an external experience happening simultaneously

Let's revisit our definition of racism:

Racism is a combination of actions, beliefs, and policies
which perpetuate and normalise the discrimination
and therefore the disadvantaging of one race, and the
simultaneous advantaging of another race.

As we discussed in chapter three, structural racism is perpetuated via inequity and the transfer of energy, in the form of benefits and advantages, from one race to another. Embedded within these dynamics of inequity is the implicit message that one race belongs to a lesser extent in comparison to another race. So, it's not just the benefits themselves that are crucial to recognise; it's also the messages embedded within these benefits. When based on someone's race, there are particular advantages and privileges which they are not routinely granted, the message they receive is loud and clear, even though, paradoxically, it is rarely ever stated explicitly: *You are not worthy. You are not welcome. We don't want you here.*

If we think back to our two friendly fish from the previous chapter. Their environment (the water) benefits the swimming outcomes of the two fish in ways that are not equitable. Therefore, it would only be natural for that 'less capable' fish, at some point in time, to equate the difference in benefits they receive to them being less worthy of belonging, and their environment to being less welcoming. None of the other fish in the pond, like (hopefully) nobody in an organisation, is literally saying, 'You are not worthy. You are not welcome. We don't want you here.' Yet, there is an unspoken narrative that arises out of the inequity. This narrative is baked into the system, in the way the system perpetuates those currents which favour some races whilst creating barriers for others. And although this narrative is rarely ever spoken aloud, its impact is definitely felt as it penetrates the souls of BIPOC and lands viscerally upon their bodies.

This is one of the more insidious and harmful consequences of structural racism, as well as other forms of structural discrimination. Over time, this narrative, which usually exists slightly below those conscious or identified aspects of the culture, becomes internalised within people's psychological landscapes and as part of their inner dialogues. Once this narrative takes residence within us, it feels a complacency being unencumbered by the constraints of political correctness and the restrictions of social niceties. As a result, it goes from being unspoken to being raucous, opinionated, and interminable.

Many of us with a lived experience of racism will be familiar with the internal battles which need to be fought, sometimes on a daily basis, for us to really believe and feel as though we belong and are truly welcome within a team, a community, or an organisation. And while an inclusive culture might be sufficient to initiate a ceasefire which temporarily quells this inner battle, it is rarely ever sufficient to negotiate an armistice so that peace and tranquillity permanently presides over the internal turmoil. This is because, irrespective of whether we are welcomed and valued in the current context, there have been countless instances where in other environments and contexts we have felt actively excluded, invisible, and like we were an intrusion of sorts. And this has created an indelible story that has subsequently been internalised and reinforced over time.

So, as we move towards a more inclusive culture, we need to be mindful that inclusivity is a lived experience that happens at two levels simultaneously. Firstly, at the cultural level, organisations need to be open to exploring those subtle, less conscious aspects of the culture that send messages implying that some people are more worthy of belonging than others. And, secondly, on a more personal level, we have to remember the messages that many BIPOC have internalised, where they are required to confront the inner voice that invalidates their experience and excludes their very humanity. Addressing inclusivity only at the cultural level will be insufficient to build an antiracist organisation. This is because it excludes, and so fails to acknowledge, the reality of those people who have internalised their historical experiences of exclusion. Paradoxically, this goes against the very premise of inclusivity itself.

This is one of the many complexities of this work, because it requires organisations and their leaders to grapple with the following dilemma:

What role, if any, do we have in supporting the professional development of team members so that they are able to have more awareness of, and therefore start to dismantle,

*those dynamics of inclusion and exclusion that they
have internalised and that now play out across their
psychological landscape?*

Hence why building an antiracist organisation is a process that should not be undertaken lightly. For while the benefits in culture and performance are significant, the pathways we are required to take in order to reap those benefits are by no means straightforward.

Developmental focus for sticking point #1: Work on increasing psychological safety so that openness, vulnerability, and the sharing of stories and experiences become the cultural norm

Connection is built through belonging, and people feel they belong when their experience matters to others. Hence an organisation or team will frequently outperform its competitors when one of its cultural norms is that another team member's experience is equally, if not more, important than your own. In creating a culture where connection and belonging make up the foundation, being able to share stories and experiences is an essential ingredient. This is because stories shared and stories heard transform cultures – they remind us of who we are; anchor us to our intrinsic natures; and help to contextualise and explain individual traits and idiosyncrasies.

When it comes to the process of building an antiracist organisation, it is especially important that people are able to have conversations, in particular about their experiences of inclusion and exclusion – of feeling like they belong or of feeling unwelcome. This is because one of the consequences of structural racism (as well as other forms of structural discrimination) is that it pushes people's experiences, including their reactions to racism itself, further to the margins, where they remain unheard and unvalidated. This further contributes to their experience of feeling unseen, and like they do not belong.

Another reason why these conversations are so important, perhaps even healing, is because that internal dialogue where BIPOC incessantly navigate between an experience of being welcomed and a sense of being excluded gets externalised when it is actively discussed and explored by their organisation or team. This provides BIPOC with a reprieve, albeit temporary, from that tiresome internal dialogue. This reprieve is an opportunity to repair and restore from the exhaustion that results from fighting this battle primarily against oneself.

For these kinds of essential conversations and stories to occur, we are required to develop a specific cultural capability. This capability enables us to facilitate and deepen an understanding of those perspectives which are less familiar to us by being as, if not more, interested in the experience of a different viewpoint as we are to bolstering and defending our own perspective. We are therefore required to modify (or upgrade) the usual orientation which dictates how we converse; this is the practical application which creates the kind of culture that cultivates belonging, because people feel their experience matters to others.

The power and potential embedded in this kind of conversation is that, even if it does not result in team members changing their point of view, it creates more connection between the holders of those diverse, perhaps even opposing, perspectives. This is because for most people, the need for their experience to be validated and witnessed, is far more important for their sense of belonging, than their need for their opinion to be agreed with.

The interesting thing is that, even if connection gets strengthened through a conversation about inclusion, diversity, or racism, this connection is transferable across to more functional and performance-based parts of the organisation. We have all had the experience of a coach or teacher who we felt really saw us, or the team that we felt really connected to, because we believed we belong, and how that improved our performance. I have facilitated numerous sessions where an atmosphere of psychological safety was created that enabled team members to share their experiences on quite a personal level. The connection created in these sessions gets organically transferred into the boardroom, or the sporting field, in a way where it results in clear up-ticks in performance.

Connection is difficult to quantify, and therefore challenging to measure. But we all feel it; we feel when it is there, and we also notice its absence. But make no mistake: just because we can't measure it, it does not mean that it is not a significant driver of performance.

These kinds of conversations necessitate that team members engage in a more personal way. This requires a certain level of authenticity, openness, perhaps even vulnerability. However, corporate cultures pride themselves on being resilient, tough, impervious – and, in many ways, they have to be. Business is demanding and cutthroat, and in a competitive market economy there is no space for weakness or vulnerability. Additionally, people fear that any demonstration of weakness or vulnerability will be associated with a lack of confidence, competence, or character, and that, in the future, that vulnerability will be used against them at a critical moment – for example, being denied a promotion, or not being selected for a team.

The developmental focus required in order to address sticking point #1 is to foster a culture where people feel sufficiently safe to share on a more personal level. This requires cultivating psychological safety within the organisation. Psychological safety, much like trust or even love, cannot be enforced or mandated. It is something which must be built and then fortified over time. And much like a muscle, it requires regular work to maintain and strengthen its effectiveness. We will discuss psychological safety in greater depth in chapters twelve and thirteen.

For many people, being immersed in a psychologically safe culture – one that is truly inclusive – is a potent antidote for the hurts and wounds resulting from the exclusion they may have experienced in other (previous) environments and contexts. This is because the messages embodied by a psychologically safe and inclusive culture present a compelling rebuttal to the narratives which BIPOC and people belonging to other marginalised social identities may have internalised. In contrast to the message, 'You are not worthy, you are not welcome, we don't want you here', the narrative characterised by an inclusive culture is:

You are welcome. We see you. And we value the totality of your humanity and your experience.

When this is people's day-to-day experience of the culture, it fosters a profound yet unspoken bond between team members, which in turn cultivates connection and belonging and, thus, performance. This is one of the powerful benefits of an inclusive culture.

Alisha's [pseudonym] story

'I can't think of just one experience, because they are accumulative. There are daily events that you experience all the time. Some of them are overt – for example, being called racist names – but others are not as obvious,' Alisha responded when I asked her about her experiences of racism in her work environment.

Alisha is a cisgendered woman of colour of South Asian heritage and is a social worker in the Australian community services sector. She went on to say that, when she started as a social worker, DEI was not even called DEI, it was called 'cultural competency'. And as a person of colour you were always given the cultural competency portfolio, so it was your job to drive cultural competency in your workplace. With a wry smile, she recalled that even bringing traditional food to the workplace was considered a cultural competency, because it was something that exposed the predominantly White workforce to other cultures.

Alisha spoke about the lack of representation of BIPOC at the senior levels of the organisations that she has worked for. 'I have only worked with one Indigenous person in a mainstream workplace. Most of the Aboriginal people I have worked with are in specialist Aboriginal organisations because it is just not safe anywhere else. In my workplace now, it's probably only 15% people of colour, and none of us are at the top. Once you get past senior workers and managers, there are no people of colour in executive positions.'

Alisha gave an example of the racism she and her colleagues get exposed to, and the complexity of having to deal with it. She recalled the experience of her colleague and the family of the young person he was supporting saying, 'We don't want no fucking Black man in our house.' Her colleague was left thinking, 'How can I use myself as a resource to try to shift this family's perspective?'. Alisha's main point was that no one could even help him think that through, because nobody else in his team was a person of colour.

As she continued to reflect, she commented, 'It is hard. And there is a cost, but nobody talks about the cost, and nobody acknowledges that cost. The cost comes from me using myself as a tool to help this person work through their racism. I think, if I can get this person to see me as a human being, then the next time they come across another Brown woman, they just don't think, "all Brown women are [insert racial stereotype]," because there was this one Brown woman called Alisha who they kind of liked.'

Alisha went on to say, 'That is as much as we can hope for, but you are putting yourself in a position where you are under siege all the time. And there is a cost to all this, and somebody needs to help us think about if we are up to paying the cost or do we need to sit it out sometimes. But who helps you to think that through? And what does the organisation do to support you to say, "I don't want to work with this family, I am not up for it."'

As a result, there is a significant impact on Alisha and her BIPOC colleagues. 'As a social worker, when you work with people who have multiple and complex needs, and who are marginalised, you experience racism from your client group on a daily basis. And your workplace is accommodative of that. That is a challenging thing to reconcile.'

Alisha spoke about how, when she experiences racism, her White leadership never knows what to do to support her, and although it's part of her job, that doesn't negate the impact that it has on her. She said, 'The tendency of social workers, youth workers, and community development workers is to always place the problem in the environment and not the person, but that doesn't change the impact. And your White leadership don't know how to supervise it. What I have found is that it is just not talked about. Another person of colour in my workplace said to me, "I don't bother raising this with my supervisor because I know they don't know what to do with this."'

Alisha also spoke about the defensiveness of [White] people when it comes to acknowledging and addressing racism, and how the board and leadership of her organisation do not see it as their role or their responsibility. 'In [her organisation], nobody is talking about racism. The defensiveness in White populations, including *the community services sector, is immense. The last time the organisation did a DEI survey, less than 20% of the staff responded and they were mostly all the happy White people, who commented how wonderful the organisation is in terms of DEI.'*

Alisha commented that, 'Staff who are people of colour did not even bother responding to the survey because they believe management doesn't listen to them anyway. But management took the 20% of people who did respond as confirmation to say how well we are doing in terms of DEI. Ironically, around the same time the survey was being conducted, the organisation had completed an antiracism training with frontline staff, but the board and senior leadership team refused to do it.'

Finally, she commented on where Australia as a country is positioned in its commitment to addressing structural racism. While she is referring to an Australian context, I believe her perceptions are equally valid across various countries and in many organisational contexts. 'When organisations, like many organisations in the community services sector, have been set up by White people and are run by White people, there is a massive element of White supremacy. It is in the DNA of the organisation. The feminist sector, as well as the LGBTQIA+ community, has been amazing in advocating for more inclusion and equity. But there has been no push around racism, so it has not shifted at all.'

'This country [Australia] is not ready, has never been ready, for a conversation about racism. We don't even have plaques at [Aboriginal] massacre sites across Australia; we still have Captain Cook [who colonised Australia on the behalf of the British] everywhere. I don't even think Aboriginal history is taught in Australian schools. I don't know a single school where you can learn an Aboriginal language as your choice – we are still teaching French. The community services sector, while left-leaning, is still indicative of Australian culture and organisations generally.'

Developmental Sticking Point #2:
Unleashing latent energy through racial equity

I feel tired a lot. Not so tired that I can't go to the gym, make dinner for myself, or do what I need to fulfil my professional obligations, but rather more of a low-grade, sometimes barely perceptible, kind of tiredness. It has become far more noticeable in recent years. I have attributed this fatigue to some combination of my erratic sleep patterns, the need to better curb my sweet tooth, that I should do more cardio in the gym, and, perhaps most notably, my middle-aged body. All these reasons, no doubt, contribute to my tiredness to some extent. But what I am becoming increasingly aware of is how exhausting structural racism is for those of us who have Black and Brown bodies.

For many BIPOC, just living, existing, functioning, let alone pursuing one's goals and performing at a high level in workplaces and other environments where dynamics of structural racism are still prevalent, is exhausting. This is partly because of the cultural load that BIPOC carry in these settings.

Cultural load is a direct consequence of structural discrimination.[22.] It Is the additional, and frequently unseen, work that BIPOC are required to do within workplaces. More obvious examples of cultural load are where there is the expectation that BIPOC are the representative and/ or an advocate for their entire race, particularly at various cultural awareness events or in discussions about racism.

---

22 I have used 'structural discrimination' rather than 'structural racism' because cultural load refers to the 'load' carried by *any* minority or socially marginalised group. Therefore, apart from BIPOC, people who identify as LGBTQIA+, differently abled, neurodiverse, from a working-class background, etc., will also experience some version of a cultural load.

We see numerous examples of cultural load in Alisha's story. Firstly, in how it was assumed that she, as the person of colour, would be responsible for the cultural competency portfolio. But then also in the immeasurable cost of working in an environment where she is consistently encountering racism, with little or no support in how to think through these experiences and attend to the impact they have on her. There are many examples of cultural load where the work being done is less obvious, primarily because it is being done internally, and so oblivious to most people it. Here are just a few examples.

The first is the perpetual battle that plays out within many BIPOC in order for them to feel welcome. We discussed this in developmental sticking point #1. This internal tug-of-war, between people's intrinsic need to belong and their tendency to emotionally evict themselves, epitomises actual experiences they have endured so many times. Irrespective of their momentary position on either side of the rope, such a tug-of-war creates an ongoing depletion of energy, much like a slow leak in a tyre. This is because, once this pattern becomes internalised, it takes on a life of its own and gets played out incessantly regardless of the dynamics of inclusion and exclusion that are occurring in the external environment or the culture.

Then there is the constant assessment of, 'Was that racist, or am I just imagining it?' We see this in Christina's story (page 63), where she must constantly question if her lack of career advancement is due to racism, particularly when she is not getting feedback that there are deficits in her technical knowledge or skills, or other performance indicators which might otherwise explain it. One of the impacts of structural racism is that it minimises or negates the lived experience of BIPOC. It does this by decentralising their emotions and pushing their reactions further into the shadows where, away from the focus of the spotlight, they remain largely unvalidated and unwitnessed. This creates a kind of paranoia where BIPOC second-guess, perhaps even negate, their own reactions. When there hasn't been a pattern or a lived experience of your emotions being validated, it feels all the more foreign to validate them for yourself. So, when faced with a racist transgression, subtle or overt, intentional or unintentional, BIPOC frequently have to interrogate their own responses, searching for evidence to justify their reaction whilst simultaneously scanning for signs of an overreaction to verify their paranoia.

This is exhausting!

And, finally, there is the naming of racism in the attempt to bring it to people's awareness, because sometimes advocating for your own rights, your own dignity, and your own experience of equity, feels like a matter of life and death. Where there is structural racism in a particular environment or culture, people need to shine a light on it by calling out what is happening. And yet, unsurprisingly, in these same environments, often this message is not particularly well-received or appreciated. As a result, there is the propensity to kill the messenger as a way of invalidating, minimising, or deflecting the message itself. BIPOC are therefore placed in a painful no-win situation. Speaking out means they will almost invariably encounter some hostility and resistance to their message, perhaps even retribution at a future point, but staying silent means having to deal with the internal hostility and the self-interrogation that accompanies the belief that they may have 'sold out'.

All of this takes energy – depleting, exhausting, sometimes soul-shattering energy. This is one of the many contributing factors to the inequity in outcomes for BIPOC in comparison to non-BIPOC when it comes to longevity, chronic disease, addictions, mental health challenges, and other key measures.

This is what contributes to the effectiveness of structural racism, and why it has been so successful in perpetuating itself over so many centuries. Inequity is perpetuated by a transfer of energy from one race to another. And when BIPOC have less energy, they are less able to fight against and challenge the system and to advocate for themselves. Furthermore, there is a propensity to overlay stereotypes and use racial tropes to frame as dysfunctional or irrational what are in fact normal and justifiable reactions to inequity and oppression. This means that the fear of being perceived as the angry, crazy, or lazy Black or Brown person creates a further barrier to fully advocating for themselves and giving voice to the frustration, the rage, and the despair that gets constellated in response to these experiences.

The exhaustion and depletion that people do or don't experience, based on their race (or another dimension of their social identity), is a function of privilege:

> *Privilege is the rights, benefits, and advantages granted or available only to particular groups. Within the context of race and racism, privilege is the rights, benefits, and advantages granted to groups based on their race. The belief of the privileged group purport that these benefits and advantages are available to all people, when in fact they are only consistently available to the privileged.*[23]

If we once again think about our two friendly fish, privilege means living a life where, for the most part, the current flows in the same direction that you want to go. The current assists you to get there faster and to expend less energy in how you do it. Of course, utilising some hard work and desire will get you there even faster, but the key point is that the current itself is providing you with a degree of assistance that you might not always be aware of.

---

23   Adapted from: Robin DiAngelo, *What Does It Mean to Be White?: Developing White Racial Literacy* (New York, NY: Peter Lang Publishing, 2012), 52

In contrast, our other friendly fish has the current flowing in the opposite direction to where they want to go. This means they must work twice as hard to make half the progress. If the current against them is particularly strong, even maintaining their status quo requires an enormous expenditure of effort and energy. Christina alludes to this when she comments, *'It feels like we have to do extra just to get to the same place as a White person. We [Black people] cannot do the bare minimum at all, there is no bare minimum for us.'*

> *What makes structural racism exhausting is the lack of privilege that BIPOC have relative to their non-BIPOC counterparts, which manifests as the need to swim against the current on an ongoing basis.*

But privilege is an interesting concept ...

On a recent run (working on my cardio) I faced a stiff headwind on the way out. I could really feel its resistance and how hard I was having to work just to counteract the force of the wind as it was pushing me backwards. I remember thinking, *After my turnaround point and, on my way home, it's going to feel so much easier with the wind at my back.* But once I turned around, the force of the wind was nowhere near as noticeable. I knew it was still there, I could feel the assistance it was giving me. But if I didn't focus on it, I could easily forget the benefits and the relative ease (in comparison to running into a headwind) that I was experiencing with the wind at my back.

My run that day is very much how privilege works. When we haven't got privilege and we are continuously running into the headwinds of life, we can't help but notice the resistance we are required push against; it consumes our energy and our focus because it demands so much of us simply to counteract its effects. On the other hand, when we have the tail wind of privilege at our back, it is much more difficult to notice its beneficial effects, even though it is the exact same force that we experience as a headwind. As a tailwind, the presence, and also the benefits, of privilege are much more easily overlooked.

Deconstructing (and de-pathologising) White privilege

Part of the current zeitgeist has resulted in 'White privilege' being an insult. We have become so polarised around race, so incapable having constructive and meaningful discourse about it, that saying someone has White privilege is tantamount to inflicting upon them a vicious insult. The resulting narrative creates a propensity to see privilege as sociopathic. Yet, one of the complex aspects of White privilege is that the advantages and benefits it bestows are most often not conscious, intentional, or personal choices. White privilege is a set of biases and advantages that have been normalised by structural racism; its foundational elements, therefore, are more systemic than they are personal.

If you belong to a race that benefits from certain entitlements and advantages, a natural, almost predictable response to the notion of privilege is to vehemently make the case that everything you have achieved, you have worked hard for. And that, as part of this process, you have had to develop essential skills and knowledge, make sacrifices, and work hard to overcome personal obstacles. You should therefore be credited for the totality of your success and be allowed to enjoy the benefits of that success, free from the scourges of guilt and shame.

Firstly, it is important to notice the defensiveness in this response, and then to believe that there must be a good reason for this defensiveness. And this reason is most likely that, for the person holding this viewpoint, their perception is that they are being attacked or judged, or that their sacrifice and hard work are being dismissed or refuted.

If what I just said elicited a defensive response, then you have my apologies for being clumsy in how I framed the concept of privilege, which resulted in you feeling personally attacked.

In which case, please allow me to try again ...

It is not justifiable, perhaps even reasonable, to hold an individual person personally responsible for the privileges they enjoy, or to blame them for where they are less identified with, or less conscious about, those privileges. This is in the same way that our friendly fish who benefits from a favourable current cannot be blamed for the fact that the current favours them. A bit like running with a tailwind, they are probably unaware of the benefits they reap because of their privilege (apologies for the mixed metaphors).

Part of the challenge of dismantling racism is that words like 'privilege' have been weaponised and used to attack those who have privilege, which is usually non-BIPOC. This overlooks the fact that privilege and its many expressions are themselves a consequence of structural racism. Additionally, trying to discuss and address something as complicated as privilege in an atmosphere of combativeness and blame erodes the psychological safety necessary to have meaningful and productive conversations about the subject.

Furthermore, in naming privilege, there is the assumption that those who have it, are expected to somehow give it up, to benevolently donate it to those who have less privilege. However, somebody cannot give away privilege because it is not theirs to give. People can give away privilege to the same extent that those fishes control the current in which they swim, or that I can conjure the wind so that what was once a tailwind now becomes a headwind. Therefore, being critical or punitive of those with privilege, even those who are less conscious about their privilege, is not justified. Nor is it helpful in our quest to build an inclusive and high-performance culture.

The critical aspect of working with privilege is simply acknowledging its existence. It's acknowledging that some people, based on nothing they have worked for or earned, and due mostly to a combination of luck and the genetic lottery, happen to be swimming with the current. Yes, in all likelihood they have worked hard and made sacrifices, but their privilege has contributed to some extent, even minimally, to the success and the benefits they now enjoy.

The strong, almost visceral, reaction that some people, particularly BIPOC, have to the notion of White privilege is probably driven less by the fact that it actually occurs, and more likely a result of people who enjoy the benefits of that privilege, denying its very existence. In other words, most people are okay with the fact that a portion of the success, the happiness, and the sense of ease that someone has is because they happen to belong to a race whose journey through life has been assisted by the current.

What makes people angry is when those same people apportion *all* their success and achievements to their own intelligence, capability, and work ethic. This is because of the implication that, if somebody has not had the same levels of success, they must be lacking in the intelligence, capability, and work ethic required to achieve that success. Many of us will see (and feel) the racial stereotypes and tropes to do with intelligence and work ethic that are entrenched within, but also perpetuated by, this kind of thinking.

> *It is the activation of these racist stereotypes and tropes that, in part, contributes to privilege being inflammatory and offensive when it remains unacknowledged.*

But for BIPOC to outwardly express a reaction, some kind of uninhibited defiance, to these stereotypes is complicated because it runs the risk of them personifying the very stereotype they are already branded with. In not wanting to react and become the angry, irrational, or disruptive BIPOC, they have no choice but to dampen down their reactions; reactions which are reasonable and natural responses to unacknowledged White privilege and the stereotyping it precipitates. When there is neither the freedom nor the safety to express these reactions externally, BIPOC are required to manage these reactions internally. This demands enormous amounts of psychological and emotional energy, which ideally would be better utilised in the pursuit of organisational outcomes.

Developmental focus for sticking point #2: Develop our 'energy intelligence' so we can start exploring performance through the lens of energy

The way we humans think about and approach life is largely informed by our basic drives and instincts. It takes considerable emotional and psychological energy to transform these drives from being primarily biological and centred around our own survival and comfort – for example, I want, I must have (food, shelter, sex, security, control, etc.) – into ways of thinking and behaving that are in service of the broader culture and about something beyond ourselves. In a similar vein, it takes an organisation intentionality and a great deal of energy to transform its basic survival needs, its tendency to be seduced by the frenzy of day-to-day deliverables, into more conscious and functional patterns of thinking that not only support inclusion and belonging but also drive sustained performance.

Additionally, apart from transforming these basic drives and survival needs, everything else we do also requires energy! Energy is the fundamental ingredient needed to make things happen.

To move around the office, to strategise, to think, to create shared accountability, to collaborate, to resolve differences, to align team members, to strongly express your viewpoint, or to listen intently to another's viewpoint, all require energy. So, whether it is the energy of capital; the energy of innovation; the energy of motivation; or the literal physical, emotional, and mental energy that people require to perform optimally in their roles, the availability of energy and how efficiently organisations utilise that energy are critical determinants of success.

However, the amount of energy in an organisational system is finite. There is a finite number of staff; a finite amount of funds available in the budget; a finite number of hours in the week; and individual team members have a limit and a finiteness in the amount of physical and mental energy they can expend. Organisations can increase the number of staff, but this will obviously cost more money; they can increase working hours, but this will further deplete team members' physical and mental energy. Because energy in the system is finite, increasing input in one element results in a trade-off where there is a reduction in output in another element.

If these finite resources get depleted, misused, or abused – resulting in there being pockets of energy that are left unharnessed and/or underutilised – apart from simply being wasteful, this undermines the ability of the organisation to perform optimally. In order to perform optimally, an organisation is therefore required to harness and then leverage the entirety of the finite energy within its system.

High-performance organisations and their leaders are adept at thinking about performance through the lens of energy utilisation.

They have developed an intelligence around energy that enables them to utilise every kilojoule of energy available to them in a way which is aligned to, and supportive of, the purpose and vision of the organisation. So, while the resources, in the form of energy, available to an organisation may be finite, its ability to be resourceful in how effectively it utilises this energy is, in theory, infinite.

Why is this relevant to our task of building an antiracist and high-performing organisation?

When structural racism perpetuates inequity, there is a transfer of energy away from BIPOC; this is commonly experienced as an energetic cost or a depletion of their vitality. This is partly due to continually performing against the current of privilege. But there is also an energetic drawdown for BIPOC when they bear the weight of projections and biases fuelled by stereotypes, that results when White privilege remains unacknowledged. Additionally, and as we have previously discussed, having to carry a cultural load due to the internal tug-of-war to feel included, the ongoing assessment of, 'Was that racist or am I imagining it?', and the cost of calling out racism, often in the face of resistance and hostility, is also exhausting.

The performance benefit of moving towards an antiracist culture is that stopping the depletion of energy that BIPOC experience due to structural racism can unleash significant amounts of latent energy. This energy now becomes available to the broader organisational system. This is because, while the impacts of unacknowledged privilege and cultural load are experienced by BIPOC personally, the foundational elements which give rise to these dynamics are in fact systemic.

The organisation now has the opportunity to re-purpose this energy. One of the ways it can be used is to transform the organisation's basic survival needs – its compulsion to only focus on its most rudimentary or urgent deliverables – into the higher-order thinking required to pursue organisational excellence and sustained performance.

Additionally, as this transformation continues, key drivers of performance, such as motivation, engagement, and collaboration, which run alongside energy levels, become much better funded. For example, in a culture littered with unchallenged stereotypes about the intelligence, work ethic, and education levels of BIPOC, it is less likely that teams will function harmoniously and collaborate seamlessly. After all, nobody wants to work alongside, risk their reputation for, or step onto the (sporting) field of battle with someone they believe is inferior to them in some capacity or will let them down in critical moments.

Acknowledging the existence of privilege provides a powerful rebuttal to these narratives and stereotypes about BIPOC; this begins to transform those cultural barriers to collaboration, which in turn provides teams with a significant performance advantage. This is because, in a team where there are subtle and unspoken barriers to collaboration, there will never be optimal performance.

Building a high-performance culture also requires a re-evaluation of those systems of thinking – the cultural operating systems – that may be out of date. For example, understanding that the foundational elements of White privilege are, in fact, systemic allows organisations to explore the dynamics of motivation, engagement, and collaboration from the perspective of their cultural enablers and barriers, as opposed to only individual capability. For some organisations, this change in thinking may represent a significant 'systems upgrade'.

When underperformance in these crucial areas is not scrutinised, at least in part, through a framework of privilege and structural discrimination, it places the weight of responsibility, perhaps even the blame, solely on the shoulders of the individual. As a result, forged by stereotypes, biases, and scapegoating, beliefs can emerge purporting that a BIPOC colleague is the weak link or the person having the issue; this belief can eventually morph into the dominant narrative. For BIPOC already grappling with a cultural load of swimming against the current, this additional burden can jeopardise not only their performance but also their wellbeing.

Addressing cultural and performance gaps via an approach only focused on individual capability diverts our attention away from a more systems-based analysis where we are open to also seeing the issue with the system itself. How can we upgrade operating systems when part of our analysis does not include an evaluation of the extent to which the system engenders an experience of inclusion, belonging, and connection for the people who are required to perform within that system? Without a commitment to regularly assess and upgrade cultural operating systems, we are destined to keep utilising antiquated or ineffective cultural systems. This results in an inefficient use of energy, possibly an incompatibility of essential 'programs', and a cultural fragility that is antithetical to a high-performance culture.

So, in order to address sticking point #2, the developmental focus requires us to change the way we think about energy and those aspects which run alongside it, such as motivation, engagement, and collaboration. It also requires us to develop our energy intelligence so that we appreciate the finiteness of energy and also explore the ways that the culture, systems, and processes of the organisation deplete, underutilise, or waste energy. This applies for the organisational system in general. However, given our task of building an antiracist organisation, we need to explore how those behaviours and narratives that are subtly embedded in the lived culture of the organisation result in a depletion of energy, specifically for BIPOC. This includes working to better understand how White privilege manifests itself, including how, when it remains unacknowledged, there is the perpetuation of racial stereotypes and tropes. And then being able to frame and acknowledge its existence, whilst at the same time doing it in a manner which does not denigrate or shame non-BIPOC.

Developmental Sticking Point #3: Re-visioning our approach to confidence and self-doubt

For the most part, systems of oppression are impersonal; they are not intending to target or create advantage or disadvantage for any individual person. This is one of the many complexities of this work: while structural racism itself is largely impersonal, it's difficult not to personalise its consequences because the way it impacts people occurs in such an intensely deep and personal manner.

(Continued from page 50)

I had received those messages so many times – that I did not belong, and that what I was feeling, my experience, and perhaps even my life did not matter – that I now believed those messages …

This is because the external messages we receive about our worth, at some point in time, become part of our psychological landscape and therefore contribute to our inner dialogue; these are the origins of internalised oppression.

Internalised oppression is when the way the external oppressor or oppressive system views, values, and treats people, becomes the way they view, value, and treat themselves.

This internal dialogue determines how we see ourselves, what we think we are capable of, and what we believe we are worthy of. American author, theologian, and civil rights activist Howard

Thurman once said, 'If we are despised long enough, we eventually despise ourselves'. What he is describing is the process where, if we experience abuse and oppression, over time we will internalise the oppressor. Internalised oppression can be seen in Christina's story (page 63) in the way she continually questions her worth and her position in the company: 'When I was younger, I think it really affected my self-esteem. It affected my confidence levels. I had to constantly ask myself, "Do you belong here? Do you deserve this? Did they make the right choice when they hired me?" There was an overarching feeling, all the time, of not deserving something.'

This is what makes abuse, discrimination, and bullying so insidious and damaging. When the world outside sends us the message, in multiple ways, that we are not important or that our life does not matter, we can hopefully retreat to the safety and sanctuary of a house, our bedroom, or perhaps even a family – a space which buffers us from the hurtful voices of the world around us. But once this oppressive voice takes residence within one's own psyche; there is no escaping its impact because there is no longer a buffer. It sits deeply within us and, with skill and precision, drip-feeds its venomous narratives into our internal dialogue, much like a slowly leaking tap—

drip … drip … drip …

Each droplet is infused with self-doubt and self-loathing that, over time, erodes our dignity, self-esteem, and self-confidence. And because we cannot help but take ourselves with us wherever we go, those messages become an ongoing and consistent aspect of our internal narrative. Once that voice has made itself comfortable and has resided there long enough, we eventually cannot distinguish that voice from our own thinking, because, in reality, that voice is now part of us.

And it doesn't just have to be the messages from our own personal experience of abuse and bullying; we also internalise the messages from broader society and the cultural soup in which we all swim. Through their repetitive and subliminal nature, these messages also, in due course, get lodged within our psyches. And in some way, we cannot help this. The cultural context we exist in, both societal as well as organisational, has an undeniable and pervasive influence on how we value and see ourselves.

As such, a woman within a culture where elements of structural sexism and misogyny are still present is going to internalise some sexism into her inner dialogue, and then sometimes assess her own worth through a lens of objectification. In a society where anti-Semitism and White supremacy are tolerated, a Jewish person can't help but absorb some of these thoughts of existential threat, and so feel the need to continually justify their existence. When we rarely see same-sex couples, trans, or gender diverse people represented positively (as opposed to stereotypically) in mainstream media, TV, and movies, individuals from the LGBTQIA+ community will internalise the viewpoint that they are not valued and welcomed as part of mainstream culture. These are just a few obvious examples, but similar dynamics will play out for all types of structural discrimination.

For each of us, this internalised oppressor will have a different voice and a distinct tactical approach in the way it undermines our confidence and self-esteem. But the underlying messages that it assaults us with are remarkably similar: 'You don't belong here. You are messed up and broken beyond repair. You are worthless. We hate you, get out of here. You are ugly/stupid/insignificant. We are more important than you. We don't even consider you to be human, so your feelings and your pain do not matter.'

And while, as in my case, we are not always aware or fully conscious of that voice, the way it manifests in our day-to-day existence will be all too familiar: anxiety, stress, self-doubt, eating disorders, depression, feelings of isolation and loneliness, self-harm, etc. Others deploy what, on the surface, at least, looks like a more functional strategy: a driving ambition to succeed. Behind this drive and ambition is the need to feel a sense of power, belonging, and self-assurance; experiences that, because of structural discrimination and/or what we were deprived of in our formative years, we may not have a sturdy psychological pattern for. We are desperate to believe that this success will deliver the ammunition to combat the inner voice that continually whispers into our ear: 'You will never amount to anything.'

But of course, no amount of external validation and success is sufficient when what we really need is a balm for those hurts and wounds we carry inside and rarely allow others to see. This need can give rise to a compulsive, almost addictive need for success, which of course is not sustainable and is often decoupled from other important areas of life and well-being. The balm we really need to sooth and abate these feelings of insecurity and self-doubt is to build the links of causality between these debilitating feelings and the system or the culture which gives rise to these harsh criticisms.

These experiences feel so personal, so directly attributable to our own inadequacy; however, building these links of causality begins to explicitly address and debunk the peddled illusion that we have adopted and then taken on as fact: that there is something inherently and intrinsically wrong with us.

Developmental focus for sticking point #3:
Work on understanding and addressing the causal links between structural racism
and confidence

Resilience, courage, composure, and self-assurance form a cluster of traits that fall loosely under the umbrella of 'confidence'. Confidence is the extent to which people believe in their ability to effectively apply their knowledge and skills through the requirements of their role and within the particular context they are required to perform. Whether it be in the boardroom or on the sporting field, the confidence and ability to apply your skills and knowledge, especially in those critical moments or under pressure, is an essential ingredient of high-performance.

For the most part, confidence and its associated cluster of traits have been explored and then addressed from the perspective of personal psychology. The underpinning assumption of this work has been that an individual's ability to access and then demonstrate confidence resides primarily within the sphere of their individual psychology. However, what this approach fails to acknowledge is the impact the cultural context has on someone's confidence. Therefore, understanding the dynamics of how people internalise certain aspects of the racial hierarchy is essential not only in building an antiracist organisation but also to effectively address challenges of confidence and self-doubt.

Internalised oppression occurs when those narratives embedded in the culture of an organisation, but also in the broader culture, about someone's relative position in the racial hierarchy get internalised to the point where those narratives now become a regular contributor to that person's internal dialogue. Therefore, for a BIPOC who is living and working within a context where there are elements of structural racism, there is a high likelihood that these internalised narratives will eventually lead to periods of insecurity, self-doubt, perhaps even self-loathing. Obviously, these severely impact someone's self-confidence and therefore their ability to take up their organisational role in an optimal manner. The crucial point here is that internalised oppression is a direct manifestation of structural racism. In other words, while internalised oppression itself plays out deep within the psychology of the individual, its origins are from structural racism embedded in the culture, and therefore beyond personal psychology.

Of course, personal traits such as confidence and self-belief are complex in their origins and have multiple factors which contribute to their development. So, suggesting that someone's entire sense of confidence, or lack thereof, is based purely on internalised oppression is obviously over-simplistic. However, the reverse is also true. Underestimating the impact cultural norms and dynamics of structural discrimination have on an individual's confidence means we may not be addressing the underlying causes of someone's lack of confidence. This is what is most likely occurring in those team members where the usual support and coaching approaches, which are tailored primarily around their personal psychology, are not delivering the desired outcomes in building the confidence they require to perform at optimal levels.

Understanding and then appreciating that what, on the surface, might look like self-doubt or a lack of confidence actually has its roots (partially) in dynamics of structural racism is a key driver of performance.

Furthermore, when we disregard the impact of internalised oppression, we place the totality of responsibility for that person's confidence onto them; we imply that it is somehow their fault, and that their lack of confidence is indicative of some personal deficiency. This places an incredible burden on the individual themselves. In situations where they may already be grappling with the complexities and experiences of devaluation because of structural discrimination, this additional burden not only further undermines their confidence and their ability to perform optimally, but it also jeopardises their mental health.

A more effective strategy is to frame an aspect of their deficit in confidence as having nothing to do with their personal psychology or where they are inadequate in some way, but rather is a direct consequence of the narratives they have internalised due to structural racism. This can be incredibly relieving for their mental health, and supportive of them building strategies that reinvigorate their confidence.

An antiracist culture understands the structural underpinnings of someone's lack of confidence *as well as* those elements related to their personal psychology. As such, it integrates both these elements into how that person receives support, therefore creating a more complete solution to these challenges. This philosophical approach to addressing self-doubt and confidence acknowledges the impersonal nature of systems of oppression, but it also appreciates that the impact is experienced as an assault on one's humanity.

The more clearly we can understand and address the underlying dynamics that result in a lack of confidence or self-doubt, the better we can harness latent capabilities by enabling team members to believe in, and therefore access, their skills and knowledge in a more consistent manner.

But this process of internalisation does not only apply to BIPOC; it also applies to non-BIPOC. The same system of oppression that perpetuates the narrative that BIPOC are inferior and therefore less deserving of certain advantages and benefits also reinforces that non-BIPOC are naturally superior and are therefore deserving of those benefits. This is known as internalised domination or superiority:

Internalised superiority is when members of the privileged group are conditioned to see their positions as natural and earned, and to therefore internalise that they are more entitled of the resources of society. As a result, the members of this group are affirmed, made visible, and represented in diverse and positive ways.[24]

This automatic affirmation and positive reinforcement of one's identity creates a degree of complacency which is not always conducive to optimal performance. If we once again go back to our two friendly fish, that 'more capable' fish will have a tendency to assume that their superior swimming ability is based entirely on their own intrinsic capability, talent, and work ethic. They therefore attribute their success purely to themselves, whilst diminishing, or perhaps ignoring, the inherent benefits they receive from the favourable currents.

Part of human nature is, when we are granted success that we have not fully worked for or earned, we overestimate our ability and therefore underestimate the work it may take to achieve similar outcomes in the absence of the supportive currents of privilege. In this way, while structural racism provides certain benefits and advantages for non-BIPOC, it is not always supportive of their overall development. While internalised oppression and internalised superiority are both consequences of structural racism, neither of them are particularly conducive to high performance.

---

24 Adapted from: Robin DiAngelo, *What Does It Mean to Be White?: Developing White Racial Literacy* (New York, NY: Peter Lang Publishing, 2012)

So, in order to address sticking point #3, the developmental focus requires to us continually challenge ourselves in the way we think about and approach confidence and self-doubt. It is only natural that we will slip back into our traditional way of thinking, which is to explore them primarily through the framework of personal psychology. In these moments, it is crucial that a developmental focus is re-applied to exploring how narratives of structural racism, and other forms of structural discrimination, may have been internalised and so contribute to someone's lack of confidence. This requires leaders, coaches, and facilitators to continually exercise discipline and discernment in seeking more structural solutions to challenges which on the surface appear to be personal.

Developmental Sticking Point #4:
Walking a mile in the shoes of BIPOC

There is a common thread which runs through almost every aspect of structural racism and goes to the core of its most foundational narratives. This is the belief that the feelings, the experiences, the humanity, and indeed the lives of BIPOC, do not matter or, at a bare minimum, they matter less than the lives of non-BIPOC. The whole #BlackLivesMatter movement has been constructed as a direct and powerful rebuttal of this narrative.

In a survey of 222 White medical students and residents, Hoffman et al found that about half endorsed false beliefs about biological differences between Black people and White people.[25] And those who did, also perceived Black people as feeling less pain than White people and were more likely to suggest inappropriate medical treatment for Black patients. In a separate study, Sabin

---

25   Kelly Hoffman, Sophie Trawalter, Jordan Axt and M. Norman Oliver, 'Racial bias in pain assessment and treatment recommendations, and false beliefs about biological differences between blacks and whites' *Proc Natl Acad Sci USA.* 113(16): (April 2016): 4296–4301. Published online 2016 Apr 4. doi: 10.1073/ pnas.1516047113

and Greenwald found paediatricians' implicit (unconscious) attitudes and stereotypes were associated with treatment recommendations.[26] The correlation between unconscious bias and a patient's race was statistically significant for prescribing a narcotic medication for pain following surgery. As paediatricians' implicit pro-White bias increased, prescribing narcotic medication decreased for African American patients but not for the White patients.

One could be forgiven for believing that these findings were representative of something which occurred in the distant past; however, these studies were completed in 2016 and 2012 respectively. One would also be justified in assuming that these kinds of archaic beliefs were more prevalent amongst those with less knowledge about human anatomy and physiology, and who did not have the education to know that, irrespective of our race, our biology is remarkably the same. However, this thinking was evident in medical students, residents, and paediatricians – people who have dedicated years to studying the science of medicine. This is demonstrative of the pervasive power and influence of structural racism. Even in modern times, and amongst those who have been educated to know better, the story that BIPOC are somehow different, and that the pain they feel is less pronounced, manages to infiltrate how medical practitioners think about and approach the treatment and pain management of BIPOC.

These attitudes are the modern-day versions of 19th-century beliefs which suggested that, 'Black people's nerve endings are less sensitive than White people's', or that, 'Black people's skin is thicker than White people's'. However, these beliefs are also a harbinger of something more sinister.

---

26 Janice Sabin and Anthony Greenwald, 'The influence of implicit bias on treatment recommendations for 4 common pediatric conditions: pain, urinary tract infection, attention deficit hyperactivity disorder, and asthma.' *Am J Public Health* 102(5) (May 2012) 988-95

These kinds of beliefs begin to subtly socialise the idea that BIPOC are different, that the supposed differences in the thickness of their skin or the sensitivity of their nerve endings makes them different to non-BIPOC. This is how the process of 'othering' gets initiated. Once we start to accept that another race is different to ourselves, perhaps even not quite as human as ourselves, we have already started to construct the justifications for treating them in a way which pays less attention to the pain they feel. This is because once we deem that another race is different or inferior in comparison to our own, it provides us with the permission to morally disengage from the impact of our actions, whilst simultaneously establishing a belief which we barely notice being assembled.

This belief intimates that they must be less deserving of the same levels of consideration, and of being treated with the same degree of care and humanity that non-BIPOC are automatically entitled to. Therefore, for a BIPOC, being immersed in an environment where structural racism is not being addressed, i.e. where we are not actively moving towards an antiracist culture, means that on a regular basis there is an invalidation of their feelings and a diminution of their experiences. This is a central aspect of the lived experience of structural racism.

For example, there was little regard for the feelings, indeed for the life, of George Floyd in the manner that Derek Chauvin nonchalantly kept his knee on George Floyd's neck until his life literally expired in front of him. Similarly, although nowhere near as extreme, the impact on my feelings and sense of humanity was not considered by those people who spat on me, called me names, and graffitied 'Go home (n-word)' on my textbooks during those first few years of high school. When game after game, month after month, throngs of people booed indigenous AFL (Australian Football League) player Adam Goodes every time he ran onto the field or went near the ball, to the point where he retired from the game he loved, there was clearly very little consideration for his feelings or the impact of these behaviours on his wellbeing. And there was absolutely no value at all placed on the life of African American man James Byrd Jr. when, in 1998, in Jasper, Texas, three White men dragged him behind a pickup truck for 5 km along an asphalt road.

And I am being intentionally confronting in this last example because the only way that people can justify in their minds committing such a heinous act is where there is an underlying belief that that person's life and their humanity has little, if any, value. And apart from my own personal example, these are just a smattering of incidents that have made their way into the public domain, and in no way represents the enormity of ways and times that the experiences and the emotions of BIPOC have been devalued or not considered.

For many, if not most, BIPOC, there will be some resonance, perhaps even a deep familiarity, with receiving the message, sometimes via people's words, or, more commonly, disguised within the subtext of their actions, that, 'Because of your race, your feelings are not quite as important in comparison to those who belong to a more privileged race.'

And herein lies the challenge ...

Because for those of us who don't have a lived experience of structural racism, the idea that there is less value placed on the feelings of BIPOC might come across as a foreign, perhaps even preposterous, suggestion. In a society which purports to value all its citizens equally, surely there cannot be such a large discrepancy in the legitimacy it places on people's feelings as well as their inherent value as a human being?

When we have not experienced racism firsthand, this can be a difficult concept to relate to, or to even accept. But when we deny the actuality of this experience, we are inadvertently embodying its intent, and therefore unintentionally validating its existence. When we are not even open to or, at a minimum, curious about the idea that this is a fundamental feature of BIPOCs' day-to-day experience, we have temporarily become the very thing that we are denying exist: the one who places a lesser premium on the feelings, emotions, and the overall experience of BIPOC.

But what is happening within us that is so challenged by this notion that we diminish, perhaps even deny, its existence so vehemently?

Firstly, for those of us without a lived experience of structural racism, acknowledging that this is a reality for many BIPOC requires us to walk a mile in their shoes. And what is critical is to walk that mile not just from an intellectual or rational perspective, but to also imagine and feel into the physical and emotional impact of your emotions being seen as invalid, dysfunctional, or irrational. This kind of walk requires a degree of open heartedness and, dare I say it, vulnerability.

However, the extent to which we are able to be truly present with the vulnerability of another person is determined by the extent we are able to be present with our own vulnerability. For some of us, being vulnerable challenges our personal comfort zones. This is because it threatens our identity and the sense of imperviousness and toughness which forms the foundations of how we see ourselves. Additionally, and as we discussed in developmental sticking point #1, being vulnerable is usually not part of the cultural norms of our organisation. This is where exploring these sticking points with a developmental focus becomes so critical.

When we individually or collectively get stuck at the limitations of our vulnerability, it often indicates the need for more psychological safety. In a culture where psychological safety is actively fostered, people feel safer to speak from their vulnerability, without fear of being judged or of it being used against them in the future. This is why one of the keys to building an antiracist organisation is having a strategic focus on fostering a psychologically safe culture.

The second reason that it might be difficult to accept the notion that the experiences and feelings of BIPOC are valued less is our personal sense of guilt, responsibility, or perhaps even our shame that somewhere, somehow, we may have contributed to this occurrence. This doesn't necessarily have to be a conscious thought; thoughts like these most often reside in the darker recesses of our subconscious. But whether it is conscious or not, for many of us, the thought that we have contributed, even unintentionally, to the pain of another elicits a trauma reaction.

Yes – and bear with me here – even those with privilege when it comes to racism experience trauma. This is because they experience a kind of moral injury. This is an injury which cannot be seen from the outside because it resides deep within our being and comes about from perpetrating, failing to prevent, or bearing witness to acts that transgress deeply held moral beliefs. These deeply held moral beliefs are more a function of our common humanity and a collective conscience, than of social politics and cultural norms.

The trauma that gets activated because of these moral injuries simultaneously creates a barrier to acknowledging how structural racism invalidates the emotions of BIPOC. This is because to acknowledge this reality, and that we might be even slightly complicit in its furtherance, only adds salt to this pre-existing moral wound. So, the resistance to acknowledging that there is a tendency to invalidate the emotions of BIPOC is as much a function of self-preservation and the need for our own healing as it is a consequence of unconscious privilege. We will discuss the idea of moral injury further in chapter thirteen.

Finally, being able to lean into taking personal responsibility is an essential ingredient in the creation of an antiracist organisation, as well as being potentially relieving for those who do experience racism on a regular basis. However, accepting this burden (of contributing to the invalidation of BIPOC's emotions) purely on our own (non-BIPOC) shoulders once again misjudges the pervasive influence and impact of structural racism. Alternatively, understanding and then actively addressing how structural racism itself influences how we think and behave is perhaps a more critical step in building an antiracist organisation. This is because most of us tend to underestimate the power of the informal cultural norms that are deeply embedded in the psyche of an organisation.

Developmental focus for sticking point #4: Work on optimising discretionary effort by welcoming the totality of people's experience and emotions

Cultivating psychological safety expands cultural comfort zones, enabling people to be sufficiently present with their own vulnerability so they can, in turn, walk a mile in the shoes of BIPOC. This allows them to get a sense of, and therefore develop greater understanding about, an experience which otherwise might be unfamiliar to them.

Secondly, those people who have not had a lived experience of structural racism, and therefore may feel challenged in acknowledging the reality of that experience, may require support in the way that their moral injury is also acknowledged, validated, and then steps taken towards its resolution. This needs to be done in a manner that is free of judgement, shame, and guilt, because, as we have previously discussed, I don't believe these are effective vehicles for sustainable change in either an individual or a collective context. From this perspective, both BIPOC and non-BIPOC need support, validation, and some version of healing. And while I am not making an equivalence between the respective experiences of BIPOC and non-BIPOC, when it comes to structural racism, there is something about our shared humanity and the vulnerabilities we all face which needs to be acknowledged and worked on.

But this is challenging work! This kind of work demands a lot of an organisation and its leaders because its cost is significant, both in the emotional labour as well as the financial and time demands. So, what is the upside to doing this work?

*How is this work in service of the purpose
and vision of the organisation?*

One of the main challenges that organisational cultures face is team member engagement. The degree to which team members are fully engaged correlates very closely with the performance of their team or organisation. But team members can only fully engage with their organisation when their organisation fully engages with the entirety of who they are.

When team members feel they can only bring certain acceptable aspects of their identity and their lived experience to their role, they feel bound to jettison the parts of themselves they believe are less welcomed by the culture. Therefore, building psychologically safe cultures where people can turn up to work and bring with them the various components of their life experience, including those aspects that may be painful or challenging, is a potent driver of employee engagement.

This is because, when people feel psychologically safe, they are inclined to engage more deeply with their work, their teammates, and with their role in general. This in turn drives performance, because greater levels of engagement enhance discretionary effort. Discretionary effort is the difference between what people have to do and what they actually want to do; it is more commonly referred to as 'going the extra mile'. Research shows that engaged individuals deliver an extra 30% in discretionary effort in comparison to disengaged individuals. This can be seen in elite sports where, based on their talent and experience, teams out-perform expectations because they have created a psychologically safe culture where team members feel naturally inclined to deliver discretionary effort. Because discretionary effort is such an effective driver of performance, it is often the X-factor that high-performance teams are continually seeking.

So when organisational cultures are able to validate the emotions of BIPOC and welcome their experiences with tenderness and respect, it creates a persuasive counter-narrative to the one that gets disseminated by structural racism. Moving towards an antiracist organisation creates a culture which, by its words and actions, declares that we welcome the diversity of people's internal experience, including – perhaps even especially – their turmoils and tensions and those experiences that have been a consequence of structural racism.

When this narrative is embedded in the culture and then actively demonstrated via people's behaviours, it embodies, in very pragmatic ways, the essence of inclusion.

In order to address sticking point #4, the focus needs to be on developing organisational capability and cultures so that those people who have a lived experience of structural racism, as well as other forms of discrimination, feel that their emotions are validated and their humanity is seen and respected. This requires us to directly address and transform those dynamics which create barriers to this happening.

These are the four developmental sticking points that organisations are most likely to encounter as we move towards an antiracist culture. What I have hopefully been able to do is to frame how, rather than being a distraction, antiracism is synergistic with building an inclusive and high-performance culture. Done properly, antiracism absolutely provides a performance advantage and commercial benefits to organisations. But in order to realise these benefits, we must continually approach the organisational challenges we are confronted by with a developmental mindset. This commitment to continually seek out the developmental opportunities within every challenge is as important an aspect of our culture as any other.

Reflection #4A:

Assessing capability of the four developmental sticking points

1. From these four developmental sticking points, which one was of most interest to you and/or provided you with the most insight?

2. Which one of the four developmental sticking points does your organisation currently demonstrate the most capability in? How can you leverage this capability further in order to build an antiracist organisation?

3. Which of the four developmental sticking points does your organisation currently demonstrate the least capability in? How can you develop capability in this area in order to build an antiracist organisation?

4. What are the ways that insufficient capability in any of the four developmental sticking points is perpetuating structural racism within your organisation? And how might this insufficient capability also be affecting performance?

5. Given these reflections, what changes can you to make in how you take up your leadership role, informal or formal, in order to address and build capability around these developmental sticking points?

Reflection #4B:

Working on your privilege

For non-BIPOC leaders:

1. Think about the achievements that you are most proud of, and some of your greatest professional successes.

2. Take a moment to celebrate these achievements, knowing that your intelligence, capability, and work ethic were part of the reasons for this success.

3. Now challenge the assumption that the *totality* of your success is due to your own intelligence, capability, and work ethic.

4. Look for ways that your privilege, based on your race, contributed even minimally to your success. For example, you may have experienced more supportive workplace cultures where your contributions were more readily appreciated; or the absence of being stereotyped and facing racial micro aggressions may have created less stressful environments, allowing you to focus more on career growth; or you may have had easier access to influential professional networks due to shared cultural backgrounds and social circles. (hint: if you are not even aware of these or similar benefits, or assumed that these benefits are available to everyone, this might be a good place to start)

5. Imagine how much harder you would have to work, or the additional sacrifices you might have to make, in order to achieve the same levels of success in the absence of your privilege and its associated benefits.

6. How might this additional work and sacrifice negatively impact other areas of your life? For example, your health, your relationship, your family life, your social life, or your overall wellbeing.

7. In your leadership role, informal or formal, how can you use your privilege to support the creation of an inclusive and high-performance culture?

For BIPOC leaders:

1. Think about the achievements that you are most proud of, and some of your greatest professional successes.

2. Without the advantage of White privilege and its associated benefits, what is the hard work and additional sacrifice that you have had to make in order to achieve your success?

3. How might this additional work and sacrifice be negatively impacting other areas of your life? For example, your health, your relationship, your family life, your social life, or your overall wellbeing.

4. In order to achieve your success, are there areas where you have a different kind of privilege? For example, your ability to build great relationships; or the psychological

privilege that comes from being self-aware and having emotional intelligence; or a kind of spiritual privilege where you have deep faith and belief in a force greater than yourself that looks after and guides you.

5. Take a moment to acknowledge that there are also benefits to these privileges that are not consistently available to everyone.

6. How can you use these other forms of privilege to support the creation of an inclusive and high-performance culture?

Part Two:

A practical guide to building an inclusive and high-performance culture

Chapter Five:

The fundamentals of performance – an overview

Performance is a complex phenomenon

For every organisation, performance is imperative. Without some kind of explicit focus on performance, the very survival of the organisation is in jeopardy. This is equally true for a not-for-profit or a social enterprise as it is for a for-profit organisation.

Most commonly, and perhaps most simply, performance can be measured by how well an organisation aligns itself to its purpose and is tracking towards the realisation of its vision (we will discuss purpose and vision in more depth in the following chapters). For a sporting team or organisation, this is relatively clear: to win a certain number of games in the season or to walk away with the premiership cup. In the corporate sector, performance can be measured by annual revenue, EBITDA (Earnings Before Interest, Taxes, Depreciation, and Amortization), or the growth of the business by a certain percentage. Not-for-profits also have performance measures, even though they may not be as obvious. For example, it might be to increase the number of beds in a homeless shelter by a certain number, or to have greater public awareness of domestic and family violence. Or, in the case of a social action organisation, performance might be measured by the extent to which it creates change in legislation or increases political advocacy. These are all ways in which performance can be tracked, and for the most part they are relatively clear and concise. However, while measuring performance itself might be relatively clear, the fundamental elements and principles which drive that performance reside in far murkler waters.

Performance is a complex phenomenon. After working with individual athletes and leaders, teams, and organisations for many years, all with the goal of improving some aspect of their performance, what I can say for sure is that nobody knows the secret recipe which guarantees a consistent and sustainable level of high performance. So many variables go into performance – some of these are sector- or industry-specific, whilst others are more generic. Some of these factors are known to us, such as effective leadership, a great culture, motivation, innovation, discretionary effort, shared accountability, knowledge management, acquisition and retention of key personnel, and talent/skill development. However, it is likely there are also additional factors which influence performance that are unknown to us or are more ephemeral or intangible in nature, therefore making them more difficult to be quantified and codified.

Furthermore, sometimes we can do all the right things which would normally be conducive to reaching our objectives, yet our performance falls short of expectations. I have worked with sporting teams who have done everything right in their physical conditioning, preparation, pregame strategy, etc; however, come game day, the sporting gods deem the other team will be the victor. This unpredictability is one of the things we love most about sport. This level of unpredictability also exists in business. If performance was a perfect science, it would make picking winners on the share market a much simpler process. The inherent volatility of the share market and its unpredictable nature is a function of the uncertain performance of any individual company or the market and broader economic environment, represented in the fluctuating dynamics between buyers and sellers or the bulls and the bears.

Despite our combined efforts to capture and clarify those organisational elements that are essential for performance, there is something unknown, perhaps even mysterious, about how performance can emerge out of the most unlikely situations. And at the same time, even with doing all the right things, which on paper should guarantee us optimal performance, it remains elusive.

Having said all that, and perhaps now being contrarian to my own thesis, there are certain things that organisations can do to increase the probability of performing at a high level. And if these elements are done in a certain way, and in a certain order, it further increases that probability. While doing these things does not guarantee success, very few organisations are able to achieve consistent success and sustainable high performance when these elements, or some version of them, are not in place. In this chapter I will provide a brief overview of these elements and highlight the relationship between them. In subsequent chapters, we will discuss each of them in more detail, as well as exploring how to integrate antiracist initiatives with these elements in order to build an inclusive and high-performance culture.

If we go back to those key measures of performance such as winning titles, EBITDA, or increasing the number of beds in a homeless shelter, it is important that we see them for what they are: they are the outcome or the result of the process an organisation or team utilises to deliver that performance. So while they might reflect the success of that process, the results themselves do nothing to elucidate the process itself. To do that, we need to take a step back from the results and think about the process that was applied to achieve those results, whether they be good, bad, or indifferent. This is challenging because the results themselves are so seductive; we tend to get caught up on and consumed by how many games we won (or lost) or how much profit we made (or didn't) that we don't focus on and deepen our understanding of the process that delivered that particular set of results.

Constructing a clear and simple process which, when followed, maximises an organisation's probability of performing at a consistently high level is the key. A useful way to approach this challenge is to start at the desired end point and then reverse-engineer the process. At Bluestone Edge, we have found there are four key interconnected elements, and to optimise the likelihood of delivering high performance on a consistent basis, organisations must clarify and then build capability around these elements.

Figure 3: The fundamental elements that drive high performance.

Deployment of skills and knowledge drives consistent high performance.

If our desired endpoint is consistent high performance, we must first clearly define what high performance is. If we fail to adequately understand and define that endpoint, then the steps we take to achieve that outcome will be inherently flawed.

From an organisational perspective, high performance is defined as:

> *The ability to consistently deploy skills and knowledge in a way which drives the vision and is in alignment with the strategy, and to do this across the variety of situations and contexts in which the organisation is required to operate.*

So in the case of a mining company, high performance involves being able to execute an agreed-upon strategy, and to do this, given the operational, environmental, economic, and social challenges the organisation may face. For example, where there is resource depletion and more easily accessible deposits are exhausted, companies may be forced to delve into more remote or technically challenging areas, increasing costs and risks. Environmental concerns such as pollution, habitat destruction, and water usage are also critical, and can lead to regulatory pressures and community opposition. Also, given the inherently hazardous nature of mining operations, safety remains a paramount concern. Maintaining high safety standards requires substantial investment in training, technology, and infrastructure. Economic volatility, including fluctuating commodity prices and geopolitical instability, poses another set of challenges, that potentially impact profitability and investment decisions.

Additionally, social license to operate is increasingly crucial, necessitating engagement with local communities and addressing their concerns regarding employment, land rights, and environmental impacts. Finally, political instability and regulatory changes in host countries can further complicate operations, introducing uncertainties and potential disruptions.

For a sporting team, high performance requires being able to execute an overarching strategy, as well as in-game strategies, and to do this given the various contextual challenges it faces. For example, managing athlete injuries, whilst also maintaining peak performance, requires sophisticated and well thought out training and recovery strategies. Balancing demanding training schedules with personal lives and athlete well-being, presents significant challenges for athletes and coaching staff alike. Additionally, financial pressures, including securing sponsorships and managing budgets, add another layer of complexity. And finally, navigating media scrutiny and managing fan expectations, all whilst upholding team morale can be incredibly challenging.

These examples remind us of the multifaceted demands that contribute to the complex nature of organisations and teams achieving sustainable high performance. And why consistently deploying skills and knowledge within the context of such varied challenges is far from straightforward.

How we see high performance from an individual perspective is slightly different, but still follows the same fundamental principle:

*The ability to consistently deploy the skills and knowledge
relative to one's role, in a way which drives the vision and is
in alignment with the strategy, and to do this across
the variety of situations and contexts in which that
individual is required to perform.*

Therefore, for an individual athlete on a sporting team, performance can be assessed by how well they deploy their skills and knowledge while navigating the highs of success and the lows of setbacks. From a mental perspective, they need to maintain composure as they grapple with pressure, focus, and decision-making under stress. They also need to adapt to unpredictable situations, opposition strategies, and environmental factors like weather conditions, all while dealing with the pressure and scrutiny they face from fans, coaches, and media. And they are required to do all this whilst playing their respective role within the overall game strategy, with the aim of supporting their team to achieve the vision for that game, which is presumably is to win.

An effective culture enables an organisation or team to consistently access its skills and knowledge.

We have all witnessed or even been part of a sales team that had an amazing month where they achieved and exceeded all targets and then, for some unknown reason independent of market forces or macroeconomic conditions, have a terrible following month where they dramatically underperform.

Equally, we have seen a sporting team spend the first half of the game playing in the zone and go into the half-time break with a considerable lead, only to emerge from the change rooms and play so dismally that their opposition overruns them in the dying minutes of the game.

We need to ask ourselves, what is more likely: that at the change in month or half-time break those teams suddenly lost all their skills and knowledge, or that at that change in month or half-time break something happened which resulted in them having *less access* to those essential skills and knowledge? I find it difficult to believe that the skills and knowledge seasoned salespeople and elite athletes have spent years, perhaps even decades, learning, honing, and developing, suddenly and for no obvious reason disappear out of their minds and bodies.

Most of us are familiar with and understand the importance of psychology and mindset for individual performance. A strong psychology and effective mindset enables an individual to access their skills and knowledge, particularly under pressure or at crucial moments in the performance cycle. Culture is the team or organisational equivalent of an individual's psychology or mindset. Culture is how the collective thinks and feels. Culture determines 'how we do things around here'. Culture determines the extent to which people feel safe, included, like they belong, and supported; and this in turn impacts how they are able to try new things, push the boundaries, and be creative. This is why culture enables organisations to consistently access the skills and knowledge they require to drive high performance and deliver on their vision.

Strategy and role clarity enable an organisation to clarify the culture.

How does an organisation decide what kind of culture it needs to create and embed?

A clear, explicit, and integrated strategy informs and clarifies the culture. Once the strategy is determined, organisations can then explore what kind of culture will enhance the execution of this strategy. While there are some fundamental components that all cultures require to be effective, the real nuancing and fine tuning of the culture is informed by the strategy the organisation intends to execute, the various contexts the organisation is required to operate in, and the nature of the business itself. The strategy of an elite sporting organisation will look very different to that of a mining company, which will look very different to that of a university. Therefore, because the strategy clarifies the culture, each of these organisations will require their own distinctive version of an effective culture once it is customised to their specific context and needs.

There are two key aspects which inform the creation of a strategy.

Firstly, given an organisational strategy is a long-term (at least 2–5 years) plan that plots a course from its current position towards its vision, an effective strategy should narrow the focus to 4–6 strategic drivers. These are the aspects of the business that the organisation is going to focus on for the duration of that strategic cycle. This requires the organisation to resist the urge to be all things to all people. This results in diluting its focus across too many strategic drivers and spreading its resources too thinly; consequentially, the strategy underpinning most of these drivers is not able to be executed to high-performance standards.

Secondly, an organisation must define what roles, responsibilities, and accountabilities are required for it to deliver on its strategy. This ensures that there is the necessary functionality in the organisation's structure for it to effectively execute its strategy.

Purpose and vision give meaning and direction to and therefore sustain the strategy.

A strategy that is not in service of something deeper and more enduring is more of a plan than a strategy.

A compelling purpose and a unifying vision provide the meaning which enables an organisation to sustain its strategy. Purpose is the deepest why of an organisation or its reason for existence – it goes to the very heart and soul of an organisation and illuminates something more expansive than its products or services. Vision provides the focus so that the organisation can clearly see what it is going to look like in 10 or 20 years. It is the driving force, which steers and informs every decision we make, every dollar we spend, every person we recruit, and every initiative we launch.

Purpose and vision sustaining the strategy is essential because organisations will inevitably come up against challenges and what feel like insurmountable developmental sticking points. At this point, if the strategy is not fortified by the organisation's purpose and vision, there will be a greater temptation to abandon the strategy and replace it with something less challenging and demanding, something which conveniently lets us off the hook from having to face the current dilemma head on. However, if the strategy is being underpinned and sustained by purpose and vision, organisational leaders are more likely to see the resistance and the challenges they face as catalysts to build the capability needed so they can live out the purpose and deliver on the vision. And if the strategy does need to be adapted or changed, this decision can be explored through a developmental lens and in a considered and non-reactive manner.

Whether an organisation survives, thrives, or fades away into irrelevance is very much contingent on its approach to clarifying and then building capability around these fundamental elements that drive performance. These same principles must also inform how we go about the process of building an antiracist organisation. This is why any antiracist initiative must be integrated with the organisation's purpose, vision, strategy, and culture.

An antiracist initiative cannot sit off to the side or be constructed as a tick-a-box project. There needs to be a symbiotic relationship between antiracism and organisational performance, otherwise the process of building an antiracist organisation will not be sustainable. An organisation's fundamental priority has to be its own success and survival, and performance sits at the very heart of these. Indeed, when directors of companies have a fiduciary responsibility to grow a successful company and deliver shareholder value, then organisational leaders need to position performance with the centrality required so they can fulfil these legal and ethical obligations.

Additionally, when antiracist initiatives are not clearly aligned with the success and performance of an organisation, they will always compete with its core business for resources and focus. And of course, in this contest, antiracism will always come off second best – and this is the way it ought to be! Any initiative, including one as important and as righteous as antiracism, should not have valuable resources devoted towards it if it is not in alignment with and supportive of the overall direction and success of the organisation.

Finally, when an antiracist initiative does not also support those fundamental elements of performance and organisational success, it will set up those driving the initiative and/or BIPOC for a cultural backlash. This is because if such an initiative is not clearly beneficial to success of the organisation and all its members it will create the perception of political correctness or tokenism. This will have the tendency to only deepen division along racial lines and therefore perpetuate the very thing that antiracism is attempting to remedy. The remaining chapters will discuss a practical guide for how organisational leaders can develop and implement an initiative that drives an antiracist and high-performance culture.

Reflection #5:

Exploring the fundamental elements of organisational performance

1. To what extent does you organisation understand and evaluate the essential elements that enable it to perform at a consistently high level?

2. How often does your organisation stop to reflect on the process it is employing to generate its performance levels? Is there sufficient focus on clarifying and then building capability around these fundamental drivers of performance?

3. How successfully does your organisation deploy skills and knowledge in a way which drives the vision and is in alignment with the strategy?

4. To what extent does your organisation's lived (actual) culture enable team members to consistently access the skills and knowledge required to perform at a sustained high level?

5. Does your organisation's current strategy clarify and inform the culture that will optimally drive the desired outcomes? Are the number of strategic drivers small enough so there can be a dedicated focus on each of them? And is there sufficient role clarity, including responsibilities and accountabilities, that ensures there is the necessary functionality to execute the strategy?

6. Is your organisation's strategy informed by, and built upon, purpose and vision? Or is the strategy more like a plan which is variable and reactive and so can be altered in the face of challenges?

7. Which one or two of these four elements presents the greatest opportunity for growth for your organisation to increase the probability of performing at a high level more consistently?

8. In your role as leader, formal or informal, what can you do to increase clarity of and capability in these one or two elements?

Chapter Six:

Organisational purpose

Purpose aligns attitudes and behaviours in service of something greater

Purpose is the deepest 'why' of our existence, our reason for being; it is what the French refer to as our raison d'être. Purpose goes beyond who we are, what we do, or even how we do it. Clarity of purpose enables us to move through life and explore the breadth of our experiences, from the uplifting to the most challenging, from the perspective that we are continually being provided opportunities to bring into sharper focus what really matters.

In this way, purpose represents a compelling force that enables us to find meaning and fulfilment even within the most mundane of tasks or during particularly difficult times. The notion of purpose can be applied to an entire organisation as well as an individual; the principles are exactly the same. However, given that we are talking about building an antiracist organisation, this is the framework through which we will commence our discussion on purpose.

A powerful organisational purpose contains three essential elements. Firstly, it needs to capture the hearts and minds of those within the organisation. This means people not only get excited about what they do, but perhaps more importantly why they do it. As a result, they find greater levels of meaning and fulfilment in how they take up their organisational roles. Thus, purpose enables people to form an emotional connection and a deeper engagement with their respective roles.

Secondly, it needs to be sufficiently compelling so that it aligns people's attitudes, behaviours, and actions to being in service of that purpose. When people find and are then moved by purpose, it creates an internal clarity, a resoluteness, that enables them to put things into perspective and focus their energy and resources on the things that really matter.

Thirdly, and perhaps most importantly, some aspect of purpose has to be about the greater good. It just can't be about what the organisation gets out of it. But rather how, by living true to its purpose, the organisation can be in service to something greater than itself and beyond its own fences and, in doing so, make a difference in the local community, the country, perhaps even the world.

Stan Slap says it beautifully:

> *'The purpose of leadership isn't to increase shareholder value or the productivity of work teams, though effective leadership does these things. Rather, the purpose of leadership is to change the world around you in the name of your values, so you can live those values more fully and use them to make life better for others. The process of leadership is to turn your values into a compelling cause for others.'*[27]

---

27 'Revealing your moment of truth' McKinsey & Company, accessed September 23, 2022, https://www.mckinsey.com/featured-insights/leadership/revealing-your-moment-of-truth

Purpose is intrinsic and best explored retrospectively

Contrary to popular opinion, and unlike mission and vision statements, purpose is not something that is created at a senior management off-site via a strategic planning discussion or a brainstorming session. Rather, purpose is already intrinsically within the organisation, and so is intertwined with its identity. Therefore, purpose has to be discovered rather than created, excavated rather than designed. Some may call it karma, others destiny; I see it more like the spirit the organisation was infused with the moment it came into existence.

Let me try to explain, because it is a concept that can be a little hard to grasp.

If with an attitude of open-minded curiosity we look back throughout the history of our organisation, through its various phases of growth, its peaks and troughs, as well as those critical events that have shaped its identity, we will most likely discover some common threads or a consistent theme. These themes will be exemplified in the organisation's most significant and greatest accomplishments where it has built the capability and operational excellence which have served it well. They will also be represented in the guiding principles, values, and ideals that are cherished by those within the organisation.

Consistent themes may also be evident in the challenges that the organisation has encountered, especially those that appear to be recurrent and particularly problematic. Sometimes these themes will be less literal, more metaphorical, and therefore disguised within the symbols and iconography of those celebrated and legendary stories which have been passed down through the generations. It is these recurrent themes which are interwoven with the very fabric of an organisation's story and its identity that shine a light on its purpose.

For example, we may look back at the history, as well as those formative experiences of our organisation, and see a recurrent thread around connection and a sense of community. In other words, there have been times when the lived culture resulted in team members experiencing meaningful connection and a profound sense of belonging. And yet, at other times, despite being in the midst of a busy workplace, team members may have the experience of feeling alone and isolated. Hence, while connection and belonging are applauded as elements of the lived culture, they simultaneously represent a 'work in progress' for the organisation.

Despite all the striving and the various cultural change initiatives intended to foster connection and belonging, the organisation continues to grapple with the task of prioritising these experiences and embedding them as part of the norm. And while we are valiantly grappling with the complexities and challenges of creating more connection within our own organisation, we are also acutely aware of how much the world around us, perhaps even our personal world, is in desperate need of more connection and a consistent experience of deep belonging.

This may well chronicle the story and accompanying narratives of an organisation whose purpose has something to do with connection and community. Obviously, each organisation will have its own version of those themes, those consistent threads which are woven throughout the central experiences, good and bad, powerful and painful, which stand out in its history and have been critical in shaping its identity. But as we, step-by-step, follow and unravel these threads, it will begin to illuminate and unearth an organisation's reason for existence.

Even though an organisation may uncover a set of themes that appear more generic in nature, further exploration and unpacking of these themes will likely reveal they have a particular tone which is representative of that organisation's distinctive purpose. It is important we remember that no organisational purpose is any more or any less important than that of other organisations. Each organisation will have its own unique version of its reason for existence, and therefore what it is contributing to the community and the world around it. As such, the world needs each organisation, its particular purpose, and that inimitable thread it is contributing to the greater good, as together these various threads make up the rich and complicated tapestry that is essential to business as well as life.

Purpose is also embodied in our biggest challenges

One of the common misconceptions about purpose is that it is evident only in those aspects where organisations are already thriving; purpose, however, is also characterised by the areas where organisations feel the most challenged.

I have found that, whatever an organisation's purpose is as evidenced by where it excels in terms of the products and services it delivers to its external stakeholders, is also paralleled almost invariably by its most recurrent and significant internal challenges. For example, a mining engineering company with expertise in assisting their clients in the most effective ways to mine precious metals and other resources, were continually challenged to mine the valuable potential buried in their team members via a strategic emphasis on their professional and personal development. And the most pressing challenge for a board of a Steiner school, which is all about providing individual learning based on what is most appropriate for a student's stage of development, was board members feeling like their own individual voices were not heard and validated.

In order to live and operate with greater congruence to their purpose, organisations are required to continually build capability in strengthening certain cultural and psychological muscles; therefore, embedded within each of these challenges lies the incentive to build that capability. These recurrent and complex challenges serve an important function and are in themselves purposeful. This is because they shine a light, sometimes agonisingly, on previously unacknowledged opportunities for growth, and in doing so highlight the developmental workout needed for those cultural muscles that support an organisation to continually illuminate and align more closely with a 'deeper why.'

Purpose can also be seen as a mythical quest

In *Built to Last*, Jim Collins and Jerry Porras refer to purpose as follows:

> *'Purpose (which should last at least 100 years) should not be confused with specific goals or business strategies (which should change many times in 100 years). Whereas you might achieve a goal or complete a strategy, you can never fulfill a purpose; it is like a guiding star on the horizon – forever pursued, but never reached.'[28]*

What I like about the way they frame purpose is that they refer to it as something which is 'forever pursued, but never reached'. In this way, the journey to fully embody our purpose is very much like an arduous voyage or a mythical quest.

Most mythical tales, which many successful Hollywood movies are based around, contain a few key elements. Firstly, there is a hero or heroine who goes on their quest to fulfil some kind of destiny

---

28 Jim Collins and Jerry Porras, *Built to Last: Successful Habits of Visionary Companies* (New York, NY: Harper Collins Publishers inc., 2002) 224

that is actually in service of the greater good. Think of heroes like Superman, Frodo Baggins, and Jerry Maguire. They are all very different, especially in how their characters are portrayed in their respective movies, but what is similar is that they each embarked on a journey, not necessarily of their own undertaking or conscious decision, but rather by following an unlikely quest or challenge that came across their path. Superman's journey to Earth was not his choice. Frodo stumbling across the ring was not something he chose to do. And perhaps my favourite, Jerry Maguire's late-night manifesto was something which just came to him, rather than a carefully thought-out strategic plan. Like these three characters, our quest often turns up in the form of a challenge, a painful experience, or a moment of great insight and clarity.

Another key element of most mythical tales is the theme of good versus evil, where our hero or heroine does battle against an antagonist or arch enemy. We see it in Superman's battle with Lex Luther and Frodo's struggle with Sauron. We also see it in the competition between Jerry Maguire and the big market sports agents who are more focused on money than the relationship with their clients. This battle with their arch enemy or the primary antagonist also mirrors an inner struggle our heroes must surmount. Frodo has to resist his own inclination towards evil and greed and the lure of the ring, and Jerry Maguire's view (at least at the start of the movie) on relationships is much like those big market sports agents in that they are regarded as transactional and disposable. In this way, their quest is not only an outer battle with the antagonist but also an inward journey of discovery, where our hero has to struggle with their own demons in order to fulfil their destiny.

Similarly, organisations and their respective leaders are on an unlikely quest, whether they realise it or not. This quest entails battling the collective antagonist in the form of external challenges such as advances in technology and digital transformation, macroeconomic factors, changing customer demographics, an ageing workforce, labour restrictions, and competition for market share, just to name a few. But in the relentless quest for optimal performance, organisations and their leaders are also required to journey inward. Here they will invariably encounter and be required to grapple with the antagonist that resides within. And as crucial as successfully overcoming these external challenges is, the ultimate determinant of creating a high-performance culture – one that is underpinned and driven by purpose – is how they show up on the battlefield within.

For leaders, these internal battles are almost invariably with those influential figures and the belief system they have internalised. These are the barely perceptible whispers that run riot across their psychological landscape, purporting the narrative that their life is devoid of purpose and lacking in meaning. Therefore, supporting organisations and their leaders with the armour and weaponry needed to triumph on these internal battlefields is essential in building the capability required to not only discover purpose, but to also live true to it. These encounters, both external and internal, represent aspects of organisational life that challenge and reinforce our understanding of purpose by revealing what enshrines us with a sense of meaning and fulfilment.

Personal purpose supports inner alignment essential for leaders building an antiracist organisation

Any organisational change initiative, particularly one as complex as building an antiracist culture, has to be driven, endorsed, and also modelled by leadership. Any kind of mixed messaging from leadership in their commitment to such an initiative, or its importance, will not be conducive to success. When it comes to tackling structural racism, absolute clarity and alignment of purpose is required. This is because, as we discussed in chapter three, leaders are attempting to dismantle a system of oppression that has powerful and nuanced mechanisms by which it preserves and perpetuates itself. Although up till now we have discussed the notion of purpose primarily from an organisational perspective, the same principles can also be applied to an individual in terms of their personal purpose.

An awareness of, and alignment with, one's personal purpose is an essential ingredient for leaders embarking upon the task of building an antiracist organisation for two essential reasons. Firstly, clarity of personal purpose adjusts the flavour of how people lead because it encourages a style of leadership that is more authentically themselves. As such, leaders are not wasting time and energy comparing themselves or their approach to leadership to others. This makes for a more sustainable approach to leadership. Importantly, this more-comfortable-in-one's-skin style of leadership is better able to foster the kind of connectedness and care that are essential in building an inclusive and high-performance culture.

Additionally, an awareness of one's personal purpose means that leaders are more able to find the meaning and the opportunities for growth that are embedded within the challenging times they will inevitably encounter. People tend to feel hopeless, even depressed, if these events are seen only as life's attempt to beat the crap out of us. The wounds and the bruises that life deals us obviously need to be tended to and cared for, for that is an essential part of the process. However, even amid the most challenging of times, meaning and learning can also be discovered, if as part of their quest to continually deepen their understanding of purpose leaders can ask themselves, 'What attribute, internal resource, or aspect of myself is this challenging, perhaps even agonising, experience attempting to bring out in me and/or compelling me to develop?'

The insights which arise from this reflection provide a much-needed balm in the form of meaning and self-awareness. As Viktor Frankl said, 'There is nothing in the world, I venture to say, that would so effectively help one to survive even the worst conditions as the knowledge that there is a meaning in one's life.'[29] Leaders can begin to see the rightness or even the benefits of such adversity and discomfort when as part of this reflection they can also ask themselves, 'How is this capability, that I am being compelled to develop, essential to me fulfilling and being of service to my personal purpose?'

In this way leaders can start to see that in a perverse kind of way, there is also an elegance to life. Because contained within what they originally thought of as their biggest, most recurrent and painful challenges, are potentially powerful doorways to the substantive gifts of meaning, resilience, and self-awareness.

The second reason that an awareness of personal purpose is essential for leaders building an antiracist organisation is that a deeper 'why' is forged when leaders can find a strong alignment and symmetry between their personal purpose and the purpose for an antiracist culture. Obviously, when there is insufficient understanding and awareness of one's personal purpose, it is less likely that these connections will be explicit. In contrast, consolidating the connection between their personal purpose and organisational initiatives, such as building an antiracist culture, can mobilise leaders to achieve extraordinary things because they are guided by the mantra, 'I see my role in leading this initiative as an opportunity to further align to, and be in service of, my personal purpose.'

---

29 Viktor Frankl, *Man's Search for Meaning: An Introduction to Logotherapy.* (Boston: Beacon Press, 1962)

This is particularly important in the context of building an antiracist organisation. Clarity of purpose, both organisationally and personally, provides the emotional funding required to commit to and prioritise an antiracist initiative as something that really matters to the organisation. In the absence of this alignment, leaders will almost invariably demonstrate mixed messages, for example as part of their non-verbal communication, about the priority, urgency, and commitment to an antiracist initiative. And this will undermine the likelihood of success because, 'After all,' team members will think, 'if leadership is not committed to this project, why should we be?'

The building of an antiracist organisation requires leaders to take full ownership of the challenge of structural racism. In this context, ownership isn't about blame; it is more about an empathetic desire to create connection and belonging. An alignment to their personal purpose enables leaders, regardless of their race, to see racism as 'my problem', so their leadership can be informed by an inner attitude of, 'If anybody in my organisation is suffering or feeling disenfranchised because of racism (or any other form of structural discrimination) then I too am suffering.'

Attempting to foster an antiracist culture with the underlying premise that racism is 'their' problem immediately fractures the culture because it creates an 'us and them' dynamic, which in turn initiates the process of othering those that already feel marginalised. The importance of embedding antiracism as part of an organisational strategy so as not to constellate a dynamic of othering is discussed further in chapter eleven.

As leaders continue to refine their understanding of their purpose, and their reason for existence comes into sharper focus, it gives greater meaning, direction, and a sense of contribution to the way they take up their respective roles in general, but also within the context of building an antiracist organisation. Purpose, therefore, enables leaders to be more aware of their potential legacy, but also the legacy they may already have left in the journey they have travelled thus far.

Reflection #6A:

Organisational purpose via personal purpose

There are two ways to explore the purpose of your organisation.

The first way is based on the perspective that there is a common thread which runs through the individual purposes of those people within the organisation. This is initially an individual reflection to be done by people within the organisation, but particularly by people in senior roles within the organisation.

Part 1: Illuminating personal purpose
(to be done individually)

1. What achievement in your life are you most proud of?

2. What is one of your most ongoing and painful challenges?

3. Who is your hero or heroine, someone that you look up to and admire?

4. If you were to live a long and fulfilling life, how would you want to be remembered?

5. If all of these experiences are meaningful and are there to illuminate and align you to your purpose, what is the common thread through these experiences that might inform you about your purpose? Based on this thread, what might be your purpose? (hint: play around with the idea until it meets the three criteria described on page 168)

6. How can you see your role within [your organisation] as an opportunity to be of service to your purpose?

Part 2: Finding the consistent theme which represents the organisational purpose (to be done as a group)

1. Once individuals have greater clarity on their personal purpose, they should share these with the rest of the group.

2. What is the consistent theme which runs through each of the individual purposes?

3. Play around with this consistent theme until it is representative of the collective and individuals can also see their own purpose reflected within the organisational purpose.

4. Make sure the organisational purpose satisfies the three criteria described on page 168.

Take your time as you ponder, reflect, and feel your way through each step. I would also recommend that you do this exercise on a regular basis. As we have discussed, our understanding of purpose is an ongoing exercise. Therefore, each new experience not only provides us with an opportunity for reflection to see how it is linked to our purpose, but also to further explore, unfold, and illuminate purpose itself.

Reflection #6B:

Organisational purpose via first principles

The second way is to unearth the organisational purpose from 'first principles'. This is by telling stories of those iconic and historical moments from the organisation's history. This might include how and why it was founded, weird or unusual events that occurred throughout its history, and critical moments of survival and growth. One way to do this is to create a fairy tale about your organisation. While fairy tales may seem childish, Indigenous and First Nations people have been telling such stories for millennia. These stories pass on the knowledge of where their people have come from, where they are now, and the journey that they have taken to get there. This starts to shine a light on who we are and something that is more timeless and deeper in terms of understanding the reason for our existence.

Such stories typically feature magic, enchantments, and mythical or fanciful beings. Every fairy tale has five components: it starts with 'once upon a time', it finishes with 'happily ever after', there is a hero, a heroine, or a protagonist and a villain or antagonist. And finally, there is a moral to the story. This is why elders and parents tell us fairy tales – because the moral of the story reveals critical insights about who we are, how we came to be, and what really matters.

To be done in groups of 4-6:

1. On a large sheet of paper, draw a circle in the top left corner and call this 'Past island' and also draw a circle on the bottom right corner call this 'Right now island'

2. The task for the team is to make up a fairy tale about the organisation's journey or from Past island to Right now island, this story is in the form of a mythical sea voyage. The story commences at Past island. The timeframe for Past island is the time when the person in your group who has been with the organisation for the longest time started, or when the organisation was founded, if the stories and events from the early days of the organisation are well-known to the group. Right now island refers to the current times.

3. As you construct a fairy tale, try not to be too literal, but rather be creative and have fun.

4. Your fairy tale might include tales of pirates coming to take your treasure, ferocious sea monsters, mad captains, ice bergs and other hidden dangers, times we fell asleep at the wheel, storms, and whirlpools.

5. Make sure your fairy tale has the following components:

   • It starts with: 'Once upon a time'.

   • It finishes with: 'Happily ever after'.

   • There is a hero, heroine, or a protagonist.

   • There is a villain or a challenge to overcome that serves as the antagonist.

   • Once the fairy tale is completed, you find the moral to the story.

6. Unpack the moral to your story. Use this moral to explore the purpose of your organisation and the deepest why of its existence.

7. How have all those crucial events and occurrences throughout the organisation's history served the function of further illuminating the purpose of the organisation?

Chapter Seven:

Purpose and the antiracist organisation

How much are we prepared to tolerate?

When it comes to structural racism within an organisation, leadership is required to ask, 'How much [racism and racial inequity] are we prepared to tolerate?' This question is crucial because it forms the foundation of the purpose or the rationale for an antiracism initiative, and as such, it informs our 'why'.

Structural racism involves the normalisation of inequity relative to race. If we permit the process of normalisation to progress, at some point in time, perhaps without us even realising, we succumb to acceptance. And this acceptance lulls all of us into a kind of paralysed complacency.

The momentum that gets generated by being purposeful in our actions is essential if we are going to disrupt the inertia of acceptance and the stupor of complacency that systems of oppression, such as racism, leverage in order to preserve themselves. 'Perturbation' is the deviation of a moving object, process, or system (for example, a system of oppression) from its normal state or path, caused by an outside influence. In this case, 'purpose' is the outside influence that produces the perturbation necessary to disrupt the normal state of racial inequity.

Furthermore, the work of building an antiracist organisation is not only challenging, but it is also costly; it requires an investment of time and money, as well as emotional labour. Clarity of purpose is therefore crucial, because it galvanises the connections and commitment that will fund this work emotionally. When we believe and feel that building an antiracist culture is aligned to purpose, and we are therefore doing something that really matters, we are naturally inclined to invest our hearts and minds into this righteous pursuit. Vision (discussed in chapters eight and nine), on the other hand, is more representative of the commercial imperative of an organisation. So, as long as we can connect an antiracist initiative in a causal way to the commercial and performance benefits for the organisation, the vision funds the work in a more literal sense, i.e., a strategic investment of resources such as time and money.

In terms of a practical guide to creating an antiracist culture, this is the first step. Everything we have discussed up until now has been a precursor to this moment. Unpacking the dynamics and impacts of structural racism, as we did in part one, now permits us to make an informed and educated choice when it comes to this question of tolerance. If we are still prepared to tolerate structural racism, we can no longer plead ignorance when its consequences, almost invariably, have an impact on our organisation's culture, the individuals within that system, and the performance of the organisation itself.

Aligning the purpose of antiracism with organisational purpose

So ... why *do* we want to create an antiracist organisation?

Each organisation will have its own version of why building an antiracist culture is imperative. This 'why' will be shaped by many factors, including, but not limited to, the organisation's current cultural and strategic direction; where it is situated along its overall process of maturation and evolution; how strongly it sees the commercial benefits of moving towards a more diverse, equitable, and inclusive culture; and the degree to which it feels a responsibility to shape and influence the broader community.

The following are some examples of what the 'why' of building an antiracist organisation might look like.

We care about our people, and want everyone in our organisation to feel included, valued, and cared for.

We understand that by moving towards an antiracist culture, we are more likely to attract and retain talented people, in particular talented BIPOC.

We can see the direct benefits to our performance by moving towards an antiracist culture.

We believe we have a role to play in terms of influencing the society and broader culture in which we work when it comes to racial equity, and DEI in general.

What is essential in terms of practical steps is spending the necessary time unearthing or exploring your organisation's purpose for building an antiracist organisation. There is a reflection at the end of this chapter which will help you to clarify and deepen your understanding of this purpose. I would suggest that you take some time and complete that reflection prior to returning to the rest of this chapter.

Once we have clarity of purpose relative to an antiracist initiative, the next step involves ensuring there is alignment between this purpose and the overall purpose of the organisation. This step is critical. For this work to be successful and sustainable, it must be supportive of, and aligned to the overall purpose of the organisation. In the absence of this alignment, the emotional connection to the work that purpose fosters will be less compelling. As a result, those driving the antiracist initiative and/or BIPOC may well experience a cultural backlash. This is because if all team members are not emotionally invested, the work of building an antiracist organisation will not be seen as a shared responsibility that belongs to everyone.

Consequently, those who are yet to reach the threshold of emotional buy-in get placed in an impossible position: do they go along, perhaps begrudgingly, with an initiative they are not emotionally invested in, or do they resist such an initiative and then risk being perceived as not a 'team player', or even worse, a 'racist'? This is really a no-win situation. And as a result, those team members will invariably resent being placed in such a position; they will resent those leaders who have initiated such a project; and they will resent the BIPOC who they believe such an initiative is designed to support. This has the potential of creating stress and division within the culture, perhaps even rupturing it along racial lines, which is obviously the very thing such an initiative is intending to address.

Therefore, if finding alignment between the purpose of an antiracist initiative and the overall purpose of your organisation is proving to be challenging, my suggestion is that you press pause on such an initiative. I suggest you stay in this pause mode until such point as you decide that either this is not the right time in your organisation's developmental process for such an initiative, or you are able to find that alignment.

I know it might be frustrating to have read this far, only to now realise that this work is not for your organisation. But I would rather this realisation happen now, instead of attempting to implement an antiracist initiative that is in conflict with the purpose and overall direction of the organisation. This will only serve to distract the organisation from its core business, divert resources away from strategic imperatives, and potentially destabilise the existing culture.

A clear organisational purpose reminds people that they matter

Up till now we have discussed how important it is that the process of moving towards antiracism is aligned with, and also supportive of, an organisation's purpose. However, the reverse is also true – being in service of an overarching purpose, to the point where people's attitudes and behaviours are aligned accordingly, starts to address some of the consequences of structural racism.

As we discussed in developmental sticking point #4, in chapter four, one of the ways that structural racism impacts BIPOC is when messages they receive and consequently internalise over time insinuate that their feelings do not matter, their lives do not matter, and therefore they do not matter. This is the internal psychological landscape that many BIPOC, as well as people from other minority and socially marginalised identities, must battle with on a regular basis.

When it comes to structural racism, I believe this is the fundamental psychological wound that gets perpetrated. It needs to be clearly and explicitly framed that this injury should not be associated with any kind of psychological deficit or problem within BIPOC. Associating the outcomes of such an injury to some deficit or dysfunction is the kind of reasoning that only serves to reinforce and collude with those messages embedded within structural racism. These messages suggest, sometimes directly, sometimes more indirectly, that there is something fundamentally wrong with BIPOC; and as we discussed in chapter three, this is how stereotypes and racist tropes get created and disseminated.

When the purpose of an organisation is emotional and emotive, it activates and stirs something deep within us, both as individuals and collectively as an entire organisation. An organisation's purpose is a persuasive reminder that what we do does in fact matter; that what we do makes a difference in the world. For BIPOC, this is in itself antiracist because that sense of contribution and meaning rebukes the internalised narrative which suggests something to the contrary. Therefore, for those in formal leadership roles, it is crucial that they are constantly reinforcing and reminding people of that purpose. From this perspective, leaders need to over-communicate in the way the organisation's purpose is continually clarified and socialised within the culture.

Purpose fosters a sense of belonging that counteracts existing on the fringes

Human beings are hardwired to belong, to feel like we are part of something larger than ourselves. This goes back to a biological imperative that is based on our intrinsic need to survive. Please allow me to explain.

Way back in time when we were a bunch of cave people and early adopters of animal-print fashions, there were two broad kinds of people. For the first kind, there was no strong desire to belong to a group or tribe, for the most part they were content being by themselves – lone wolves, if you will. For the second kind, there was a much stronger drive to belong to something and to create strong social connections, so those people naturally gravitated towards forming groups, tribes, and societies. We can imagine these two broad kinds of people both going through life and doing their best to survive, perhaps even thrive, given the unpredictability and the numerous life-threatening dangers that they faced. But then something happened: natural selection.

The theory of natural selection was first expounded by Charles Darwin, who suggested that organisms that are better adapted to their environment tend to survive better and therefore produce more offspring. This means that those genetic traits and tendencies which avail greater survival get selectively propagated throughout a given population, while those genetic traits that decrease survival over time get selected out and therefore occur less frequently in a population.

Back in the times when we were cave people, belonging to a group or a tribe came with many obvious benefits. For example, hunting in a group yields a far greater chance of success than hunting by yourself. Therefore, those people with a tendency to stay in groups gained significant advantages in terms of the availability of food. This in turn provided sustenance and energy, as well as protein for muscle development, which meant they were physically stronger and fitter, and this further increased their probability of survival. Also, when it came to protection from potential threats, be it a hungry sabre-toothed tiger or a competing tribe, being part of a connected and cohesive group provided a significant survival benefit. As a result, through the process of evolution, shaped by natural selection, the need to belong became increasingly forged as one of our basic drives and instincts.

Today, we can still see aspects of both these tendencies in terms of a continuum. There are still those people who are naturally drawn to being in groups, and those who, for the most part, prefer their own company. The difference today is that the benefits of belonging to a group or being part of a tribe are nowhere near as obvious. For most of us, there is no need to go out and hunt in order to eat; we simply go to the refrigerator or use Uber Eats. And we have no consistent extinction level threats in the form of sabre-toothed tigers or marauding neighbouring tribes. So, the reasons we initially evolved with a basic drive to belong as a way of enhancing our survival no longer exist in the way that they used to.

However, despite the drastic changes in our external environment (and frequency of extinction level threats) since the days when we lived in caves, the research demonstrates that there are still better outcomes for those people who feel a sense of belonging and have strong social connections. For example, Cacioppo and Patrick found links between social isolation and loneliness to a variety of health outcomes, including cardiovascular disease and stroke, dementia and cognitive impairment, and depression and anxiety.[30] A similar study found that social isolation and loneliness was associated to a 29% increased risk of heart disease, and a 32% increased risk of stroke, and that social isolation was also associated to higher rates of depression, anxiety, and suicide.[31]

Kurnia et al found that loneliness is a significant predictor of sleep fragmentation.[32] Loneliness has been shown to predict poor health, and sleep is an essential ingredient for good health. Kurnia et al hypothesised that one possible mechanism for the relationship between adequate sleep and good health, or conversely insufficient sleep and poor health, is that lonely individuals do not sleep as well as individuals who feel more connected to others.

One of the impacts of structural racism is that it pushes BIPOC towards the fringes of society (and organisations). The messages

---

30   John Cacioppo and William Patrick, *Loneliness: Human nature and the need for social connection* (New York, NY: W.W. Norton & Company, 2008)

31   31 National Academies of Sciences, Engineering, and Medicine, *Social Isolation and Loneliness in Older Adults: Opportunities for the Health Care System*. (Washington, DC: The National Academies Press, 2020) https://doi.org/10.17226/25663

32   Lianne Kurnia et al, 'Loneliness Is Associated with Sleep Fragmentation in a Communal Society' *Sleep*, Volume 34, Issue 11, (November 2011) 1519–1526, https://doi.org/10.5665/sleep.1390

embedded in dynamics of racial inequity actively exclude BIPOC and their experiences, and this undermines their sense of belonging. This was discussed in developmental sticking point #1, in chapter four. Obviously, belonging and connection are complex phenomena, and people from all races will organically form communities, teams, and tribes, which are beneficial in terms of people's experience of belonging. But it is the pervasive nature of the narratives embedded in structural racism that incessantly echo through the internal dialogues of BIPOC that continually remind them that their place in society is far more at the fringes than it is at the centre.

The disparity in health outcomes for BIPOC in comparison to non-BIPOC is exceedingly complex and there are multiple factors contributing to it. However, one additional reason is the narratives embedded in structural racism which, when internalised, place under duress, sometimes to the point of fracture, BIPOCs' sense of belonging and connection.

In contrast, an organisation with a clear purpose beckons all its people to align around those fundamental tenets in order for the collective to be in service of something greater than the individual. Purpose, therefore, invites people to relocate from the fringes, and incrementally move more towards the centre. For many BIPOC this narrative is less familiar, they are far more accustomed to the narrative which pushes them further towards the periphery. Therefore, when organisations are able to unearth and clarify a compelling purpose, one that evokes an emotional connection, as well as inclusion and unity, it is a powerful demonstration of antiracism. An overarching organisational purpose cannot change those dynamics of structural discrimination within the broader culture. However, by giving people a place and a reason to belong, purpose can provide a sanctuary of belonging and community to those who may not have a reliable experience of these outside the four walls of their workplace.

Reflection #7:

Finding the purpose of an antiracism initiative in your organisation

1. Within your organisation, to what extent has structural racism become acceptable? (keep in mind that structural racism is perpetuated primarily via inequity, which can be seen in objective measures as well as in subjective experiences)

2. Are these levels tolerable to you?

3. If not, what are the impacts and consequences for the organisation in the way that structural racism gets manifested?

4. What would be the benefits to the organisation of addressing these consequences of structural racism?

5. How important is it that, within your organisation, people feel like they, and the work they do, matters? How might fostering an antiracist culture give people, particularly BIPOC, an increased sense that they matter?

6. How important is it that, within your organisation, people feel like they belong? How might fostering an antiracist culture give people, particularly BIPOC, an increased sense that they belong?

7. To what extent does your organisation have an ethical and moral responsibility to influence and demonstrate leadership to society and the broader culture when it comes to racial equity, and DEI in general?

8. Given your above responses, what is the 'why' or the purpose of an antiracism initiative for your organisation?

Chapter Eight:

Organisational vision

Vision presents a compelling case for possibility

If purpose is the 'why' of the organisation, then vision is the 'what'. While purpose is representative of the 'soul' of the organisation and what ultimately, perhaps even altruistically, it is in service of, vision is deeply rooted in the commercial imperative of the organisation.

There are different ways that leaders think about and perceive their organisation's vision. Here is what I have found to be the most effective and impactful in terms of delivering sustained high performance.

An organisation's vision is the dream or the goal of what is ultimately possible for an organisation; vision elucidates where an organisation is going, and what it will look like when it gets there. It is therefore essential that an organisation's vision is formulated around a long-term time horizon, at least 5 years, but preferably 10 or 20 years. The vision should primarily address the question, 'What will we [the organisation] look like in 10 or 20 years?'

This 'what' needs to be a stretch goal so there is only a 10% chance of the vision being achieved given the current capability. The vision represents a precise target that beckons an organisation towards what it can be at its best, by presenting a compelling case for possibility; the vision therefore provides a focal point for initiatives that support the growth and development of the organisation in a particular direction. In other words, underpinning the very notion of the vision is the unrealised potential within an organisation if it has the right leadership, if it builds an outstanding culture, if it is effectively structured and 'right sized', if it can execute a well thought-out and tactical strategy, and if it assembles a team of talented people who are passionately aligned to the purpose. From this perspective, without the driving force of a clear and unifying vision, optimal performance is virtually impossible.

Crucially, an organisation's vision should also be specific and measurable. This then raises one of the challenging aspects when it comes to clarifying an organisation's vision: defining the single metric which encompasses and reflects an organisation's overall success. For for-profit organisations, this might be relatively straightforward; the vision might be to increase revenue or profit by X% in 10 years. For other organisations, especially those with multiple and diverse deliverables, this can be more complex. For example, a state sporting organisation (SSO) may have key deliverables which include growing membership numbers, increasing the number of participants in junior sport, and having its high-performance/elite teams performing well. It is therefore complex to decide which of these, if any, is the one metric against which the performance of the entire organisation can be measured.

Sometimes it is impractical, perhaps even impossible, to distil the performance of an entire organisation, particularly one with multiple key deliverables, down to one metric. In these cases, leadership needs to take the time and have the discipline to sit with the tension of the undetermined while the various options for this one metric can be explored and evaluated. Resisting the urge to diffuse the tension by prematurely settling on a metric, or a set of metrics, that do not fully capture the overall performance of the organisation, will ensure that the vision is robust and unifying.

Importantly, a specific metric that enables the organisation to track its forward progress towards the vision provides team members with clarity in terms of the essential components of their role. This is supportive of improved decision-making, because it helps to ascertain what is truly important, and therefore where people should be focusing their time and energy. When organisations are genuinely committed to their vision, every component of the business, each aspect of the strategy, as well as the day-to-day decisions, will be stress tested and justified through the filter of this vision. For example, if we are recruiting a new CFO, which applicant will be most likely to drive the organisation towards the vision? Is how we currently approach the professional development of our people supportive of the organisation in realising its vision? If we are re-evaluating our strategy, what are the 4 to 6 strategic initiatives or drivers which are going to propel us towards the vision most effectively? And if we are considering acquiring another company, is this going to take us further away or towards our vision?

Once the vision is clarified, it needs to be socialised throughout the organisation. This means that organisational leaders make a clear and compelling case for that vision. Socialising the vision also starts to introduce it into the everyday vernacular of the organisation. The more that team members are thinking about the processes, policies, and cultural components which are supportive of the vision, the more it informs and gets built into everyday decisions and behaviours. A critical driver of optimal performance is when everyone is pulling in the same direction because team members take up their respective roles in a manner which is cognisant of, and committed to, doing what is needed, even if what is needed is difficult, to maximally drive the vision.

This is what supports organisations to achieve the extraordinary.

Reflection #8:

Constructing an organisational vision

1. Think about all the various measurables and metrics which reflect the success and performance of your organisation.

2. Decide on one which most accurately captures the performance of the entire organisation in terms of its success in achieving its key deliverables. Take the time here to really explore and evaluate the options in terms of this metric. If this is challenging, be mindful of the tendency to diffuse the tension by settling on a metric that does not fully represent and capture the overall success of the organisation.

3. Decide on the timeframe for your vision. This should be a long-term time horizon, so at least 5 years, but preferably 10 or 20 years.

4. What will this key metric look like in that timeframe? This needs to be a stretch goal, one that can only be achieved via a sustained focus on the growth of the organisation and if the organisation is able to execute on those key drivers of performance. Remember that organisations tend to overestimate what they can achieve short-term, but underestimate what they can achieve in the long term.

5. Make a plan to socialise this vision, so that over time it becomes embedded in the everyday vernacular,

thinking, and decision-making of team members. In the plan to socialise the vision ensure that, how it is aligned with, and supportive of, the organisational purpose is clearly communicated.

Chapter Nine:

Organisational vision and the antiracist organisation

Integrating antiracist initiatives with the vision is essential for success

One of the main reasons most diversity, equity, and inclusion (DEI) programs do not yield the desired results is because they are not integrated with the vision of the organisation. Rather than capitalise on DEI programs as vehicles that directly drive commercial success, organisations more commonly embark upon diversity initiatives in order to maintain optics for shareholders and other key stakeholders; to grant them increased legal protection in the event of a discrimination lawsuit; or to satisfy the demands of being seen as socially progressive and politically correct. Sometimes DEI programs are also launched as a way of repairing the brand after a well-publicised event that reveals shortfalls in the organisation's approach to diversity and inclusion. For example, in May 2018, Starbucks put 175,000 workers through a one-day diversity training in response to the widely publicised arrest of two Black men in a Philadelphia store.

When DEI programs are not clearly and explicitly integrated with the vision of the organisation, they will be delivered as something 'on the side', and as a result are unlikely to achieve the desired outcomes. This is because, over time, rather than an initiative which provides the organisation with a competitive advantage, these programs prove to be a distraction from core business and the success of the organisation, because they divert resources and focus away from the organisation's performance imperative. In the absence of an explicit commercial benefit, the organisation will find it increasingly challenging to justify and fund the program, and as a result, it will peter out with the potential and hopes that the program initially held remaining unfulfilled.

Therefore, any initiative to build an antiracist organisation must be approached in an integrated way. We cannot compartmentalise the organisation's commercial reality and its need to perform as we go about this process, so our approach must be aligned to, and also supportive of, the commercial imperative rooted in the organisation's vision. Anything else is ethically questionable, because it goes against the very premise on which the organisation was founded and currently operates. So please let me be clear: building an antiracist organisation *should not* be the organisational vision itself. The vision still needs to have a stand-alone commercial imperative that engages and inspires management, staff, shareholders, as well as other relevant stakeholders. After all, at the end of the day, we are still running a business.

Leaders must objectively evaluate the commercial benefits of DEI programs

DEI work, when done properly, is costly in terms of an investment of time and money, but also emotions. The key question that organisational leaders need to address is, 'Is there sufficient commercial benefit in building an antiracist culture that such an initiative is directly and causally supportive of the organisation's vision?'

There is an abundance of research available which validates the commercial benefits of more diverse and inclusive cultures. This research is readily available, so I won't go into too much detail with those. But some of the most frequently cited benefits include:

Greater variety of perspectives: if there are more people with diverse backgrounds and different life experiences, there is a greater likelihood that they will have different perspectives.

Better innovation and greater creativity: diversity fosters a rich tapestry of perspectives, experiences, and ideas within organisations, which fuels innovation and creativity. This is because varied backgrounds and viewpoints challenge conventional thinking and encourage dynamic problem-solving. Additionally, inclusive environments empower diverse talents to collaborate, resulting in groundbreaking solutions that cater to a broader range of needs and preferences.

More effective decision-making: when team members come from a more diverse range of backgrounds, they are able to gather information from a wider range of sources and experiences. This supports a more sophisticated and effective decision-making process.

Improved attraction and retention of talent: if there is greater acceptance of people from diverse backgrounds to the point where they feel more included, talented team members are more likely to join and stay with the organisation.

Brand reputation: when businesses genuinely create more inclusive cultures and advocate for diversity, they are perceived as more relatable and socially responsible. This will improve the brand's reputation, increase customer loyalty, and attract new markets and partnerships.

Like any other aspect of strategy, the decision to implement an antiracist initiative needs to be evaluated specifically through the lens of an organisation's vision and current context. In other words, 'Is there a clear and explicit commercial benefit, in terms of driving us towards our vision, derived through the process of building an antiracist organisation?'

If there is no clear alignment between the performance and commercial benefits of an antiracist culture and the organisation's vision, leaders need to reassess such an initiative. In this case, as we discussed in chapter seven, temporarily or permanently discarding such a program will most likely be in the organisation's best interest. Proceeding with an antiracism initiative in the absence of its synergy with the vision jeopardises the success and wellbeing of the organisation by allocating resources to an area which is not a key driver of commercial success.

Echoes of racial capitalism manifest as barriers to maximal engagement

Given that a vision, by definition, is a 'stretch goal', in order to generate the levels of performance required to bring to fruition such a lofty ambition requires team members to be fully engaged and emotionally invested; there is no room for passengers on such an arduous journey. And because the process of driving towards the vision is deeply rooted in a commercial imperative, we also require team members to be supportive of a set of capitalistic ideals which are foundational in that imperative. But how can BIPOC fully engage in, and endorse, a capitalistic direction, when historically and currently aspects of capitalism have been weaponised and used against them as elaborate apparatuses to further structural racism?

This may be a surprising concept to many of us, so please let me elaborate.

The notion of 'racial capitalism' was first coined by Cedric Robinson in 1983. He asserted that exploitative work practices, primarily pertaining to BIPOC, and the process of capital accumulation for people with privileged racial identities are mutually reinforcing.[33] In other words, decoupling capitalism and racism is complicated because, in some ways, capitalism has been built and has subsequently thrived on the foundations of structural racism.

For example, in the United States, between 1934 and the 1960s, the practice of 'redlining' withheld essential services from customers who resided in neighbourhoods classified as 'hazardous' for investment purposes. These areas were often inner-city neighbourhoods with a high proportion of Black people and other ethnic minorities, as well as low-income families. The process of redlining included, but was not limited to, the denial of financial and credit services, mortgage availability, and healthcare. Additionally, the impractical positioning of supermarkets in Black neighbourhoods contributed to the development of food deserts in many of these areas. Reverse redlining also occurred when predatory lenders and insurers took advantage of the lack of competition and targeted the mostly minority groups in these neighbourhoods with inflated interest rates and insurance premiums. Blacklisting was another related strategy employed by redlining institutions to keep track of areas, groups, and people that the discriminating party intended to exclude.

As a direct consequence of redlining, there was a lack of investment and development in these neighbourhoods, and, as a result, there was relatively less appreciation in the house and land value in these areas. In comparison, White neighbourhoods – where these services were more readily available – benefited

---

33 Cedric Robinson, *Black Marxism: The Making of the Black Radical Tradition*. (NC, USA: University of North Carolina Press, 1983)

from a greater investment in services and infrastructure. This has resulted in a greater appreciation in the value of the land and property owned in these areas.

Racial capitalism in the United States is deeply intertwined with the historical legacy of slavery. From the colonial era through the 19th century, the exploitation of African American slaves served as a foundational element in the development of American capitalism, as enslaved people were systematically subjected to forced labour, particularly in southern states.

The commodification of human beings and the extraction of labour without compensation laid the groundwork for racialised economic structures that have persisted even after the abolition of slavery. The exploitation of Black labour during slavery contributed to the accumulation of wealth that, over time, became a structural advantage for White Americans. The repercussions of this historical exploitation continue to shape socio-economic realities, emphasising the inseparable connection between racial capitalism and the enduring impact of slavery in the United States.

These examples highlight how capitalism has been weaponised, and only those with the privilege of having the appropriate racial background have been able to benefit from the supposed free-market system. The legacy of racial capitalism is evident in racial economic disparities, limited access to resources, and systemic inequalities that disproportionately affect Black communities and perseverate to current times.

Data from the 2019 Survey of Consumer Finances in the United States showed that long-standing and substantial wealth disparities between families in different racial and ethnic groups were little changed since the previous survey in 2016.[34] White families have

---

34 'Disparities in Wealth by Race and Ethnicity in the 2019 Survey of Consumer Finances', Board of Governors of the Federal Reserve System, September 28, 2020, accessed February 17, 2022, https://www.federalreserve.gov/econres/notes/feds-notes/disparities-in-wealth-by-race-and-ethnicity-in-the-2019-survey-of-consumer-finances-20200928

the highest level of both median and mean family wealth – of $188,200 and $983,400, respectively – while Black and Hispanic families have considerably less wealth than White families, with Black families' median and mean wealth less than 15% that of White families, at $24,100 and $142,500. In 2021, according to the United States Census bureau, households whose head was classified as White had median incomes of $77,999, in comparison to households headed by someone classified as Black who had median incomes of $48,297.[35]

From the time Australia was colonised in 1788 until the 1960s, Australian Aboriginals and Torres Strait Islanders were exploited as unpaid or cheap labour. They were used in sectors such as the pastoralist industry, pearling, and marsupial eradication. These were all early versions of industry and the dawning of capitalism in Australia. Trade in Aboriginal children and adolescents also occurred, as children were often taken from Aboriginal campsites and used as either personal servants or as labour by the colonists who took them.

In the late 1830s, as it became apparent that the transportation of convicts from England to Australia was about to cease, colonists expressed a need for an alternative form of cheap labour. In 1837, a Committee on Immigration put forward the idea of importing coolie labourers. 'Coolie' is a slang term referring to a low-wage labourer, most commonly of South Asian or East Asian descent. For the next two decades, until the mid-1950s, coolie workers were frequently imported to Australia, primarily from China and India, to work in low-wage jobs in various areas of industry throughout Australia.

---

35 'Income, Poverty and Health Insurance Coverage in the United States: 2021', United States Census Bureau, accessed March 26, 2023, https://www.census.gov/newsroom/press-releases/2022/income-poverty-health-insurance-coverage

As discussed in chapter three, one of the South African government's rationales for instituting the system of apartheid was to support South Africa's emerging economy by creating a class of people that could be easily exploited as cheap labour in industries such as mining. As a result of apartheid legislation, and in one of the biggest mass evictions in modern history, 3.5 million Black Africans were removed from their homes and forced into segregated neighbourhoods.

One of the common themes in these examples in the United States, Australia, and South Africa, is the dispossession and/or the inability of BIPOC to own and acquire land. Owning land is one of the most effective forms of capital accumulation. Without the ability and/or the right to own land, people's ability to participate fairly as part of a capitalist system by accumulating wealth over generations is significantly impeded. Moreover, historical and current exploitative forms of labour such as slavery, sharecropping, indentured servitude, convict labour, and sweatshops are integral features of capitalism that also most commonly exploit those from BIPOC backgrounds. Finally, using strategies such as those discussed in chapter three, structural racism can also manifest as exclusionary tactics that create barriers for BIPOC to enter higher-level and better paying jobs.

And although many of us might think that these kinds of examples occurred only in the past, the echoes of slavery continue to reverberate into current times. By most objective measures, BIPOC continue to be underrepresented within C-suite teams and boards. In Fortune 500 companies, BIPOC make up 31% of the frontline workforce, yet only 17% of the C-suite[36], and in 2021, 465 (93%) of these companies had a White CEO.[37] And based on

---

36 'Women, BIPOC face roadblocks to C-suite, Gartner report' HRDive, accessed March 4, 2023, https://www.hrdive.com/news/women-bipoc-promotion-c-suite/602584/

37 Richard Zweigenhaft and G. William Domhoff, *Diversity in the Power Elite (3rd ed.) Ironies and Unfulfilled Promises* (Maryland, USA: Rowman & Littlefield Publishers, 2018)

the aforementioned statistics, there is still a significant wealth and income discrepancy between BIPOC and non-BIPOC. So while all of us who work in organisational settings are partaking in some version of a capitalist expedition, not all of us are reaping the benefits of capitalism in equitable ways.

These examples are not to suggest that *every* aspect of capitalism has been constructed on a foundation of structural racism; that would be an oversimplification. However, we also need to acknowledge that *some* of the fundamental tenets of capitalism have been underpinned by structural racism. This is because when the need and ability of those with privileged racial identities to acquire wealth is prioritised over the basic rights of BIPOC, their dignity, and their right to a 'fair day's wage for a fair day's work', we can start to form connections between capitalism and structural racism.

Antiracism is aware of dynamics [of racial inequity] and works actively to address them

The disenfranchisement and oppression that many BIPOC have experienced at the hands of capitalism can manifest at both the collective and personal levels as a kind of resistance to fully engage in the vision. The nature of this resistance will be subtle and usually less conscious in its expression. It will also convince us to explain it purely through the lens of personal psychology; those BIPOC will therefore be perceived as disengaged, difficult to manage, not a team player, or having a poor work ethic. This perspective once again underestimates the impact of structural racism and the 'cultural soup' people are swimming in on an individual's behaviour. And it also once again creates a fertile ground for the formation and propagation of racialised stereotypes and tropes.

BIPOC's barely perceptible defiance to capitalism is a natural reaction to the system of capitalism itself that has thrived, in part, because of its mutually beneficial relationship with structural racism. And some version of this resistance may well occur irrespective of the extent to which an individual identifies with an experience of being personally oppressed and/or disadvantaged by capitalism. This is because there are some experiences that are so injurious to the psyche that they are transferred between people through a combination of learned behaviours, vicarious suffering, and intergenerational trauma. Hence, it is possible that many, if not most, BIPOC will have some inkling of this experience, even if it resides on the fringes of their consciousness.

Critically, this is the dynamic that needs to be attended to and unpacked before BIPOC can fully engage, heart and soul, with an organisational vision. Until this happens, the underlying narrative of BIPOC is going to resemble, 'Sure, I can invest in and work really hard in the pursuit of an organisational vision, but at the end of the day, like it has always been, it is going to be the people in power (which is most likely non-BIPOC) who are going to benefit from my labour, sacrifice, and toil.'

This is the modern-day version of slavery. And while it is nowhere near as obvious or as extreme in its manifestation, the underlying principles are analogous: BIPOC work; however, they are not permitted to fully benefit from and enjoy the fruits of their labour, yet these fruits are enjoyed disproportionately by non-BIPOC.

If you have not guessed already, I am being intentionally provocative and challenging in drawing this analogy. I expect a degree of defensiveness and denial on the behalf of some readers. I have learnt that speaking about painful parts of our shared history in a manner which sugar-coats their consequences is not beneficial to our collective growth in this area, let alone supportive of building an antiracist organisation.

This brings us to a critical point in our journey:

How do we fully engage the hearts and minds of BIPOC in a capitalistic pursuit, such as an organisational vision, when historically, aspects of capitalism have been used against them?

Even though structural racism is driven by a system (of oppression) that is impersonal, the way it impacts people in a physical, emotional, and visceral manner is experienced very much as a personal assault. Therefore, for a more complete solution to the above challenge of how to engage the hearts and minds of BIPOC in a capitalistic pursuit, we need to simultaneously address these dynamics at both the personal and the systemic levels.

Re-visioning capitalism

Addressing the personal component of this challenge requires us to be slightly paradoxical in our thinking. Because although we are focusing on an organisation's vision, to fully engage BIPOC in the pursuit of that vision requires leaders to utilise a different sense: hearing.

BIPOC cannot truly buy into and deeply engage with a capitalistic endeavour until the historical and current ways that capitalism has been weaponised against them has been acknowledged. Structural racism involves the minimisation, silencing, and decentralisation of the BIPOC experience. This was discussed in chapter four as part of developmental sticking point #4. To summarise Ken Hardy from his article, *Healing the Hidden Wounds of Racial Trauma*[38]:

---

38 Kenneth Hardy, 'Healing the Hidden Wounds of Racial Trauma.' *Reclaiming Children and Youth*, 22(1), 24-28 (Spring 2013). http://reclaimingjournal.com/node/1412/

'Systemic oppression causes "internalized devaluation," which leads to an "assaulted sense of self" and "internalized voicelessness" that "erodes the ability to defend against a barrage of unwelcomed and unjustified negative, debilitating messages."'

Being actively heard and affirmed is a powerful antiracist intervention, as well as a potent antidote to the pain BIPOC undergo because of structural racism; this is because centralising their experience acts in direct defiance to those dynamics propagated by structural racism. Telling stories and sharing history, particularly about the impact of racial capitalism on themselves and their family and on their ancestors, is a critical step required to bring to light the psychological wounds which are both individual and collective. These wounds, when left unvalidated and unattended to, will at some point manifest as a barrier, even a subtle one, to a BIPOC's full engagement with the organisation's vision.

Additionally, believing that the vision also applies to themselves is essential if people are going to engage with that vision. The complexities and challenges of how BIPOC experience and internalise dynamics of exclusion and inclusion was discussed as part developmental sticking point #1 in chapter four. Once again, being heard and these experiences being witnessed begins to unravel and directly rebuke the internalised narratives which resemble, 'You are not worthy. You are not welcome. We don't want you here.'

Therefore, a critical step in the process of building antiracist organisations is designing and running antiracism forums. These forums, where BIPOC can discuss their experiences of racism, particularly their experiences of racial capitalism, challenges the strategies utilised by structural racism by doing the exact opposite. The purpose of these forums is twofold.

Firstly, to ensure that people feel heard, witnessed, and validated in terms of their organisational experience of racism. This is of particular importance if those at senior levels of leadership do not identify as BIPOC. As we discussed in developmental sticking point #4, in chapter four, for those without a lived experience of structural racism, developing an understanding and walking in the shoes of those people within your organisation who have experienced racism is a crucial component of the process. The second purpose of these forums is to collect data which will be helpful in how we go about re-visioning capitalism at the systemic level; more about this shortly.

The nature of these forums is variable and will depend on the cultural context of the organisation and its maturity in terms of being able to have constructive conversations about race. For some organisations, having these discussions in affinity groups – where BIPOC and non-BIPOC share their experiences in separate groups – will be most appropriate, whilst, for other organisations, mixed groups will be more effective. The format of these forums is also variable. For some organisations, town halls will be the best fit, where hundreds of people come together, and have their views and experiences heard. For other organisations, roundtables will work better, where small groups of 15 to 20 people gather to exchange experiences and ideas. Alternatively, some organisations may prefer smaller focus groups of sizes 8 to 12. Obviously, organisations can do a combination of the above. The key is to find the format that is most suited to the culture of the organisation and where it is situated along its journey towards antiracism.

Of paramount importance in how these antiracism forums are constructed, or even in the decision whether to conduct them, needs to be a consideration of the cultural load on BIPOC.

Revisiting our understanding of cultural load:

> *Cultural load is a direct consequence of structural
> discrimination. It is the additional and frequently unseen
> work that BIPOC are required to do within workplaces.
> More obvious examples of cultural load are where there is
> the expectation that BIPOC are the representative
> and/or an advocate for their entire race,
> particularly at various cultural awareness
> events or in discussions about racism.*

Not being mindful of the cultural load which may occur as a result of these forums risks racial capitalism being repeated, albeit unintentionally – where BIPOC are responsible for doing the work on the behalf of, and also potentially for the benefit of, non-BIPOC.

We all have psychological barriers and boundaries when it comes to what each of us feels comfortable and permissible to share in the content and the style of our communication. These barriers are a combination of the belief systems that have been constructed as a result of our personal history; the conditioning we have internalised from those that are close and influential to us; and the cultural norms of the context we are currently operating in. Facilitation, when done skilfully, notices when individuals and teams arrive at the psychological barriers that are vigorously defended by espoused narratives that sound like, 'Don't say any more. Don't reveal any more about yourself. Don't tell that aspect of truth. Don't be vulnerable,' and gently supports people to venture one or two steps further outside of their comfort zone. Every time this happens, and people are supported to be slightly uncomfortable, capability is built in our ability to sit with, hold, witness, and validate those stories and experiences that up till now may never have seen the light of day. This is also a significant step in building psychological safety, which we will discuss further in chapters twelve and thirteen.

In how these antiracism forums are facilitated, we need to be mindful of what constitutes racism: racism is a combination of actions, beliefs, and policies which perpetuate and normalise the discrimination and therefore the disadvantaging of one race, and the simultaneous advantaging of another race. Therefore, we need to keep sharpening our ability to see racism as something which perpetuates the disadvantaging of one race and the advantaging of another, and so to continually challenge the belief that racism is only what is obvious in terms of overt physical violence, harassment, or vilification. Unfortunately, racism is founded upon dynamics that are much more subtle than its most obvious expressions, and the ones that most of us associate to racism. These include pathologisation and/or the minimisation of people's natural reactions to the pain and suffering caused by racism, which may include rage, anger, frustration, grief, and hopelessness.

This process might have to be repeated multiple times and in various formats. The indicator that leaders need to monitor this process is the extent to which BIPOC can fully and unreservedly engage emotionally with the organisation's vision. A lack of engagement and emotional buy-in to the vision should be seen as symptomatic of the need for more listening as a way of continuing to acknowledge and witness the painful experiences that many BIPOC have endured at the hands of racial capitalism. When people feel sufficiently heard and validated so that enough of their history of discrimination has been resolved, engagement in the vision will be a natural, almost organic, consequence.

Of course, there will always be those people who no matter how much they are heard and validated, for various reasons, will not fully engage. For those individuals, a different conversation needs to be had of re-evaluating their role within the organisation. As I said previously, when it comes to the realisation of a unifying and compelling vision which is also a stretch goal, there is no room for passengers.

Addressing the systemic aspects of racial capitalism is a little more complicated.

Capitalism as an ideal is deeply ingrained in the belief systems of most organisations. In turn, these beliefs shape the processes, policies, and culture of that organisation's operating system. And this is the way it ought to be! The spirit of capitalism is an essential driving force that is needed to propel an organisation towards its vision. Woven into the aspirations of capitalism is a desire and a hunger to satisfy a commercial imperative; so in the absence of this drive and hunger, organisations are less likely to find success.

However, in the way capitalism *functions*, there are also certain tendencies which have a mutually beneficial relationship with structural racism. This does not mean that we need to eradicate capitalism entirely or admonish every aspect of it; however, to build an antiracist organisation, it does require us to re-evaluate how we think about capitalism. The question we need to ask ourselves is, 'What might capitalism look like if it is not able to advance itself through racial inequity and the exploitation of BIPOC?'

Revisiting the definition of an antiracist organisation:

An antiracist organisation is one that, through its culture, systems, policies, and processes, works to actively dismantle racism and therefore create equity within the workplace.

Re-visioning capitalism therefore requires us to untangle those manifestations which represent the purest form of capitalism and are essential in impelling an organisation towards its vision, from those elements of it that have thrived because of the way it has taken advantage of BIPOC through exploitative work practices and cultures. These dynamics of racial capitalism may not always be obvious in our own organisation, even though imperceptible remnants of old or habitual ways of thinking and working may well echo into the present-day. This makes the untangling process complex, because these dynamics may possibly fall below our conscious recognition, making them subtle and difficult to identify. This requires us to scrutinise capitalism within the context of our own organisation by exploring those aspects of it that tend to normalise racial inequity and/or are exploitative of BIPOC. Not only is this a critical step in building an antiracist organisation, it is perhaps also the ethical responsibility of leaders.

This is where the experiences that BIPOC share, and the data that is collected as part of the antiracism forums, is particularly valuable. Each monetary experience of racial inequity, each microaggression, every feeling that one's career progression has stalled due to race, if traced back far enough, potentially has its roots somewhere in racial capitalism. And it is the processes, policies, and culture that are built on this foundation that contribute to people's experience of racism within an organisational context.

Objectively evaluating these experiences is akin to being a sleuth, seeking clues which indicate that buried within the drive to fulfil a commercial imperative are also vestiges of racial capitalism. Further illumination of these clues occurs when the experiences people share as part of the antiracism forums are validated and unpacked so the underlying dynamics which gave rise to their experiences come more into our direct line of sight. This is where having these conversations facilitated is usually beneficial. Therefore, the framework with which we need to hear and witness the experiences shared at the antiracism forums is, 'How might these experiences of racial inequity be symptomatic, or a manifestation, of ways of thinking and working that are founded upon, even slightly, dynamics of racial capitalism?'

Moving towards racial equity by addressing racial capitalism potentially takes away a powerful lever that capitalism uses to advance itself. Therefore, even the very intention of addressing racial inequity within an organisation puts us on a collision course with capitalism itself. So we need to be mindful, as we discussed in chapter three, that when a system feels under threat, it will find creative mechanisms by which to shore up its own survival.

Through the process of unravelling the clues, we may well encounter further evidence revealing the existence of racial capitalism. When this occurs, the system of racism, in an attempt to perpetuate itself, will tamper with this evidence by constructing sophisticated ways of denying and justifying the evidence, or normalising it, by making it appear acceptable or commonplace. These strategies need to be seen as a system of oppression's attempt to convince us that it does not exist, and that racial capitalism is a fairy-tale dreamed up by woke hipsters determined to overthrow the power structure.

Make no bones about it: as we get closer to being cognisant of the sophistication of its methods, structural racism will conjure up significant resistance. The resultant risk is that we overlook or minimise the degree to which structural racism is deeply rooted in how the driving force of capitalism is utilised in order to fulfil an organisation's commercial imperative.

When we encounter these moments of resistance, reminding ourselves of the purpose of the organisation is vital. The 'why' that elucidates our organisation's reason for existence is also a powerful force that, when fully leveraged, delivers the clarity as well as the power required to combat this resistance. This is why, as discussed in chapter seven, aligning an initiative to build an antiracist organisation to the purpose of the broader organisation is so essential. Because every time we revisit and continue to illuminate the purpose of the organisation, we are reminded why it is so important we stand firm in the face of this resistance, and not be deceived by the clever and sophisticated ways structural racism will attempt to deny, minimise, deflect, and normalise the existence of these racist elements of capitalism.

Reflection #9:

Evaluating the performance benefits of building an antiracist culture

1. Revisit your organisation's vision from reflection #8.

2. Review the commercial benefits of a more diverse and inclusive culture, with a particular focus on an antiracist culture.

3. For your organisation, *at this point in time*, do the commercial benefits of moving towards an antiracist culture sufficiently support the organisation's vision so that it justifies such an initiative?

4. Should you and other key personnel conclude that the commercial benefits of moving towards an antiracist culture *do not* justify such an initiative, re-evaluate and reconsider if now is the most opportune time to deliver such an initiative.

5. If the commercial benefits *do* justify such an initiative, what might your organisation's version of antiracism forums look like? Make sure you take into account:

    a. The cultural context of the organisation – the culture of the organisation and where it is situated along its journey towards antiracism.

    b. The maturity of the organisation in terms of being able to have constructive conversations about race and racism.

c. The cultural load which BIPOC may have to carry as a result of these forums.

d. Given the above, the most appropriate format for these forums. Town halls, round tables, or focus groups? And 'affinity' or 'mixed' groups?

Chapter Ten:

Organisational strategy and role clarity

Purpose, vision, and strategy have an interdependent relationship

If the purpose of an organisation illuminates its reason for existence or its 'why', and the vision clarifies the 'what' [we are going to look like in X years], then the strategy and the optimal culture determines the 'how'. We will discuss culture and its role in creating an antiracist and high-performance organisation in chapters twelve and thirteen, but for the time being let's explore the importance of organisational strategy and role clarity.

The ultimate objective of an organisation's strategy is to explicitly state, from a high-level perspective, how the organisation is going to deliver its vision. From a functional point of view, strategy is the sum of the actions the organisation intends to implement to maximise the probability of achieving its long-term goals and vision.

These elements — the purpose, the vision, and the strategy of an organisation — are interdependent in nature. This is because an effective strategy is built around, and informed by, the purpose of the organisation. Thus, in the way it approaches its strategic objectives, organisational members are able is to find greater meaning and fulfilment because they are aligned to the purpose. And when there is a concise and unifying vision, it enables the organisation to construct a strategic plan with a single clear goal in mind: to deliver on that vision. In this way, by informing the direction, the structure, and the 'why' of the strategy, the purpose and vision sustain the strategy.

There may be a perception that constructing an organisational strategy is a straightforward exercise. However, to optimise the strategic plan's ability to propel an organisation towards its long-term goals, it needs to be crafted so that there is a balance between a simplicity of implementation and execution, and being sufficiently rigorous so it withstands the test of time and shifting business environments and macroeconomic conditions. This can be a complex and nuanced process.

An effective organisational strategy is constructed around multiple levels

An effective strategic plan needs to be integrated with the purpose and vision of the organisation. Ideally, it also needs to be multi-levelled, where the initial level clarifies the strategy from a high-level perspective, and each subsequent level drills down, documenting increasing levels of detail. Therefore, one way to approach the construction of a strategic plan is as follows.

Level one: What are our 4–6 strategic drivers?
These strategic drivers can be distilled down by starting with the question, 'What are the most powerful levers we [the organisation] have at our disposal that are going to maximally propel the momentum of the organisation towards the vision?'

Organisations need to resist the temptation to have more than 6 strategic drivers. Sometimes organisations, driven by a need to be all things to all people, have a strategic plan that either explicitly or informally has numerous (more than 6) areas of strategic focus. This results in the organisation diluting its focus across too many areas and thus spreading its finite resources too thinly. Consequently, very few, if any, of these strategic goals receive the emphasis and focus required to be completed in a timeframe and to a standard which inspires team members with a sense of pride and excellence. Over time, this can breed a normalisation of mediocrity, which is clearly contrary to the creation of a high-performance culture. Additionally, team members' focus can get attenuated when there are too many important strategic goals demanding their attention. This may require them to utilise inefficient thinking and processes to address these numerous demands, resulting in a greater likelihood of underperformance and burnout. This in turn can create a kind of organisational malaise, perhaps even a depression, because people feel they are working hard but nothing on the to-do list is getting ticked off, or at least being completed to a standard of excellence.

Therefore, every one of these drivers needs to justify its place in the strategic plan by demonstrating a strong and direct relationship between itself and the delivery of the vision. Organisational leaders need to stress test potential drivers and run them through the various filters required so that the final set of strategic drivers represent the 4–6 most powerful and effective levers to drive performance towards the achievement of the vision.

Level two: For each strategic driver, what are the keys to success?

For each of the strategic drivers, leadership need to decide what are the keys to success in order maximise the effectiveness of this driver. These keys to success can be considered the 'sub-drivers' of each of the main strategic drivers. In many ways, this step mirrors level one, where myriad of potential options need to be stress tested in order to ascertain which are the 3–4 most indispensable and effective keys to success for each of the strategic drivers.

Level three: For each of the keys to success, what does success look like?

For each of the keys to success, organisations need to clarify what success looks like. In other words, if each of the keys to success were executed with excellence, and in a way which maximally drives the vision, what would the specific outcomes be? Once again, it is essential that these specific outcomes are kept to a finite number, ideally between 4 and 6.

Once these specific outcomes for each of the keys to success have been clarified, the organisation can start to build an operational plan around these outcomes. The operational plan is the final level of detail which clarifies what is important to focus on and therefore where and how team members are required to direct their energy and attention on a day-to-day basis.

Level four: In order to achieve this success, what are the functionalities and roles required?

As part of crafting a strategic plan, the functionalities that are required to execute that strategy need to be ascertained and clarified. These functionalities are represented by the knowledge, skills, and expertise that the organisation requires to effectively execute the strategy. With the functionalities clear, the organisation can then ensure it is right sized in terms of its structure and the roles that are required to meet these functionalities. Creating a structure and thus an organisational chart that enables rather than creates barriers to the effective execution of the strategy is a critical determinant of success.

One of the principal functions of leadership is to continually clarify the technical as well as the cultural components of people's role

In any organisation, role clarity is one of the essential requirements for success. This is because optimal team member engagement, and therefore performance, can only occur when they have certainty regarding the expectations and obligations associated to their role, as well as clarity in terms of the boundaries of their role, relative to the roles of their teammates.

Organisational leaders, therefore, as one of the principal functions of their role, need to over-communicate when it comes to role clarity. Ideally, this involves leaders clarifying the respective roles of their team members by connecting these roles to the strategic plan and then aligning each role to the purpose and vision of the organisation. This should be done in a way that is clear and concise, so it is understandable and relatable; consistent, in that the same key messages are being delivered by management on every occasion; and continual, so these messages are ongoing and repeated. Think of these as the three Cs of effective leadership communication (or four Cs, depending on whether you count 'clear and concise' as one or two Cs). In other words, overcommunicating, 'Sam, this is your role. Given our strategy, this is why your role represents a key function within that strategy, and this is how you executing the requirements of your role is going to drive us towards our vision and is aligned to the overall purpose of our organisation or team.'

In a high-performance environment, each team member has absolute clarity around the two essential components of their role: the *technical* aspect and the *cultural* aspect. The technical component refers to the functional and/or operational aspects of their role. Whether they are a lawyer, a cleaner, an accountant, a plumber, or a footballer, each individual must fulfil a set of technical and operational responsibilities in order for their organisation or team to deliver a particular set of outcomes.

However, what is less frequently discussed and clarified are the cultural components and responsibilities of each person's role. One of the key enablers of optimal performance is a culture of shared accountability. This is where each team member believes, and behaves, as though the cultural buck stops at them. This belief is deeply engrained in the psyche of the group and is actively demonstrated regardless of whether someone is the newest person on the team or the most seasoned leader. If each person in a high-performance environment has a cultural role to play in how they contribute to co-creating the desired culture, clarifying the responsibilities associated with this aspect of their role is equally as important as providing them with the clarity they require in terms of the technical component of their role.

In chapter five, we defined high performance from an individual perspective as:

The ability to consistently deploy skills and knowledge in a way which drives the vision relative to one's role and in alignment with the strategy, and to do this across the variety of situations and contexts in which that individual is required to perform.

Therefore, a powerful driver of performance is when every team member has the clarity of role to be able to respond effectively when that internal voice enquires, 'In this moment, given our agreed-upon strategy and the current context, what does my role require of me?'

When faced with this vital enquiry, role clarity in terms of the functions of their role and a surety of the boundaries of these functions relative to their teammates enables people to align their actions and behaviours most effectively to the agreed-upon strategy. And, paradoxically, this clarity also allows people to adapt situationally and be sufficiently agile, because when the intention of their role is clear, they feel the permission and the freedom to utilise their skills, experience, and knowledge in service of that intention.

An effective strategy, therefore, needs to ensure that team members are appropriately supported in the development of the skills and knowledge required so that they are well equipped to take up both the technical and cultural aspects of their role in a manner which drives the vision and is in service of the purpose of the organisation. In this way, having a clear, explicit, and integrated strategy informs and clarifies what the optimal culture needs to look and feel like.

Reflection #10:

Stress-testing your organisational strategy

1. Does your organisation have its own version of a clear, explicit, and integrated strategy which clarifies the four levels of detail (or something similar) discussed in this chapter? More importantly, is the clear intention of this strategy to propel the momentum of the organisation towards the achievement of its vision?

2. If not, organise a time where the appropriate people can get together to start to construct an organisational strategy using the structure and process described in this chapter.

3. If yes, then go to the next question.

4. With your existing organisational strategy, stress test it using the following criteria:

   - Is the intention of the strategy clearly and explicitly driving the organisation towards its vision?

   - Does the strategy clarify the 4–6 most powerful strategic drivers in terms of the achievement of the vision?

   - Does the number of strategic drivers detailed in the strategy enable the organisation to maintain its focus on delivering these to high-performance expectations in terms of timeframes and standards? If not, be ruthless in reducing the number of strategic drivers to a number which the organisation is able to maintain a strong and consistent focus on.

- For each of the strategic drivers, are there definite keys to success which can be used to maintain direction and focus, as well as evaluate the success of delivering these strategic imperatives?

- For each of these keys to success, is there clarity in terms of what success looks like? And are these outcomes aligned with and built into the operational plan?

- Based on this operational plan, is the organisation 'right-sized', and does it have the required structure and functionalities to implement and execute the operational plan?

- Does the strategic plan clarify the optimal culture needed in order for it to be effectively executed?

Chapter Eleven:

Strategic planning and the antiracist organisation

Ascertaining and then cultivating the optimal culture needs to be included in the strategic plan

Every organisation will have a unique set of strategic drivers it is required to execute on in order to deliver its vision. This set will be dependent on multiple factors including, but not limited to, macroeconomic conditions, industry specific challenges, the maturity and developmental stage of the organisation, and of course, the vision itself.

Culture is an essential driver of organisational performance. Integrating culture into the strategic planning process ensures that the culture organisations aspire to also complements and enhances the execution of strategic initiatives. Therefore, as part of their strategic plan, organisations must also address, 'What is the optimal culture that is going enhance our strategic initiatives, and thus drive us towards our vision? And how do we cultivate that culture?' At which level of the strategic plan 'culture' is detailed, and the degree of prioritisation it receives, will once again be dependent on the particular context and circumstances of each organisation. But what is essential is that somewhere, as part of the organisational strategy, culture is clarified.

Many people will be familiar with legendary management consultant Peter Drucker saying, 'Culture eats strategy for breakfast.' Yet, despite the notoriety of his comment, it is not uncommon for organisations, as part of their strategic planning and thinking, to overlook how they are going to ascertain, and then cultivate, the optimal culture.

Building an antiracist organisation primarily falls under the banner of a cultural endeavour; as such, clarifying how the organisation intends to create an antiracist culture needs to be clarified somewhere within the culture section of the strategic plan. Furthermore, central to the outcome of creating an antiracist culture is developing the understanding as well as the capability needed to address racial inequity. Therefore, clarifying and detailing how the organisation intends to accomplish this outcome also needs to be included as part of, 'What does success look like?' and then incorporated as an actionable item somewhere within the strategy.

When we are dealing with a system of oppression that, via structural racism, has been ubiquitous and successfully perpetuated itself over centuries, overnight change and transformation is an unlikely outcome. Therefore, when it comes to designing an organisational strategy, which includes an antiracist culture as one of its strategic outcomes, leaders need to be mindful of some of the distinctive challenges and dynamics which occur as a direct consequence of structural racism itself. This is what we shall discuss in the remainder of this chapter.

Organisations and their leaders frequently underestimate the complexity of DEI work and therefore what it takes to build an antiracist organisation

The task of building an antiracist organisation is complex and challenging. And it's perhaps the insufficient appreciation and/or acceptance of this assertion that contributes to organisational leaders underestimating the commitment needed to create truly diverse, equitable, and inclusive cultures. This is why embedding an antiracism initiative into the strategic plan is so critical, because without the prioritisation and the clarity of execution this enables, organisations will be less equipped to address the challenges they will invariably encounter on the way towards antiracism.

For example, one of the cornerstones of DEI programs is working to address unconscious or implicit bias. Unconscious bias is when we have attitudes towards people, or associate them with certain stereotypes and assumptions, without our conscious knowledge. These biases are not constructed overnight. In most cases they have been created and then reinforced by a constant stream of subliminal messages we receive from those close to us, such as family and friends, but also media, advertising, and popular culture. We barely notice as these messages indoctrinate us about which social identities and experiences are more acceptable, and which we should perceive as someone different from ourselves, or 'the other'. As we discussed in developmental sticking point #4 in chapter four, these messages, which are often rooted in dynamics of structural discrimination, serve to reinforce, but also justify, the marginalisation and devaluing of certain groups of people.

These biases have become firmly entrenched in our individual and collective psyches, and are, by definition, unconscious.

Therefore, the most effective way to transform them is to make more conscious those discriminatory attitudes and behaviours which may have been inadvertently normalised, or which have flown under the radar. This requires a strategic focus, where an ongoing commitment and investment to continually confront the dynamics and impacts of unconscious bias and stereotyping is detailed. Given the pervasiveness of these dynamics, if this commitment is not made explicit as part of an overall strategic plan, transformation and success in this area will remain elusive. For example, in a 2019 meta-analysis of more than 490 studies involving some 80,000 people, psychologist Patrick Forscher and his colleagues found that most unconscious bias trainings did not result in significant changes to biased behaviour.[39]

The fact that antiracism training – or 'cultural awareness' trainings, as they are often described – are frequently delivered as one-day, sometimes even half-day, programs, is indicative of the extent to which we underestimate what is required to properly address these matters. These sessions are relatively cheap and enable organisations to tick the diversity training box. However, it is unlikely they will be effective in unravelling the conditioning that has resulted from a lifetime of messages we have received and subsequently internalised about people and groups that are different from our own. This makes it unlikely these one-and-done kind of diversity programs will be able to make any substantial difference in changing the long-term behaviours of participants, and therefore deliver the intended outcomes to the organisation.

This underlines the importance that an organisation's intentions to create an antiracist culture are built into, and made explicit as, part of its strategy. And furthermore, in how this strategy has been constructed, people have been realistic and sober in terms of

---

39 Patrick Forscher et al, 'A meta-analysis of procedures to change implicit measures.' *Journal of Personality and Social Psychology, 117*(3), (September 2019) 522 – 559 doi.org/10.1037/pspa0000160

what it takes to unlearn deeply ingrained systems of thinking, such as unconscious bias and stereotyping, which perpetuate racial inequity.

Antiracism must be seen as everyone's responsibility

We know that within an organisational context, racism is a humanitarian and a well-being concern, as well as an impediment to optimal performance. Therefore, in order to directly address racism, organisational leaders and teams must approach cultivating racial equity, and inclusion in general, like any other teamwork or cultural difficulty – where the challenge belongs to everyone.

When this does not happen, people default to believing that the responsibility for addressing the challenges of racism resides primarily with BIPOC, and it is therefore 'their' problem to resolve. For example, if BIPOC are the minority, then they should adapt to the majority's way of thinking. This 'thinking' can include a denial that racism is even an issue and, as part of this denial, BIPOC should relinquish their own reactions and the responses they have to subtle (or overt) racist behaviours and microaggressions.

When we do not see addressing racism as being everyone's responsibility, there is a tendency to assume it is incumbent on BIPOC to initiate and drive those strategies where the desired outcome is to create racial equity. However, placing the burden of strategic responsibility primarily on BIPOC fails to acknowledge the historical patterns and impacts of structural racism that we discussed in chapter three. These patterns are deeply ingrained in organisational systems and thinking, and so belong to everyone. Therefore, an essential aspect of constructing a strategy, which includes moving towards antiracism, is being aware of the cultural load carried by BIPOC, and how the dynamics of structural racism can unintentionally infiltrate into how the strategy itself gets constructed.

From this more systemic perspective, sometimes the mere presence of BIPOC, as well as others with minority or marginalised identities, brings to the surface developmental sticking points that are pre-existing within the organisation's thinking and culture. It is likely that these same developmental sticking points are impacting performance in other areas of the organisation; areas that may not be as obvious. Rather than the responsibility for driving an antiracist strategy resting solely on the shoulders of BIPOC, best practice is to explore how the developmental challenges we experience, relative to creating an antiracist culture, are also a microcosm of the organisational system itself. This is also the approach which best encapsulates a high-performance mindset. This is because fostering a culture of shared accountability in how we address these concerns, and explicitly including these in the strategy, will deliver the most comprehensive and sustainable solutions.

A critical ingredient in the construction of an antiracist strategy is that non-BIPOC team members, and particularly non-BIPOC leaders, care about the issue of structural racism. Transformation in any long-standing issue or challenge can only happen to the extent that people actually care about that issue and are emotionally invested in changing the status quo. At this point, revisiting and then realigning to people's personal purpose (see reflection #6A) may be useful:

What would it mean for how I prioritise and think about, building an antiracist organisation, if I was truly in service of my personal purpose?

And if personal purpose is about making a difference and/or doing something for the greater good, how can I, impelled

*by my personal purpose, utilise whatever power, privilege,
and influence I have in how I engage with and directly
address structural racism within my organisation?*

Making antiracism a strategic focus minimises the 'othering' effect

It is frequently BIPOC's experiences of and reactions to racism that provide the initial impetus and rationale for building an antiracist culture. As a result, BIPOC are frequently seen as disrupting the status quo of privilege and entitlement by elevating their experiences of racism to a level of cognisance where they can no longer be denied, ignored, or brushed over. When this happens, the system of racism, in an attempt to re-establish the status quo, will often construct an insidious narrative, even if this narrative is only heard as whispers in the hallways or in the rolling of eyes during a management meeting. This narrative subtly insinuates that if BIPOC are raising the issue of racism, not only is it their problem to solve, but in fact, they themselves are the problem. Because if BIPOC were not part of the organisation, there would be no need to grapple with these cultural challenges they are drawing attention to in the first place. This endeavour to re-establish the status quo uses strategy #3 discussed in chapter three, by leveraging stereotypes and racialised tropes of BIPOC being angry, aggressive, disruptive, and problematic. This is the organisational equivalent of killing the messenger.

We can also notice that almost imperceptibly embedded within this thinking are the initial stages of BIPOC being othered. Being othered is when certain people, or groups of people, are deemed to not be included or as welcomed in the cultural mainstream and are therefore perceived to be different or 'the other'. For those people experiencing the othering, they will usually feel excluded, and like they are part of an us-and-them dynamic, where they are the 'them'. They therefore feel like they are less connected and do not completely belong; but more about belonging shortly.

As we discussed in developmental sticking point #3 in chapter four, one of the consequences of structural racism is internalised oppression.

> *Internalised oppression is when the way the external oppressor or oppressive system views, values, and treats people becomes the way they view, value, and treat themselves.*

When BIPOC experience being othered, they receive the message that *they* are the problem, even if this message is couched within a strategy to address racism. This message, which originates from the culture, colludes with the rejection of self that already exists within them as a consequence of internalised oppression.

The messages BIPOC are receiving indirectly from the organisation as well as from their own experience of internalised oppression are saying a very similar thing: 'You are not welcome. We don't want you here. You are the problem.' When this happens, we are perpetuating the very thing that we are trying to address and transform via the process of building an antiracist organisation.

The cultural load this places on BIPOC cannot be overestimated. On one hand, they are thrilled, proud even, that the organisation they are part of is taking steps to directly address racism. But on the other hand, as part of the process, they have been made to feel like they are the problem, and it is therefore their responsibility to solve 'their problem'. The complex clash of realities within this moment may well serve to reinforce the belief that they do not really belong to this organisation, or at best that they belong a little less than those with more privileged racial identities. And as a result, BIPOC may start to disengage from their roles, first emotionally, then maybe intellectually, and finally, perhaps even physically, resulting in their departure from the organisation. Clearly, this will be an unintended and undesirable consequence for an organisation that is committed to antiracism.

Therefore, it is crucial that as part of building an antiracist culture the organisation does not underestimate the importance of clarifying and making explicit this element within its strategic plan. And in the way the plan for an antiracist culture is delivered and socialised, it is clearly framed like any other issue or challenge that the organisation is facing – that this is a team issue, and we are therefore all responsible for playing our respective roles in the design and then in the execution of the strategy in order to provide the best possible outcomes for the organisation.

People need developmental support in how they take up the cultural component of their role

As part of a strategic plan, having an explicit focus on building the technical ability of a workforce via ongoing professional developmental is a key determinant of organisational performance. The obvious benefit of deepening relevant skills, knowledge, and expertise is that it increases the overall technical capability of an organisation. Additionally, when people's intrinsic needs to learn, to grow, and to work towards a sense of mastery are assuaged, there is a greater likelihood that organisations will be able to attract and retain talented individuals who possess a strong growth mindset.[40]

As we discussed in chapter ten, when it comes to the implementation and execution of the strategy, role clarity is an

---

40 *Growth mindset* is a theory of motivation proposed by Carol Dweck. She suggests that people with a growth mindset believe that their most basic abilities can be developed through dedication and hard work – brains and talent are just the starting point. This view creates a love of learning and a resilience that are essential for great accomplishment.

essential ingredient for success. To drive maximal engagement and therefore performance, team members need clarity on the technical as well as the cultural components of their role. Building an antiracist organisation is primarily a cultural initiative. We therefore need to think about and prioritise the developmental support people may require to effectively take up the cultural aspect of their role, in a similar way to how we approach building capability in those more technical parts of their role.

In chapter three, we discussed how in my experience of working with organisations, the vast majority of people within them are kind, considerate, and well-intentioned people. Hence, attitudes and behaviours that are unintentionally racist and/or result in perpetuating racial inequity, usually arise out of (i) the need for more awareness of their own unconscious biases and beliefs; (ii) the need for more education in terms of the history of racism and its associated dynamics and impacts, particularly in their own geographical context; (iii) an individual's own fears and insecurities, which get externalised and/or projected as unintentional or unconscious racism; or (iv) some combination of the above three elements. Therefore, a strategy and a commitment to address the underlying drivers of those attitudes and behaviours that perpetuate racial inequity is essential in terms of clarifying the cultural component of people's roles.

Given these elements, which reinforce the status quo when it comes to racial inequity, what is the support and development people need to get better at fulfilling the responsibilities and requirements of the cultural component of their role?

Where this is similar to the technical aspect of people's role is that there needs to be a strategic focus on development, and this focus needs to be detailed as part of the strategic plan. Where it is perhaps different to the technical aspect is in the nature and methodology of development process itself.

This work is primarily psychological work. It is slow, it is deep, and at times is simultaneously challenging and confronting. After all, having our own unconscious biases revealed to us, or learning how we project our own insecurities or sense of inadequacy onto those people we see as different from ourselves requires us to recalibrate deeply held aspects of our identity.

This work therefore requires us to explore and unpack our experiences, including some of the more painful ones, so we can start to recognise how the narratives that have been created around these experiences play their part in constructing how we see ourselves. Breaking down those aspects of our identity which are no longer serving us, and then re-building those same elements with the functionalities that enable us to fulfil both the technical and cultural obligations of our role requires a certain inner resolve. And while there is no fixed recipe for what this process calls on us to find within ourselves, in my personal and professional experience, it is an alchemical combination of self-awareness, intestinal fortitude, compassion for self, and absolute clarity on the purpose or the deeper 'why' of why we would willingly undertake such an arduous inward journey.

From a practical perspective, when it comes to building an antiracist organisation, there are many responsibilities and areas of development that might be supportive in terms of the cultural aspect of people's roles. As a starting point, here are five, which if thoughtfully addressed will go a long way towards the creation of an antiracist culture.

Firstly, the requirements of their role might be to focus on building awareness of their own unconscious biases and/or tendency to form stereotypes. Secondly, it could be to educate themselves about key historical events, particularly those aspects of history that are relevant to their own geographic region and context. Thirdly, team members can work to better understand their privilege, especially those areas of privilege they are not as aware of or less identified with. Fourth could be to find ways to utilise whatever power, influence, and privilege they do have to name and address incidences of racial inequity as they happen, but also, to do this in a manner which does not shame or belittle those demonstrating the behaviours. Fifth and finally, it could be to work on their insecurities and aspects of their own psychology that they are less comfortable with. This will minimise the tendency to project those less-conscious parts of their identity onto BIPOC and other people from minority and/or marginalised groups. For example, when people are not comfortable or less identified with their own anger or rage, there is a tendency to project it onto BIPOC. Hence the common stereotype or racialised trope of the angry BIPOC.

See what I mean? Deep, psychological, and confronting work, and not for the faint of heart! This is why it is so important to see building an antiracist organisation as being aligned to and supportive of the vision and purpose of the organisation. In the absence of this synergistic alignment, there is not the commercial drive nor the deeper 'why' for individual team members to undertake the kind of development and challenging transformational processes that build the capability necessary to fulfil the cultural obligations of their respective role.

Most organisations, but in particular small- to medium-sized ones, will usually not have the internal capability or expertise to deliver these kinds of programs in a safe and effective manner. This is where engaging a specialist DEI facilitator or a 'culture coach' is worthwhile.

Many of us have heard of, or perhaps even been witness to, occasions where DEI issues and concerns which required a sensitive and refined approach were tackled with hubris and an insufficient understanding of the complexity of those dynamics at hand. These events result in ruptures to the cultural fabric of a team or organisation – ruptures which are sometimes irreparable. These incidences are once again indicative of our insufficient appreciation of the complexity of addressing and transforming the systems of oppression and resultant unconscious biases that have entrenched themselves in our collective and individual psyches. And while recommending a DEI specialist facilitator to guide you through these challenges may well be seen as shamelessly self-promotional, it is my genuine belief that if we are committed to antiracist outcomes and, more broadly, to fostering a culture of inclusion and belonging, then we need to engage people who are specialists in this area.

Reflection #11A:

Determining the strategy to develop the cultural component of people's role

1. For yourself and/or those people that you lead, what are the cultural components of your respective roles that are essential in creating an inclusive and high-performance culture?

2. What are the key capabilities that people need so they can effectively execute these cultural components?

3. To what extent has there been a developmental focus on building these capabilities? Does this 'people development initiative' have a strategic focus that is detailed in the organisational strategy?

4. Based on these responses, what might need to be included or changed in the strategic plan so that there is a consistent and appropriate prioritisation on developing those capabilities essential for people to execute the cultural component of their roles?

Reflection #11B:

Unpacking unconscious bias

1. Try to become aware of an area of unconscious (implicit) bias you have in terms of people's race. This will most likely be a little tricky because, by definition, these biases are largely unconscious. As we discussed in chapter four, even if you are BIPOC, you may well have areas of unconscious bias due to internalised oppression.

2. The subtleties of unconscious bias will reveal themselves in slight differences in the ways you think about, relate to, communicate with, and make assumptions about BIPOC, in comparison to non-BIPOC. Therefore, biases will manifest in the assumptions you make about people's capability, education, temperament, family background, and culture, to name just a few. This step might take some deeper self-reflection.

3. When you discover an area where you are making assumptions relative to people's race, firstly congratulate yourself: this is not an easy or comfortable process.

4. What is the belief or the bias which underlies the assumption you are making? For example, that BIPOC are not as intelligent, or BIPOC are angry a lot, or BIPOC are not as disciplined or hard-working.

5. How is this belief related to stereotypes and/or racialised tropes?

6. Given that this belief did not originate with you, can you see how and where you were exposed to this belief and have subsequently internalised it? (hint: for example, from those people close to you, such as family and friends, or from the media, education, advertising)

7. How might your unconscious bias be a reflection of a larger cultural bias that occurs to some extent within your organisation?

Bonus question:

8. To what extent is this bias also a projection? In other words, the bias that is being projected onto or associated with BIPOC mirrors an area of your own psychology and/or identity you might feel insecure about, are ashamed about, or have trouble fully owning and celebrating?

Chapter Twelve:

Building
high-performance cultures

The cultural context determines the behaviours that make sense to people

Culture can be simply defined as: the systems of knowledge, symbols, behaviour, and values shared by a group of people, and is more generally described as: the way we do things around here. Culture is always socially learned, shaped by people, and transferred between us. There is no culture, or no point to culture, without people.

When people turn up to work, they bring with them a personal culture – their own understanding of 'normal' that has been influenced and shaped primarily by those closest to them, most often family. That personal or individual culture exists within a team culture – the marketing team, the nightshift, or a sporting team. This in turn sits within an organisational culture – the Minneapolis Police Department, for example – which then sits within a community culture, and ultimately within the broader culture of our society. Culture is therefore multilayered, with numerous factors exerting an influence on individual and collective behaviours. And it is these various layers and influences which establish the 'cultural context'.

From an organisational perspective, the cultural context can be thought of as a collection of cultural norms.

Why is this relevant to building a high-performance culture?

The cultural context defines and dictates which ways of thinking and behaving are deemed as more acceptable. It is therefore a key determinant of the extent to which a particular organisation or team thinks, feels, and, perhaps most importantly, behaves in a high-performance manner. Additionally, and as we discussed in chapter five, the cultural context enables teams and organisations to consistently access their skills and knowledge, so they can execute the strategy and deliver optimal performance.

For any individual, their behaviour makes sense to them given the cultural context they are operating within. Behaviours, practices, and attitudes that from an objective perspective are clearly unacceptable, or perhaps even bordering on being culturally dysfunctional, may fall within the bounds of acceptability because they make sense when viewed from that individual's perspective. This is because those behaviours and attitudes have been rewarded, or at a minimum not resisted, and therefore over time have been affirmed and then normalised by the cultural context.

The acceptability of any set of behaviours and the degree to which they are seen to be 'normal' is therefore subjective and determined primarily by the cultural context. What is acceptable, perhaps even rewarded, in one cultural context, may well be considered taboo in another.

An emphasis on 'values' has become ubiquitous in most organisations. As such, organisations and teams will distil a collection of values, and then aspire to live the behaviours which epitomise these values. However, the extent to which people's actual behaviours are aligned with the stated values is ultimately determined by the cultural context and the explicit and implicit messages it invokes; for it is these narratives which dictate the behaviours that make sense to people. Hence, our ability to understand and transform less-helpful narratives are greater determinants of performance than a set of values which are not necessarily linked to specific behaviours. This is why, to some people's surprise, I have not elaborated on the notion of organisational values, but rather, focused the discussion on deepening our understanding of the cultural context.

From most perspectives, Lance Armstrong's long-term behavioural pattern of doping with the aim of improving his performance would be considered cheating and therefore should not be tolerated. However, from his perspective, this behaviour made sense given his cultural context and what had been normalised within the US Postal cycling team, and perhaps within the sport of professional cycling in general. This does not indemnify him from being personally responsible for his decisions and the resulting consequences of those actions; although it does require us to revisit a familiar complexity.

This complexity requires us to explore the extent to which any individual within a team or organisational setting is wholly and solely responsible for their behaviour. Obviously, individuals need to be responsible for their behaviour, and need to be held accountable when that behaviour diverges from the elite standards and professionalism required for optimal performance. Yet, assigning absolute responsibility to an individual for their behaviour underestimates the formidable influence and pervasive tendency the cultural context has to normalise and make sense of certain behaviours, attitudes, and practices. This is a useful reminder that an individual's behaviour needs to be explored through two different but equally valid lenses. Firstly, through the lens of personal responsibility and accountability for one's actions, and secondly through an understanding of how the cultural context influences and normalises certain behaviours, thereby making them culturally acceptable.

Another example more closely related to our topic is that, as horrendous and abhorrent as Derek Chauvin's treatment of George Floyd was, somewhere in his thinking this behaviour made sense to him and was considered to be normal. His thinking was based on the multiple layers of conditioning and the resultant cultural context within which he was ensconced. For example, his personal culture, the Minneapolis Police Department culture, as well as the broader culture within the United States.

Organisations and teams will not perform at a high level consistently until those elite behaviours which drive high performance are embedded in the culture to the point where they become norms. Therefore, building high-performance cultures requires leaders and their teams to shift the cultural context so as to cultivate those behaviours that are supportive of high performance, whilst at the same time eradicating, or at least minimising, those behaviours that detract from high performance. When the interplay of what gets rewarded and what gets resisted is left unexplored and thus unaddressed, behaviours that based on the cultural context make sense eventually become normalised, even if they are incongruous to the desired culture and organisational outcomes. Therefore, understanding the intricacies of the cultural context in how it is constructed, as well as its impact, is imperative to creating a high-performance culture as well as an antiracist organisation.

History creates and then reinforces the cultural context

Figure 4: The building blocks which construct the cultural context.

The cultural context of an organisation or team has its origins in history. History can be yesterday, it can be last week's game, it can be last quarter's earnings, and it can be a particular significant occurrence or iconic event which happened years, even decades prior. Deeply held beliefs and narratives about who we are get created around these historical events. For example, a football team loses two close games in a row, and a narrative gets created, 'We don't have what it takes to win the close games.' Or in an organisation, somebody gets promoted into a senior position because of their friendship with the CEO, which shapes a narrative intimating that, 'Career advancement in this company is based on knowing the right people, so there is little benefit in being dedicated, hard-working, and developing your expertise.' Of course, the opposite versions of history will give rise to different narratives being created.

These narratives and deeply held beliefs which construct an organisation's identity get reinforced and further entrenched in the collective psyche every time history repeats itself. And given that these narratives tend to be self-fulfilling prophecies, this is not uncommon. For example, without hard work and dedication being incentivised by career progression, team members are slightly less hard-working and dedicated. This means they are less likely to get promoted, leaving the door open for a promotion, which at least based on optics, reeks of nepotism.

These narratives give rise to a set of cultural norms which determine which behaviours are acceptable and therefore get rewarded, and which are less acceptable and so get resisted. For example, in a team meeting, someone makes a sexist comment. The meeting is short, and the team is busy, so nobody says anything. While that behaviour was not rewarded, by the same token neither was it resisted. And in that instant, sexism becomes slightly more normalised and therefore slightly more acceptable within the culture of that team. This one instant in isolation neither creates nor diminishes a cultural norm. But it is the accumulation over time of these discrete incidences that fortifies existing cultural norms, as well as establishes new ones.

This is why certain aspects of the cultural context are fluid and shift on a regular basis. History is always getting written and re-written; what happens today will be history by tomorrow. And it is this history, and the narratives which get created around an accumulation of yesterdays, that will continually recalibrate the cultural context. This is how cultures shift and transform themselves organically. But to have intentionality in this process and to move cultures in a specific, desired direction – which presumably is towards optimal performance – requires us to explore how various aspects of history reverberate into current times.

Aspects of our shared history are always playing out in current times. And while this may not be happening in a literal sense, if we pay enough attention, we can see and feel the currents of history as they ripple forward and land on the shores of the present. This is because historical events did not just occur randomly or out of the blue. They occurred because there were certain cultural tendencies and systems of thinking which gave rise to them. Until we have become sufficiently aware of these tendencies and ways of thinking, to the extent that we are able to transform or resolve them, the propensity for similar events to occur will remain.

For example, in Michael's story (page 4), you will recall there was something about the way his peers treated him which suggested that his way of being, thinking, showing up, or working did not quite fit with their way. The colonisation of Australia happened more than 200 years ago. But the fact that this aspect of Australia's history is yet to be fully processed and reconciled results in the echoes of colonisation happening in the present. If an underlying premise of colonisation is, 'Our way is better than your way,' then we can see a version of a colonialist attitude in the way that Michael was treated by his peers.

This is why, as we discussed in chapter nine, intentionally creating the spaces and opportunities that enable a deeper dialogue around people's current experiences is essential. But equally important is an exploration of how the unaddressed and so yet to be reconciled aspects of our personal and shared histories reverberate into the present. Understanding the role that history plays in moulding the cultural context is a vital ingredient if we are going to shape the cultural context with intentionality and purpose.

One of the challenges of creating high-performance cultures is that those narratives which dictate the cultural context frequently reside within the collective unconscious of the organisation or team. As a result, these narratives are like ghosts in the walls, where people *feel* their influence, but can rarely identify them. This creates a kind of 'shadow culture' that gives rise to those behavioural norms that people will seldom refer to or take ownership of. The benefit of creating opportunities for deeper dialogue is that those narratives which usually remain buried within the collective unconscious and are not aligned with, or conducive to, the desired culture, can be bought to the surface where they can be suitably unpacked and transformed.

But delving into the psychological recesses of an organisation, especially if there is a possibility that we will encounter some unresolved episodes of history, is not for the faint of heart. Additionally, while these cultural contexts primarily apply to the collective, they also reside within individuals. This is because, over time, the beliefs and narratives about those behaviours that are deemed more acceptable become internalised and so integrated into our own belief systems. As a result, these narratives also belong to us, and are personal to us. So, in challenging cultural contexts, not only are we challenging something that exists 'out there', in the culture of the organisation, we are also challenging beliefs that are deeply personal to us and have been vital in the construction of our own identity. This requires us to develop new cultural muscles: these muscles are the approaches to organisational development and ways of thinking that up till now have been largely underutilised.

If we are going to embark on this journey and do it in a way so as not adversely impact organisational members or allow less-helpful narratives to become self-fulfilling prophecies, the essential ingredient is psychological safety. I will unpack psychological safety in far greater depth throughout the rest of this chapter, but I wanted to introduce you to its relevance at this point in our discussion.

Culture is a muscle!

This is undoubtedly my favourite saying. I use it so often; I am sure my clients are sick of those words tumbling out of my mouth.

But I can't help myself, because I think the metaphor is so apt – the basic principles essential to increase muscle functionality apply equally to the development of a high-performance culture. Most of us, especially those who work in, or have an interest in, sport will be familiar with these principles of muscle development.

Firstly, we need to train regularly. Training once a week or once a fortnight will not result in elite standards of fitness. Secondly, we have to be uncomfortable. Racking the bench press bar at the first sign of fatigue or stopping running as soon as our lactate level starts to rise will not increase our conditioning. In fact, one could argue that the benefits of training only start *beyond* the point where we start to feel uncomfortable. Thirdly and finally, there is a big difference between talking about working out and going to the gym and actually lifting.

Ultimately, increasing muscle strength requires a progressive overload approach which results in slight damage to muscle fibres, and then as part of the repair process and in an attempt to adapt to the stress we place upon the muscle, there is a gain in functionality. A degree of stress and discomfort are therefore essential parts of the process – not to the point of rupture or doing serious damage, but just enough to create some damage to muscle fibres.

The principles of building a robust and resilient culture, one that is able to deliver high performance and create a professional environment, are exactly the same.

Culture is often discussed and worked on at an executive off-site or a preseason camp. And then it might be worked on sporadically, if it is done at all. When schedules get busy, or when teams find themselves under the pump, is when working on culture is frequently de-prioritised; often at a time when it is most needed. Building high-performance cultures requires a prioritisation and a commitment to build in 'culture work' as part of our everyday routines. While what culture work looks like will be different for every organisation or team, what is immutable is the dedication and frequent focus that building a great culture requires.

Strengthening cultures also requires people to be uncomfortable. The only way to improve culture is to challenge existing belief systems, mindsets, and cultural norms; challenge them not to the point of rupture, but in a way which enables them to be rebuilt into more effective versions. For example, avoiding or stopping a performance conversation at the first point of discomfort fails to resolve the issue at hand. But also, and perhaps more importantly, we discard the opportunity to exercise a particular set of cultural muscles and so fail to build capability around these competencies.

Finally, we frequently *talk about* culture, but what is more challenging is *doing* culture. Noticing, and then addressing, the changes in vibe during a team meeting; providing constructive or developmental feedback; and working on repairing ruptures in relationships in the early stages; are all examples of *doing* culture. We can talk about accountability, and about the importance of giving and receiving constructive feedback, and about the levels of trust and collaboration in our team, but ultimately, *doing* something about addressing these dynamics is what builds great cultures.

In the absence of a progressive overload approach to culture, cultural muscles atrophy, leading to a deterioration those cultural competencies that are the essential drivers of elite performance. Therefore, in thinking about cultural change, be that fostering a high-performance mindset or an antiracist approach to how we work, understanding the cultural muscles which need to be strengthened is a critical step in the process. We then need to employ a progressive overload approach to that development; an approach that does not shy away from the uncomfortable but rather seeks it out and welcomes it. But for the uncomfortable to be tolerated, let alone welcomed, the essential ingredient is psychological safety.

Psychological safety is essential for many drivers of high performance

If you ask any group of management consultants or CEOs about the most effective way to build a high-performance culture, you will receive as many answers as you have people; there is no agreed-upon way to build a high-performance culture. If there was, everybody would be doing it, and every team and organisation would be incrementally moving towards optimal performance.

One approach to driving optimal performance is via a strategic focus on creating a culture with psychological safety as one of its fundamental tenets. As we shall see, psychological safety is not only pivotal for many of the essential enablers of high-performance to flourish, but it also creates the cultural underpinnings that are supportive of building an antiracist organisation. This follows the principle that building an antiracist culture – or any kind of DEI (diversity, equity, and inclusion) work, for that matter – has to be integrated with, and woven into, the day-to-day demands of fulfilling an organisation's commercial imperative.

It should be noted that psychological safety is not necessarily the outcome, but rather a means to an end. And that 'end' is greater performance! Psychological safety is simply a vehicle which drives greater organisational performance; it is up to leadership to decide if they want that vehicle to be a scooter or a Ferrari. The rest of this chapter focuses on deepening our understanding of psychological safety, whilst chapter thirteen discusses the 'how' of creating psychologically safe cultures.

Despite experts agreeing on what psychological safety entails, agreement on a methodology to achieve this outcome remains elusive. This is because psychological safety occurs at the complicated and fragile intersection of leadership competencies, the psychological aftermath of our (painful) personal histories, and ancient survival mechanisms that have been honed and fortified through the process of evolution.

The term 'psychological safety' was coined by Harvard Business School Professor Amy Edmondson. She defines psychological safety as, 'A shared belief that the environment is conducive to personal risks.'[41] Psychological safety is founded on the belief that an individual within their workplace can raise questions, express themselves, share concerns, and even admit to mistakes, without fear of being ridiculed, judged, shamed, or belittled. It enables people to come to work and be their whole selves, without the need to compartmentalise or excessively censor particular aspects of their thinking, their personality, or their culture.

Psychological safety drives performance because it is the essential ingredient for many of the cultural competencies that enable sustainable high performance. Most would agree that in creating such a culture the following cultural competencies are essential: using coaching as a vehicle for development; innovation and creativity; a culture of shared accountability because teams are able to have uncomfortable conversations; collaboration, teamwork, and the ability to resolve interpersonal conflicts and tensions in a timely manner; the ability to acquire and retain talent; and, finally, discretionary effort, where team members are naturally inclined to go the extra mile in service of the goals (vision) of the organisation or team. These drivers of high performance are equally relevant whether we are talking about an elite sporting team, a well-established for-profit corporation, a not-for-profit, or a technology start-up. Additionally – and here is the key point – while each of these cultural competencies contains within them the potential to enhance performance, the degree to which this

---

41 Amy Edmondson, 'Psychological Safety and Learning Behavior in Work Teams' *Administrative Science Quarterly*, Vol. 44, No. 2 (Jun., 1999): 350-383

potential is fully realised is determined by the levels of psychological safety.

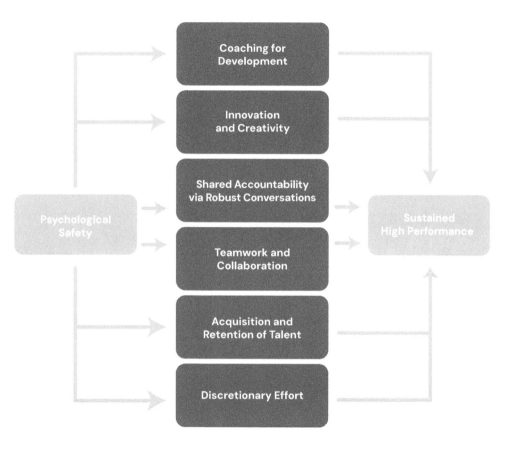

Figure 5: Psychological safety is essential for the key drivers of sustained high performance.

Coaching as a vehicle for development: whether it's an elite sporting team or an executive team, coaching is a critical and powerful driver of performance. I always find it perplexing that most people, especially those who work in or follow sport, have no reservations about the importance of the role a coach plays in supporting elite performance in athletes. Yet, despite their own desire to be 'elite', they don't engage a coach to support them in the development required to be a high-performing executive.

The coach–coachee relationship is at the centre of elite performance. The art of coaching is centred around inspiring growth and change via the emotional connection between the coach and coachee. For a coachee's relationship with their coach to be valued and nurtured so that mutual trust and respect can be built over time, a psychologically safe environment is required. In this kind of setting, the coachee feels their coach is perhaps the one person who always has their back, who they can confide in during times of stress, turmoil, and self-doubt, and who will hold them accountable with compassion and empathy. Finally, it is their coach who also has a deep knowledge of their particular set of challenges related to their context and role, but also their psychological make-up and drivers.

Additionally, intrinsic to the process of coaching is the ability for the coach to provide feedback, both positive and constructive, as a way of developing the person they are coaching. With insufficient psychological safety, there is a much greater likelihood that the coachee will take such feedback personally and/or get defensive, and as a result be less able to integrate the feedback provided by the coach.

Innovation and Creativity: cultures that are psychologically safe allow innovation and creativity to be championed, even though there may not always be a guarantee of success. True innovation requires the courage to explore territories that are yet to be traversed. Driven by a desire for excellence, and a mantra of, 'What if?' innovative teams can experiment with new approaches to business and performance knowing that, for every ground-breaking innovation, there may well be numerous failures. This can only happen in an environment where people feel safe to try new things, to take a risk, and have the freedom to fail, knowing that they will not be belittled or reprimanded.

A culture of shared accountability: having uncomfortable conversations about cultural, performance, and behavioural expectations is a critical competency for driving optimal performance. The extent to which these conversations can be productive is correlated to the extent psychological safety is present. When there are high levels of psychological safety, individuals believe that constructive feedback is given for their own development, and so for their benefit. There is less chance, therefore, that this feedback is taken personally, and perceived as an attack or a putdown.

We have all heard stories of, perhaps even witnessed firsthand, so-called 'honesty sessions' resulting in significant ruptures within teams because there were not sufficient levels of psychological safety to contain the tensions of these robust conversations. Psychological safety enables team members to examine their own behaviours, as well as the behaviours of their teammates, through a developmental lens and so evaluate how these behaviours foster or undermine performance, and the extent to which they contribute to the desired culture and outcomes.

Additionally, the trust required to withstand the crucible of these challenging conversations, not to mention the pressure and demands of an ever-changing business environment, requires deeper levels of connection. This kind of connection can only occur when team members feel safe enough to be authentic, to be vulnerable, sometimes even raw, in how they share what they are feeling and the challenges they are experiencing within their context and role.

Collaboration and teamwork: when there is greater psychological safety, team members are able to speak freely and take moderate risks both strategically and in terms of their relationships. Psychological safety means that interpersonal conflicts and tensions get proactively addressed and resolved, rather than them going underground and manifesting as passive-aggressive behaviours. Additionally, when tensions and ruptures in relationships do not get repaired in a timely manner, they will almost invariably manifest as a propensity to form silos or factions between individuals, teams, and business units.

Acquisition and retention of talent: more and more, what potential employees are looking for in an employer of choice is a culture of psychological safety. Furthermore, organisations with higher levels of psychological safety have better retention of talent. As a result, teams are more stable, thereby deepening the trust and connections between team members; minimising recruitment and on-boarding costs; and there is greater retention of industry-specific expertise and intellectual property.

Discretionary effort: when people feel psychologically safe, they will tend to engage more deeply with their work, their teammates, and their role in general. This is a powerful driver of performance because greater levels of engagement enhance discretionary effort. Discretionary effort is the difference between what people have to do and what they want to do; it is more commonly referred to as 'going the extra mile'. Research shows that engaged individuals deliver an extra 30% in discretionary effort in comparison to disengaged individuals.

Each of the above cultural competencies is essential in the creation of a high-performance culture. Can they occur in the absence of psychological safety? Perhaps. However, the extent to which these cultural competencies can flourish and thus be utilised in service of creating a high-performance culture is proportional to the degree of psychological safety present.

Psychological safety is not binary

There is a belief that psychological safety is binary – either we have it, or we don't. In fact, psychological safety exists along a continuum. On one end of the continuum is a culture that is 100% fear-based, and at the other end is a culture that is 100% psychologically safe. Organisational cultures that exist around these extremes are a rarity; far more common are cultures that are positioned somewhere in between, where there is some degree of psychological safety but it is not absolute.

Furthermore, not only does psychological safety exist along a continuum, but where it is situated along that continuum is constantly shifting and recalibrating. What shifts psychological safety is primarily people's behaviours, and then how other people interpret, make associations with, and respond to those behaviours. We have all sat through team meetings where, in comparison to the start, there was a discernible increase or decrease in psychological safety as the meeting concluded. There are innumerable dynamics and occurrences which foster or undermine psychological safety over the longer term, but also hour by hour, minute by minute.

Somebody admitting to a mistake and being supported rather than belittled or shamed will increase psychological safety. Likewise, taking a few moments to validate someone's concerns, feelings, or nervousness about an upcoming task or project, or asking a clarifying question to deepen the understanding of someone's perspective or experience, will also support psychological safety. In contrast, people getting talked over, or their viewpoint not being valued or validated, particularly if they hold a minority or more challenging perspective, will diminish psychological safety. But then, if this momentary micro-rupture in people's sense of safety is not bought to people's attention and addressed in a way where there is some degree of repair, it will undermine psychological safety even further.

Psychological safety, therefore, is cultivated as well as diminished by the messages that people receive (from the cultural context) which signal how safe it is for them to bring to the fore their inherent humanity in the form of their perspectives, ideas, concerns, thoughts, feelings, and fears.

Psychological safety is a feeling

Psychological safety is a feeling embedded in the culture. Therefore, it can be systematised, mandated, or delivered by standard operating procedures to the extent that any other personal or deeply felt experience, such as love or trust, can be mandated or systematised: minimally, if at all. And given it is a feeling, one of the most useful gauges of psychological safety is our own felt experience.

The extent to which we feel the freedom to be ourselves is a measure of psychological safety. In contrast, the degree of angst we feel due to a need for greater vigilance in filtering inherent aspects of our personality, identity, or culture should also be considered a trustworthy indicator of psychological safety. Additionally, useful clues about the shared experience of psychological safety can be gathered by paying attention to subtle shifts in the energy in our teammates, or how the atmosphere and their levels of engagement recalibrate in response to various behavioural and interpersonal dynamics.

It should be noted that psychological safety is not synonymous with comfort. Psychological safety fosters openness and risk-taking in groups, whereas comfort prioritises avoiding discomfort, thereby maintaining the status quo by inhibiting growth and innovation.

While comfort aims to foster tranquillity and consistency, psychological safety promotes growth through vulnerability and constructive feedback, enriching collaboration, and individual development.

Much like a muscle, working at the limits of psychological safety with a view to strengthening it, will invariably require people to be uncomfortable at certain points in the process. Team members, therefore, need to be able to discern between the unavoidable discomfort that accompanies growth and the reactions that arise due to a genuine insufficiency of psychological safety.

In terms of cultivating psychologically safe cultures, one of the challenges is that, in our day-to-day busyness, we don't often take the time to reflect on and thus connect these subtle feelings of freedom, engagement, tension, and fear to those behaviours that have been normalised by the cultural context. To fully realise the potential psychological safety has in the creation of a high-performance environment, it needs to be a strategic priority that is clearly and explicitly part of and aligned with the purpose and vision of the organisation.

Perhaps counterintuitively, the most effective way of increasing psychological safety is to have conversations about psychological safety. People discussing where and why they do or don't feel safe, and what it may take to increase their levels of safety, is in itself a significant driver of psychological safety. However, this is complicated because, in order to talk about and unpack the drivers of, and barriers to, greater psychological safety, what we actually need is … psychological safety.

Therefore, essential in the process of creating psychologically safe cultures is ensuring these discussions are facilitated in a way where people feel validated, valued, and witnessed in terms of the experiences they share. Every time this happens, it strengthens the 'cultural container', which is then able to hold greater levels of complexity and discomfort in terms of the conversations people feel permitted and safe enough to hold. In contrast, when these conversations are not adequately facilitated and supported, it can result in them being more detrimental than beneficial. This is because poorly facilitated conversations can cause ruptures in the fabric of the culture that, due to insufficient psychological safety, the organisation is unable to repair in an effective and timely fashion.

So the extent to which an uncomfortable or challenging discussion can be initiated, and that conversation can take place in a safe and constructive manner, is determined by where an organisation's culture is situated along the psychological safety continuum. For example, if there is a moderate degree of psychological safety, teams can have productive conversations about less-challenging subjects such as alignment of strategy, organisational values, or the importance of people development.

In comparison, more challenging subjects such as those about interpersonal dynamics, performance management, or the barriers to collaboration within or between teams, may well require higher levels of psychological safety. Finally, for organisations and teams to have conversations about complex and painful matters such as inclusion and discrimination requires even higher levels of psychological safety. This is because of the personal impact of gender inequity, racism, homophobia, anti-Semitism, Islamophobia etc., and the complicated nature of how organisational cultures, systems, and processes intersect with these individual experiences of oppression and marginalisation.

This is one of the reasons why DEI programs have such a poor success rate, and in some cases *decrease* diversity within an organisation. When the design and delivery of a Diversity and

Inclusion program requires a certain threshold of psychological safety that is beyond the current capability of the culture (based on where it is positioned along the psychological safety continuum), it is likely that the program itself will be detrimental. This is because, if people do speak openly and personally about their lived experiences of discrimination, the culture might not be able to hold, process, and start to address these dynamics. As a result, narratives about the experiences of BIPOC (in the case of racism) not being valued, and apprehensions about the sincerity of the transformation process itself, will only be reinforced. This creates an even less safe environment that brings about a collective retreat to the comfort of familiar patterns and established ways of thinking. As a result, challenges to do with diversity, equity, and inclusion are less likely to be proactively addressed. Over time this results in a workforce that is not as diverse and a culture which is less inclusive.

Painful and unresolved experiences diminish our capacity to lead for psychological safety

We know that organisational and team cultures sit somewhere along a continuum with psychological safety at one extreme and a fear-based culture at the other. Humans have very specific psychological and physiological responses to fear and threat, be they real or perceived. There is, therefore, an inherent set of developmental challenges for organisations and teams which sit more towards the fear-based end of this continuum.

Please excuse me here while I indulge my inner nerd.

When confronted with a threat and/or an environment the brain determines to be unsafe (think of walking out of the safety of your cave and being confronted with a snarling and hungry sabre-toothed tiger) a part of the brain called the amygdala automatically (i.e. without a conscious decision) activates a powerful combination of survival responses. This is what is commonly referred to as the 'fight or flight response', although we can also include two more responses – freeze, and appease – to the list of possible reactions.

At the same time, the amygdala hijacks and shuts down the part of our brain known as the prefrontal cortex. This is the part of the brain that regulates voluntary actions and executive functioning such as reasoning, planning, and decision-making. The prefrontal cortex also enables us to think and feel at the same time, thereby simultaneously processing information and emotions. It also gives us access to empathy and compassion. These survival responses that get initiated when we are faced with a threat, real or perceived, have been honed and reinforced over time, all with the specific goal of maximising our personal survival. Therefore, when they are activated, this becomes the foremost – perhaps the only – priority; care and consideration for the wellbeing of others, by demonstrating empathy and compassion, quickly become de-prioritised. After all, stopping to show empathy and support for a colleague who is struggling to keep up only increases the probability of us becoming sabre-toothed tiger breakfast.

In the moment these survival responses get activated, we lose access to many of those executive functions and capabilities that are so essential for effective leadership. Not to mention, many of these capabilities are also essential for cultivating the psychological safety that is a crucial requirement in the creation of high-performance cultures.

But here is the rub …

Painful and unresolved experiences diminish our capacity to lead for psychological safety.

Part of the human condition is that most of us will go through life and, at some point, encounter experiences that are painful, emotionally injurious, perhaps even traumatic At the time these experiences occur, a split happens. This splitting involves part of our psyche moving forward and being able to function adequately with the demands of everyday life, while another part, in an attempt to resolve and heal the painful experience, remains back at this moment in time. As a way of protecting itself from further injury and trauma, the part of our psyche that stays with this experience creates a neurological imprint (or emotional memory) of this experience, and also an accompanying set of survival responses which it can activate should something similar recur. These survival responses are a combination of fight, flight, freeze, and appease, and are stored subconsciously as latent survival mechanisms (LSMs).

These LSMs lie dormant – hence why they are 'latent' – until something happens that reminds us, even subconsciously, of that original event. In that split second, the amygdala goes into action, it activates an LSM and simultaneously hijacks the prefrontal cortex. And before we know it, we literally lose our minds and therefore our ability to access those executive functions such as reasoning, decision-making, compassion, and empathy that are so essential for effective leadership.

In those moments, when it appears as though a leader or a team member, or perhaps even ourselves, has lost the plot or is having a meltdown, this is most likely what is happening in terms of our physiological and psychological responses. Hopefully these are only 'moments', as opposed to a continuous state of affairs. While each of us needs to take responsibility for these moments, blaming and shaming either ourselves or others is misplaced and not justified. This is because of the powerful yet unconscious nature of these responses, and the fact that they have been hardwired into our systems, because at some point in time they served an essential survival function.

Most of us will have some understanding of this phenomenon, in no small part because the concept of 'being triggered' has made its way into everyday vernacular. However, this language is commonly used with a pejorative tone to it, and has a negative connotation, because it implies that having a natural and hardwired reaction to a stressful or traumatic experience is somehow your fault, and so makes you a bad person. I have taken the time to explain the basic psychology and physiology of our triggered reactions in an attempt to actively debunk this narrative. Feeling ashamed or being reprimanded will do little to minimise the likelihood of being triggered once again in the context of a similar event. Rather, to be able to address and resolve the LSMs which give rise to our triggered states, people need environments rich in the trust, empathy, and connection upon which psychological safety can be cultivated.

Reflection #12A:

Exploring the dynamics of racism within your cultural context

1. Spend some time researching the history and dynamics of racism within your specific (geographic) context. How have these historical elements and dynamics shaped the narratives which have in turn informed the cultural norms of your country or region?

2. In countries and cultures which are more homogeneous when it comes to race, these dynamics might be less obvious. For example, there could be a 'racial' hierarchy based on caste, religion, or skin tone.

3. What is the history of racism within in your geographic context in terms of the perpetuation of racial inequity?

4. Where and how has this history and these dynamics been resolved?

5. Where and how has this history and these dynamics yet to be resolved?

6. Reflect on the cultural context of your organisation in terms of how it addresses, talks about, and works with race and racism. What are the barely said narratives that do and don't give people permission to have certain conversations, experiences, reactions, and feelings?

7. What has been the impact of these narratives on BIPOC, both historically and currently?

8. How is the cultural context of your organisation a reflection of the larger cultural context in terms of the community, city, country, etc. your organisation is situated within?

Reflection #12B:

Resolving an LSM to improve your capability to lead for psychological safety

1. Think of a time in your leadership role, formal or informal, where you got activated or 'triggered' to the extent that it impacted your ability to create a psychologically safe environment.

2. In this incident, what aspect or mindset required to lead for psychological safety did you find most challenging to embody, e.g., were you not empathetic enough, too defensive, feeling tired and overwhelmed, not being open to a different/diverse viewpoint, feeling insecure? (please note: this does not mean that you are unable to embody this attribute in all your interactions)

3. What about that person/people, the context, or the situation might have triggered this reaction in you?

4. Can you think of a challenging or painful formative experience, or a series of experiences, which might have created the LSM that got activated? (this is where you may have to challenge yourself a little and do a few 'cultural reps' 😊). Recall this experience, in particular the challenging or painful aspects of it.

5. Who do you know, from a book you have read, or a movie you have seen, someone you love, a beloved pet, or any kind of mythical person or figure, etc., who could have supported you and given you what you needed throughout this experience/s?

6. What characteristics or traits does this person/figure possess that were so needed during your initial (painful) experience?

7. How and where do you already embody some of those traits, even a little bit?

8. Go back to the situation from question one. If you were to embody those traits more fully, how would you handle that situation differently? Would there be a different/better outcome?

Bonus question:

9. Can you see how this formative experience and/or the traits that were needed are linked to your personal purpose from reflection #6A? If so, how?

Chapter Thirteen:

Building high-performance cultures and the antiracist organisation

If the main goal of this book is to provide you with a practical guide to building an inclusive and high-performance culture, then this chapter brings together the principles and concepts we have discussed thus far. So in many ways, this is where the rubber meets the road. The challenge this chapter intends to address is:

How can we apply the principles and insights we have learned, in a manner which is cognisant of our organisation's context, in order to bring to fruition our goals for opening these pages in the first place?

Shaping the cultural context towards antiracism requires psychological safety

Building an antiracist organisation will almost invariably require us to transform the cultural context. As we discussed in chapter twelve, the cultural context dictates and determines those behaviours that make sense to people. One of the goals of an antiracist organisation, therefore, is to shape the cultural context so that racism and racial inequity no longer make sense. This is one of the most complex aspects of our work.

If we once again come back to our definition of an antiracist organisation:

An antiracist organisation is one that, through its culture, systems, policies, and processes, works to actively dismantle racism and, therefore, create racial equity within the workplace.

Therefore, essential in building an antiracist organisation is addressing the cultural enablers of structural racism. This is because, without a commitment to create a culture of antiracism, there will not be the impetus to scrutinise the systems, policies, and processes for how they might also sustain racial inequity. However, culture is so challenging to transform because ultimately culture is about our behaviours, and the origins of our behaviours are deeply rooted in individual and collective psychology. This chapter is a deep dive into the psychology of building cultures that are not only high performing, but also antiracist.

In chapter nine, we discussed the importance of initiating antiracism forums, where the experiences of BIPOC can be heard and validated. The purpose of these forums is to start re-visioning capitalism by initiating conversations about race and racism, and thus addressing some of the unresolved hurts and disadvantages, past and present, which have occurred at the hands of racial capitalism. Having constructive conversations about racism should not be thought of as belonging only to antiracism forums, but also embedding this capability as part of the day-to-day cultural norms which make up the cultural context. In chapter twelve we also discussed the essential components of a culture that drives high performance in a sustainable way.

The indispensable cultural feature required for both these outcomes – being able to have constructive conversations about people's experiences of racism and the creation of a high-performance environment — is psychological safety. Therefore, psychological safety must be considered an essential cultural capability to develop on the journey towards creating an inclusive and high-performance culture.

How do we create a psychologically safe culture?

The extent to which an individual feels psychologically safe in a given culture is a complex phenomenon. For a start, psychological safety is a feeling, and feelings, by definition, are subjective and personal. A meeting where voices get raised may result in one person feeling unsafe, whereas, for another person, this may be relatively less disconcerting. This is based on their personal experiences and the (largely unconscious) associations they make or don't make to those raised voices. This is why psychological safety is rarely absolute; there will invariably be people who, in comparison to their colleagues, feel more safe or less safe within the same environment or given a similar set of external stimuli.

This is also why psychological safety cannot be mandated or demanded into existence by a leader (or facilitator) saying, 'This is a safe space'. Enforcing psychological safety, much like enforcing a particular set of emotions, is problematic. This is because our emotions are complex, multifaceted responses that arise from a combination of psychological, physiological, and environmental factors, making them difficult to be enforced or mandated. Rather, psychological safety needs to be developed, crafted, and tenderly attended to. It is not a finite outcome, but rather, an ongoing process underpinned by self-awareness, compassion, and our ability to notice and then react to moment-to-moment shifts in the levels of safety experienced by ourselves and our teammates.

Despite its subjective and personal nature, there are some essential elements which need to be embedded into the culture if we are going to have any chance of developing psychological safety. You will notice the obvious interconnectivity and interdependence of these three elements. Each has a symbiotic hand in the cultivation of the other. Therefore, these three elements should not be thought of as discrete or individual components, but rather an integrated philosophical approach to the creation of environments with greater levels of psychological safety. No doubt there are other components which are beneficial in the creation of psychological safety, but these are the three that I have found to be the most influential in constructing the cultural underpinnings upon which psychological safety can be built.

Trust: Psychological safety and trust are intertwined concepts, to the point where trust is a key foundational element needed for psychological safety. In the absence of trust, and the safety and comfort which it instils, team members will almost certainly hesitate to express themselves, which in turn stifles creativity, innovation, and effective communication. In contrast, when high levels of trust are present, individuals are more likely to open up and share their thoughts and feelings, which in turn fosters a supportive and empathetic atmosphere. Colleagues who trust one another are more likely to offer help, seek guidance, and provide constructive feedback. This in turn further enhances psychological safety.

Empathy: Empathy involves understanding and caring about the perspectives and emotions of others. When people feel that others genuinely empathise with their feelings and experiences, they are more likely to feel safe and valued. Additionally, as part of developmental sticking point #1 in chapter four, we discussed how cultural components essential for optimal performance, such as connection and belonging, get enhanced when people feel their experience matters to others. The non-judgmental attitude which gets promoted by empathy and understanding encourages learning from mistakes rather than punishing them, by demonstrating it is acceptable to be imperfect and that growth is valued.

Connection: Being willing to take risk – a personal risk, an emotional risk, a relationship risk, a strategic risk, or even an innovation risk, requires connection and camaraderie. This is because the underlying narrative of connection suggests that, 'Even though it is you taking the risk, you are not taking that risk alone; because we are very clear in the belief that you are taking that risk on the behalf of us all, for our collective benefit.' In a connected environment, team members are able to express their thoughts, ideas, and concerns, knowing they will be heard and respected. This open dialogue fosters a culture of empathy, understanding, and support, where mistakes are seen as opportunities for growth, rather than reasons for blame. Ultimately, connection creates the sense of belonging and acceptance that is central to psychological safety.

Given that psychological safety is a feeling, it should not be surprising that these three constituent ingredients – those elements which are fundamental to it flourishing – are also based on our feelings. We *feel* when there is trust with teammates and colleagues; likewise, we have an intuitive and felt sense when empathy and connection are strongly present within teams.

Feelings are complex, non-cognitive, and subjective emotional states or experiences that arise in response to various stimuli, thoughts, or circumstances. They encompass a wide spectrum of emotions, including happiness, sadness, anger, fear, love, and many more. These emotional responses are a fundamental aspect of human consciousness, and are influenced by individual temperament, past experiences, and the cultural context. Feelings serve as a means of perceiving and responding to the world around us, helping us navigate social interactions, make decisions, and shape our overall wellbeing. Because of their complex and subjective nature, feelings are difficult to quantify and measure. However, this does not minimise the importance and the impact that they have in the creation of psychological safety.

But for these three components – trust, empathy, and connection – to become established as cultural norms requires something that most organisations find challenging to cultivate: vulnerability.

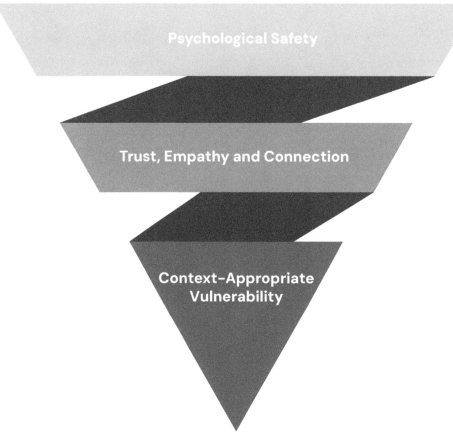

Figure 6: The foundations of psychological safety.

Building greater levels of trust, empathy, and connection requires some degree of vulnerability; these aspects of culture, and therefore psychological safety, are unlikely to occur in its absence.

This is because vulnerability is the antidote needed to rebuke those long-term and deeply entrenched cultural narratives that persistently whisper into the ears of the collective psyche, 'Don't take a risk. Don't trust your teammates, they are sure to let you down, just like [parent, friend, partner] did. Don't get close enough to people where what they feel is important to you, because you are only going to get hurt. Don't be too honest or too transparent, especially if it is going to leave you open to being belittled, shamed, or reprimanded. Revealing too much about yourself can only result in you feeling judged.'

These cultural norms belong to the individual as well as the collective, and mirror the aftermath of painful, sometimes traumatic, aspects of our personal histories. Throughout our life, but especially during our formative years, each of us, based on our experiences, will construct and then internalise a set of narratives and belief systems. Until such point where we start to understand and then, if necessary, transform these narratives, they run in the background of our lives at a mostly subconscious level, informing our thoughts, behaviours, and actions, much like the operating system on our computer.

When narratives get constructed around painful experiences, they serve as important survival mechanisms (LSMs) as their function is to protect us from re-experiencing similar painful episodes. In some cases, these experiences are obvious: being bullied, teased, or feeling like we don't fit in; experiencing any kind of physical, emotional, or sexual abuse; or growing up in a household where one or both parents were violent, had addictive tendencies, and/or mental health challenges. But sometimes these experiences are more subtle. Growing up where our feelings were never acknowledged or enquired after forms a narrative which dismisses what we feel, and any vulnerability that is associated with those feelings. This is not uncommon in high achievers, where a strong emphasis was placed on our sporting or academic outcomes. At the same time, we received the message that what we were feeling, particularly those more painful or vulnerable feelings, were not a priority or of importance, or perhaps that they were even a distraction to our success, and so needed to be pushed to the margins.

By creating a protective barrier around these experiences, such narratives and beliefs provide an important survival function. But – and here is the key – these barriers can also prevent us from connecting with the vulnerability that is so essential for the creation of psychologically safe cultures. Therefore, as we shall soon see, resolving our LSMs and the narratives that we have constructed around them is a crucial aspect in the being able to lead in a manner which creates psychologically safe cultures.

It is important to unpack the concept of vulnerability, and in the process clarify the ways that vulnerability, what it means, and how it is expressed, is different in an organisational or professional context in comparison to a more personal setting.

Firstly, the purpose of vulnerability is different. In an organisational context, its purpose is to achieve specific objectives such as teamwork, problem solving, innovation, and collaboration. Contrast this to a personal context, where the purpose of vulnerability is to strengthen personal relationships and create emotional bonds through connection, intimacy, and the sharing of one's feelings, fears, and insecurities. While vulnerability in a professional context may also involve the sharing of one's feelings, fears, and insecurities, it is done with the ultimate goal of increasing the effectiveness and functioning of teams and organisations.

Secondly, the boundaries of how vulnerability is expressed are different in a professional setting compared to a personal setting. In organisations, team members are subject to contextual boundaries, where there is an expectation that they maintain professional standards and adhere to cultural norms. Expressions of vulnerability that are slightly beyond existing cultural norms will help to incrementally shift and recalibrate the cultural context. However, displays of emotion and vulnerability that are well beyond cultural norms (as dictated by the cultural context) may incur a backlash, as these norms work to re-exert themselves if they have been extended too far, or challenged beyond their capacity to recalibrate.

In personal settings, expressions of vulnerability generally have fewer constraints, and are guided by history and relationship dynamics. In personal relationships, people generally feel freer to express their innermost thoughts and emotions with less concern for cultural norms and expectations. As a result, in personal settings the boundaries which dictate vulnerability tend to be more fluid or permeable.

Thirdly and finally, in professional environments, risk and role needs to be taken into calculation in terms of expressions of vulnerability. As such, people need to weigh the potential risks and benefits of sharing personal struggles or emotions in the workplace, and consider how it might affect their career, their reputation, or their relationship with colleagues, managers, and clients. Furthermore, assessing if and how vulnerability is in service of their role, and the effectiveness of how they take up their role, should be considered an ethical obligation. In contrast, vulnerability in personal settings can sometimes feel riskier because of its potential to directly impact important and close personal relationships. So, whilst in personal setting sharing one's innermost thoughts and feelings may lead to deeper emotional connections, it can also result in conflicts, misunderstandings, and emotional hurt.

While there are challenges and constraints in expressing vulnerability in professional contexts, most organisations will also have deeply embedded cultural norms which make this even more challenging. Remember that what we reward and what we resist determines culture and creates the cultural context. Think about, in organisational life, the behaviours that we reward, and even aspire to develop in ourselves. We reward confidence, we reward competence, we reward resilience, we reward toughness, we reward power. In the sporting industry, where I do most of my work, this is even more salient. Physical toughness, fitness, and an ability to execute skills under pressure, are rewarded, because these are more likely to deliver on-field success. While these are perhaps most obvious in a sporting environment, there will be cultural equivalencies of these which play out in most business and corporate settings. Of course, these aspects of toughness, of resilience, of competence are essential for success in any field, and as such need to be developed and appropriately rewarded.

The challenge then becomes, how do we develop and reward competence, resilience, and power in the technical or on-field aspects of people's roles, and simultaneously develop a culture where, in those moments where vulnerability is required, perhaps even essential, it is not actively resisted?

This is where leadership is crucial!

Leaders need to take into consideration the constraints of being vulnerable in a professional setting, and then demonstrate context-appropriate vulnerability in an authentic way. This models something that may be slightly outside the cultural norm, but also importantly, the messages embedded in their behaviour grants permission for others to do the same.

Psychological safety is primarily leader-driven

Leaders are the key to shaping positive cultures. Hence, any initiative which aims to transform the cultural context and/or cultivate psychological safety needs to be leader-driven. This is because leaders are responsible for setting the cultural tone, modelling those behaviours which need to be rewarded, and defending the culture against those behaviours which need to be resisted. This is a crucial leadership capability because psychological safety cannot and will not occur if leaders are not modelling the behaviours which are emblematic of psychological safety. There is no room for a 'do what I say, not what I do' approach to leadership when it comes to the creation of a psychologically safe culture.

If context-appropriate vulnerability is the foundation upon which psychological safety is built, then the extent to which this becomes a cultural norm, and thus makes sense to people, is principally dependent on leadership firstly being able model it, and then cultivate it in others. This can only happen if there is an acceptance of, and a comfort with, their own vulnerability. Leaders, therefore, need to have a fluid (adaptable) relationship with their own power states; in other words, they need to be able to access, and then lead from, both their 'low-power' and 'high-power' states.

For many of us, vulnerability can feel like a low-power state; we are less familiar with it when compared to the robustness, the resilience, and the competence we more readily identify with and aspire to. While vulnerability takes an incredible amount of courage and strength, it is the associations that we make to it that result in us perceiving it as a low-power state. These associations mirror the narratives about vulnerability espoused by societal norms and our unconscious biases.

These narratives are often characterised by the 'ghosts of history' (recall the influence history has in creating the cultural context) where painful or disappointing events from the past are yet to be fully resolved and reconciled. They therefore lie dormant within the walls of the organisation, until they get animated back to life in response to a team member demonstrating even a whiff of vulnerability that results in people feeling uneasy and less comfortable. We will all be familiar with these narratives manifesting as a joke[42] made in poor taste, or some other version of a tactless compensation concocted in an attempt to deflect or avoid our discomfort and/or our inability to simply 'be with' vulnerability, either our own or someone else's.

Therefore, when leaders demonstrate a version of authentic vulnerability, it is likely to push up against and challenge those cultural norms which advocate for invincibility and strength over vulnerability. And when these established norms inevitably galvanise to re-exert their dominance, rather than revert to the safety and familiarity of a high-power state, leaders are required to surrender not only to their own vulnerability, but also to the vulnerability within the culture that is most likely present, but rarely ever spoken for.

In contrast, leaders tend to be more comfortable with, and more identified with, their high-power states. These states are much more congruent with the cultural norms and expectations associated with leadership. This does not at all diminish their importance and the part these high-power states play in leading for psychological safety. Having the conviction to step into the authority conferred in one's leadership role is essential in terms of the power needed to set a vision towards antiracism and then be uncompromising in the pursuit of that vision. After all, in the creation of an antiracist organisation, some things need to be non-negotiable. Additionally, in order to install the desired culture, access to high-power states

---

42 I think humour and fun are important components of high-performance cultures. However, the humour I am referring to here is when it is used as a mechanism for deflecting or avoiding the vulnerability that is yet to be fully integrated as a cultural norm but is crucial for the creation of psychological safety.

is needed in how leaders reinforce those behaviours that should get rewarded and stand against those that need to be resisted. For example, creating a culture of shared accountability; being relentless in the pursuit of and then addressing racial capitalism; and, as we shall soon see, calling people out or calling them in when microaggressions occur, all require leaders with a sturdy relationship to their high-power states.

Finally, leaders are most effective when the guiding principle which determines how they take up their role is something resembling, 'Given the current purpose and context, what does my role require of me?' Therefore, not only do leaders need to be able to access their low-power and high-power states almost at will, they also need to be able to ascertain, from a situational perspective, which location on the power continuum will maximise their effectiveness.

Leaders need support to understand and resolve their LSMs so that they can better model and uphold a psychologically safe culture

It is virtually impossible for leaders to lead in a way which consistently models a psychologically safe culture when their LSMs are regularly getting activated. Leaders might notice their moodiness; their tendency to be easily overwhelmed; an inability or unwillingness to make a decision; a resistance to proactively manage poor performance by appeasing a team member; an inclination to be 'quick to temper'; or a reduced capacity for compassion and empathy. You will no doubt see aspects of fight, flight, freeze, and appease in these behaviours.

From one perspective, all of these can be viewed as the behavioural manifestations of LSMs subconsciously attempting to reconcile a perceived threat and/or insufficient safety. But without a deeper awareness of how the activation of their LSMs are resulting in these behaviours, leaders are left to simply observe their own behaviours, much like watching a movie with a predictably bad ending, without any ability to influence the outcome. Many leaders I coach talk about an out-of-body experience, where they are watching themselves behave in ways they know are not conducive to the outcomes they want to achieve, but without the agency to curtail the calamitous sequence of events.

These hard-wired[43] survival responses get initiated in present time, even though the original injury might have occurred years, even decades earlier. The whole objective of these LSMs is, when faced with the threat of a sabre-toothed tiger, or 21st century equivalent, to maximise personal survival. As a result, rather than the leader's actions being informed by purpose, context, and role, the survival and safety of that leader becomes of paramount importance, usually at the expense of those they lead. Apart from undermining psychological safety, this goes against the fundamental tenets and ethical considerations of leadership, which are about looking after the people they lead by prioritising their wellbeing and the goals of the organisation – sometimes at the expense of their own needs. As Simon Sinek, one of my favourite thinkers on leadership, says:

'The cost of leadership is self-interest.'[44]

Leading for psychological safety requires leaders to have access to power states from various locations along the power continuum, contingent on the situation and context. But unresolved LSMs

---

43   The 'hardwiring' is in reference to the response driven by an activated LSM. In contrast, LSMs themselves are anything but hardwired, because they are so amenable to change and transformation via appropriate therapeutic, coaching, and healing protocols.

44   Simon Sinek, *Leaders Eat Last: Why Some Teams Pull Together and Others Don't* (New York, NY: Penguin Group, 2014) quoting Lieutenant General George Flynn

result in them getting unintentionally and usually unconsciously trapped in power states which lack the fluidity required to cultivate the psychological safety upon which an antiracist organisation can be built. Therefore, before leaders can create psychological safety in their organisations and teams, they need to be able to create internal psychological safety by being able to regulate how they respond to the external stimuli and environments which induce fear and threat, even if these are more perception than reality.

LSMs are frequently constructed around times or experiences when, through no fault of our own, the distribution of power was not symmetrical, and this power advantage was used over us, or against us, in ways which were abusive.[45] Contained within these LSMs is usually a story about power, a story which at some stage needs to be unpacked, validated, and witnessed. But until this happens, these LSMs remain frozen moments in time, where the emotional or psychological wound sustained remains unresolved. And it is the unresolved nature of LSMs that creates the trigger which, when unintentionally activated, initiates a cascade of psychological and physiological responses which are unhelpful in the creation of psychological safety.

If, in the original injury – as is most often the case – power was used over us, then one of two broad patterns occurs when an unresolved LSM gets activated. One of the consequences of these injuries is that, without a familiar or a functional pattern of power to guide us, we become enfeebled in our capacity to reliably access the power we need, when we need it. As a result, in an attempt to recreate the familiar, we retreat to a version of the original pattern. And so, we get stuck in a low-power position, even if the context requires for us to access the power and authority conferred in us via our leadership role.

---

45 Abuse can be defined as when power is used over someone, or against someone, where they have not got the ability to defend themselves against that power in that moment.

Alternatively, there is an overcompensation which results in us being overly attached to a high-power state, and therefore be less able to access and lead from crucial low-power states, such as vulnerability. This overcompensation is impelled by an internal script resembling, 'I am never going to feel that powerless ever again [referencing the experience of powerlessness from the original injury].'

Therefore, as part of their professional development, leaders need to be supported and encouraged to find their own approach to resolve these LSMs. This aspect of leadership development is frequently overlooked. When I deliver leadership development programs, people are invariably surprised by the degree to which these programs traverse people's personal psychology and are focused on developing self-awareness. This gap in appreciating the criticality of leaders' psychology is one reason why despite the undeniable benefits of psychologically safe organisations, the developmental pathways leaders are required to tread in order to build them remain elusive and misunderstood.

We have been led to believe that leadership development is primarily about frameworks, tools, and theories. And while these are essential components, we sometimes forget that, ultimately, a leader's ability to consistently apply these frameworks and theories in a way which increases their effectiveness is largely reliant on their psychology and self-awareness. When leadership development programs neglect to address the underlying psychological drivers that enable leaders to effectively access and execute essential competencies and skills, they are not doing justice to the demands of leadership, or the complexity of human psychology.

I have found a combination of therapy and coaching to be an effective method in addressing these developmental needs. This combination approach firstly enables leaders to better understand the psychological and physiological pathways which underpin their LSMs, and secondly, to transform and find resolutions to the painful experiences which continue to sustain these LSMs. Ideally, these resolutions also contain within them strategies unique to each leader that they can utilise to maintain a fluid relationship to their power, which is also context- and role-informed.

The creation of a more psychologically safe culture should therefore not only be viewed as an organisational initiative, but also a deep and introspective journey for its leaders. It is a journey that takes them to the heart of their LSMs; perhaps even to the centre of the places where they feel most wounded and inadequate. This is not a journey for the faint of heart, or for those who are not fully committed to the process.

Of course, working at this level of development in itself requires greater levels of psychological safety. The beauty of this kind of work is that, as leaders lean into the challenge of self-reflection and taking personal inventory of their LSMs, the gaps in psychological safety within the culture quickly become evident. This enables leaders to simultaneously address those aspects of the culture that require more psychological safety, as well as their own LSMs that get activated as a direct consequence of those gaps.

If the creation of a high-performance and psychologically safe culture is considered to be a worthwhile pursuit, and nothing in life that is worth achieving is ever easy, this aspect of leadership and leadership development should be viewed as one of the fundamental requirements and challenges of organisational life.

Understanding and awareness of privilege can unlock latent energy

For leaders aspiring to advance psychological safety and build antiracist organisations, another essential capability is an understanding of privilege. This includes the ability to recognise the areas where they have privilege in general, but particularly in terms of their race. This is especially important for non-BIPOC leaders looking to create antiracist cultures.

Privilege and power are closely interconnected concepts in the realm of inclusion and equity.

If we revisit our understanding of privilege:

> *Privilege is the rights, benefits, and advantages granted or available only to particular groups. Within the context of race and racism, privilege is the rights, benefits, and advantages granted to groups based on their race. The belief of the privileged group purport that these benefits and advantages are available to all people, when in fact they are only consistently available to the privileged.*

Power, on the other hand, represents the ability to influence or control others, institutions, and resources. It can be both formal – such as institutional power; for example, political authority – and informal – such as social influence and networks. Power often determines who makes decisions, sets the cultural norms, and shapes the distribution of resources in organisations.

The connection between privilege and power is that privilege often confers power. Individuals or groups with privilege are more likely to have access to resources, opportunities, and positions of authority, which they can then use to reinforce their privilege and exert influence over others. This perpetuates cycles of inequity, as those with privilege are often in positions to maintain the status quo, while those without privilege struggle to gain access to similar advantages.

As we discussed in chapter four, what makes White privilege exhausting and infuriating for those who do not benefit from it is less about the fact that it exists in the first place but more to do with the inequity it perpetuates, and the impact that this has on BIPOC remaining unacknowledged. Therefore, before equity can be created and power redistributed, there has to be an understanding of privilege, and then an acknowledgement of where that privilege is located. But privilege has a way of perpetuating itself because unconscious and/or unacknowledged privilege concretises systems of oppression, thus maintaining the status quo.

One of the challenges of privilege, is that it can make us blind to the privilege that we do have. In fact, the more privilege we have, the less able we are to become aware of the existence of that privilege, let alone acknowledge the benefits we derive from it. For example, the 'popular' person in a team will vehemently maintain there is no hierarchy or factions which delineate the cool kids from the less-cool kids. But if you ask someone who is new to the team and/or is not identified as one of the cool kids, they will be acutely aware of the unspoken hierarchy which permeates the team, and their relatively low rank within that hierarchy. In this example, the privilege is obviously located with the 'popular' person. And it is likely that they will also be the person who has more power. Therefore, their viewpoint – that there is no unspoken hierarchy or factions – will most likely be the one with the most influence, and thus the status quo gets defended and upheld. As a result, the new person or less popular person will remain feeling on the outside, with little or no ability to access the privilege needed to challenge these dynamics of hierarchy and factionalism.

In a similar way that unresolved LSMs reconstruct those 'stuck moments' from our history in terms of our power, they can also make us blind to our privilege. This is because when unresolved LSMs keep us stuck in past experiences, particularly experiences where power was used over us or against us, we tend to identify more strongly with those states where we have less access to our power. As a result, we have much less ability and/or willingness to pick up and take ownership of those areas where we do in fact have privilege.

When those who do have privilege in terms of their race can only identify with or speak from those dimensions of social identities where they have less privilege, it can be infuriating for BIPOC. This is not to say that those areas where they have less privilege are not valid in a different context, but in the context of fostering an antiracist culture, it is essential that those who do in fact have privilege can take ownership of it.

Privilege, by its very nature, results in us being comfortable, often to the point of being complacent, or in extreme cases, apathetic. After all, even if we are aware of our privilege, why would we want to change a system when we are comfortably positioned atop of the hierarchy and reaping the benefits associated with that privilege?

At the same time, those with less privilege – which in the case of race is obviously BIPOC – can feel overwhelmed. If we think back to our two friendly fish from chapter three, when someone is continually swimming against the current, there is a greater propensity to feel overwhelmed, tired, and exhausted; continually having to work twice as hard for half the outcome eventually wears out even the most resilient of people. This is part of the cultural load that BIPOC carry within the workplace when there is not a movement towards building an antiracist culture.

So, when those with more privilege in terms of race are comfortable, and consequently are not strongly incentivised to make change, and those with less privilege are overwhelmed and exhausted as a direct result of structural racism and the cultural load they are carrying:

How do organisations unearth the hunger and the momentum to drive the work needed to build an antiracist and high-performance culture?

Firstly, we need to acknowledge our own privilege, and then understand that creating equity in the workplace does not necessarily mean we lose the advantages and benefits associated with that privilege. An awareness of privilege also decreases cultural load, if for no other reason than it reduces the fury and the frustration many BIPOC feel in the face of unacknowledged privilege. For this to occur, LSMs which keep leaders and team members trapped in low-power states need to be recognised and addressed.

And secondly, as we become more aware of that privilege, we need to ask ourselves, 'How do I use my privilege well?' And in doing so, we find ways to use the advantages and benefits we have, as a direct result of that privilege, to advocate for those with less privilege – all with the goal of creating more equitable workplaces. As we discussed in chapter six, part of personal purpose is aligning our thoughts and actions to a greater good, something bigger than ourselves. Therefore, in exploring ways to use that privilege well, leaders revisiting and realigning to their personal purpose (as per reflection #6A) is a crucial step.

When privilege gets increasingly acknowledged and we simultaneously develop those leadership capabilities that help us to use that privilege well, organisations will incrementally reduce cultural load and shift gradually towards racial equity. As we discussed in chapter four, developmental sticking point #2, when we move towards racial equity, and unspoken racial tensions subside, latent energy gets unleashed from the system. Organisations gain a competitive advantage when they are able to access energy that previously was not available to them. Team members then have the opportunity to re-purpose this energy in service of those functions that enhance organisational culture and performance. In this context, 'energy' can be thought of as what enhances collaboration, innovation, effective teamwork, giving and receiving constructive feedback, knowledge management, addressing conflict, and other key functions that drive optimal and sustainable performance.

Hence, the hunger and momentum required to drive antiracist and high-performance initiatives gets liberated from within the system as we start to address and resolve those structural and cultural dynamics that have given rise to, and then perpetuated, racial inequity in the first place. There is an elegance to the organisational system itself, in the fact that the challenge of creating racial equity contains within it an essential element to its own solution. All we need to do is liberate this latent energy by taking steps towards greater psychological safety, an increased awareness of privilege, and a reduction in the cultural load carried by BIPOC.

Doing culture – 'calling out' and 'calling in'

If an antiracist organisation is built on both humanitarian and commercial imperatives, then the humanitarian aspect asks of us, 'How important to us is it that our teammates and colleagues, regardless of their race, feel psychologically safe?'[46]

Racism is usually associated with its most obvious and overt manifestations. We believe racism is primarily about the harassment, the bullying, the name-calling – those behaviours that unambiguously fall into the category of racial vilification. These are obviously behaviours that we need to shine a light on and

---

46 While for obvious reasons the focus here is race and racism, it is equally important that we also explore this question of psychological safety through the lens of other systems of oppression, e.g. gender and gender diversity, sexuality, religion, class, ableism etc.

subsequently address if we are going to shift the cultural context towards antiracism. But what is undoubtedly more complex in terms of creating an antiracist culture are those expressions of racism which are less obvious.

These behaviours frequently originate from well-meaning people who have very little intention of being racist. In comparison to more explicit demonstrations of racism, the impact of these behaviours, when examined on a one-off basis, may be relatively innocuous. However, due to the more subtle nature of their expression, they tend to reside on the fringes of our awareness where they can flourish mostly undetected. Additionally, because of the inherent challenges of addressing such behaviours, it is possible they are occurring on a more frequent basis, and so have been normalised by the cultural context.

Unless we are purposefully moving towards an antiracist organisation, the cultural norms do not usually endorse other people, especially non-BIPOC, stepping in and bringing attention to these behaviours as they occur. And when racial stereotypes remain unexplored and unacknowledged, there is not the cultural permission for BIPOC to defend themselves, for fear of once again being perceived as the angry, aggressive, or disruptive BIPOC. As a result, being exposed to a barrage of these unwelcome and hurtful interactions on a regular basis, with little ability to defend oneself against them, is akin to death by a thousand cuts. There is undeniably an impact of these repetitive interactions that sits within the bodies, minds, and spirits of BIPOC. The cumulative impact of these interactions therefore serves as one more contributing factor to the differences in the health, social, and financial outcomes of BIPOC in comparison to non-BIPOC.

The collection of these behaviours falls under the category of 'microaggressions'.

Microaggressions are a set of behaviours, usually expressed as an action or a statement that subtly, indirectly, and usually unintentionally, discriminate against a member of a minority and/or socially marginalised group.

Microaggressions move us away from antiracism by decreasing psychological safety and increasing cultural load. They are born at the intersection of unconscious bias and the cultural context. As we discussed in chapter eleven, unconscious or implicit bias is when we have attitudes towards people, or associate them with certain stereotypes or assumptions, without our conscious knowledge. These biases begin their life as a collective narrative within the broader culture and include racialised tropes and stereotypes. But over time, they become internalised, resulting in a compilation of unconscious biases residing within an individual's psyche. And when the cultural context does not actively resist the externalisation of these biases in terms of the behaviours they give rise to, microaggressions become commonplace because, based on the cultural context, they make sense to people.

Being critical of a BIPOC's communication style as being 'too direct' or 'too loud', as Pearl (page 88) experienced, is an example of a microaggression. Commenting to a Black woman that she 'speaks so well' [for a Black person] or asking if her hair is real, as Christina (page 63) experienced, are microaggressions. This person's [talking to Christina] behaviour was most likely well intentioned. It might even represent an attempt to reach out and make a connection, despite the awkwardness born out of a yet to be resolved racial tension – a racial tension that clearly is far bigger and more complex than the individuals involved. The good intentions underpinning these behaviours, or at least the lack of nefarious intentions, means that a challenge to these behaviours in terms of them being framed as racist microaggressions is most likely to be met with defensiveness and/or being righteously aghast at the mere insinuation. However, the identification with their good intentions does little to diminish the impact of these comments. This impact is so visceral (referring back to how Ta-Nehisi Coates frames racism) because these microaggressions are so firmly and unconsciously entrenched in hurtful racist stereotypes. But also, because somewhere deep inside, the fact that Pearl and Christina know these comments are born more out of conditioning than malice makes them even more complicated to defend against.

When faced with a regular stream of racist microaggressions, it is only natural that BIPOC become a little guarded or defensive. Becoming hypervigilant – where people are continually alert and attempting to anticipate where the next microaggression might emerge from and preparing a defence against it – is an essential strategy for survival in such a culture. However, when psychological safety requires trust, connection, and vulnerability, the defensive postures that people naturally inhabit in a culture where microaggressions abound is the antithesis of the kinds of behaviours that are conducive to psychological safety.

You might recall from chapter one, when faced with the insinuation of being racist, it is a natural and biologically hardwired reaction for non-BIPOC to become defensive. So, in how we start to shift the cultural context towards antiracism, a critical challenge is how to address microaggressions, including the cultural underpinnings which gave rise to them. This also includes dealing with people's defensiveness in a manner which does not result in them being shamed or feeling reprimanded.

In the previous chapter, we discussed that many organisations talk about culture, but what differentiates a high-performance organisation is the way it places a consistent focus on *doing* culture. It is the little things we do, on a day-to-day basis, which creates the cultural context; this in turn determines the extent to which those behaviours that are crucial in driving high performance get normalised and embedded. In the same way, if and how we notice and then address racist microaggressions may seem like a minor thing, but it will be a significant determinant of the success we have in creating an antiracist organisation. Actively addressing microaggressions, as well as not addressing them, will both reinforce a particular cultural context – albeit very different cultural contexts, but a cultural context, nonetheless.

The goal of antiracism is not necessarily to create a culture where microaggressions never occur, because to some extent they are symptomatic of the narratives and stereotypes which are woven into the broader culture. Rather, that when they do occur, they are noticed, and then we are able to repair the damage they engender in a timely, effective, and safe manner. Therefore, the overarching goal of the way we deal with microaggressions is that we minimise the harm that BIPOC experience as a result of those behaviours, as well as the harm that non-BIPOC may incur as a result of their behaviours being reflected back to them. Anything else will undermine the psychological safety that is so essential to our success.

When we notice a microaggression, the key is just doing *something*; doing something, even clumsily or awkwardly, is better than doing nothing. This is one way that an antiracist organisation actively works to dismantle racism. On the other hand, the passivity of doing nothing for fear of getting it wrong gives further permission to that behaviour, which only entrenches it more deeply as a cultural norm.

Additionally, when we experience, or even witness, racism – or any kind structural discrimination for that matter – it creates an ongoing traumatic experience, irrespective of our race. And it is this traumatic experience that contributes to our tendency to feel clumsy in intervening, or to freeze and therefore not intervene at all. The concept that, whether we experience racism firsthand, partake in it, or witness it, there is a kind of trauma that gets constellated 'irrespective of our race' might be surprising to some. This form of trauma is the result of a moral injury that occurs in the face of such events.

Moral injury refers to the psychological, social, and spiritual impact of events involving the violation or transgression of our deeply held moral beliefs. These moral beliefs are both our own personal beliefs, as well as those beliefs about what is right and fair and just that belong to the collective, and therefore transcend our individual histories and perspectives. These beliefs are as much about honouring and respecting our shared humanity as they are about a personal idea of what is right and wrong. So when these beliefs are transgressed, a moral injury occurs that revolves around the guilt, shame, and inner conflict stemming from actions or witnessing events that contradict one's own moral compass, as well as the moral compass that navigates our shared humanity. When viewed from this perspective, all of us are harmed by racism. And just to be absolutely clear, when it comes to racism, I am not making an equivalency between the experiences of BIPOC and non-BIPOC; the principles of structural racism and privilege still apply. But what I am saying is that, for a more sustainable, more human-centric solution to our challenges, the impact of racism on non-BIPOC has to also be recognised in how we move forward.

There are two broad approaches in how we address microaggressions: 'calling out' and 'calling in'. Both of these are examples of *doing* culture. The capability organisations demonstrate in how microaggressions are called out and called in is a reflection of the cultural context and the maturity of an organisation in terms of its journey towards antiracism. Calling out and calling in essentially serve the same purpose: to point out that what someone is doing is inconsistent with our goal of cultivating an antiracist culture, and that we are therefore going to actively resist that behaviour. When we observe a microaggression occurring, whether we choose to call that person out or call them in is a decision contingent on the context, our role, and the nature of the microaggression itself.

Calling out happens in the moment we notice a microaggression, or an even more explicit manifestation of racism. This moment may well be in a group context, such as a team meeting. Its goal is to let that person know that a comment or action they have demonstrated is not consistent with the desired culture, and the degree of hurt and oppression they are potentially causing warrants immediate and decisive action, even if that means interrupting a team meeting.

Because calling out frequently occurs in a group or a team environment, it provides an opportunity to frame explicitly the cultural and/or structural underpinnings of that behaviour. Team members can then discuss how everybody has been responsible for co-creating the environment and the cultural context which results in an individual's demonstration of a microaggression making sense to them. You will recall from chapter eleven, the importance of approaching creating racial equity, and inclusion in general, like we approach any other teamwork or cultural difficulty: that the challenge belongs to everyone. This is not to abdicate the need for personal responsibility. However, the ideal outcome is for shifts to be made in that individual's awareness and understanding of microaggressions, as well as for the group to begin to address the cultural enablers of that behaviour. This is part of the developmental focus that we discussed in chapter four and is an example of the commitment and work that are essential ingredients in building an antiracist organisation.

Calling in, on the other hand, usually happens after the event, and in a more personal or one-on-one setting. The purpose of calling in is to take the time, in a more private environment, to explain to that person why what they did or said is offensive and potentially harmful. It may include an educational approach in terms of supporting that person's understanding of the dynamics of racism (or another form of structural discrimination) and then potentially providing coaching in terms of possible strategies of how to do it differently or better next time.

Calling in provides greater opportunity to address the resistance that occurs when the person identifies only with the intention of their actions but fails to recognise the impact – albeit unintentional – of their actions. Helping and coaching people to better understand the underlying drivers of their resistance is a critical aspect of both the calling out and calling in processes. Their resistance and defensiveness may well have its origins in their personal history and their own experiences of discrimination, in combination with internalised narratives of structural racism. This means that when future demonstrations of microaggressions are called out or called in, they will hopefully be met with less resistance.

While context and approach for calling out and calling in may be different, ideally both need to be approached with a developmental focus, for there is no other way this works. So, essential as part of the process is an intention of doing it in a way which does not shame or belittle the person demonstrating the microaggression. Particularly, given the group nature of calling out, and therefore the propensity for public shaming to occur, the true art of calling out is to do it in a way where the person feels supported and challenged in terms of their development, rather than shamed or belittled. This aspect of the process is crucial, because if people are called out or called in in a manner where they feel belittled or shamed, it will undermine the psychological safety that is essential to making this process successful. This in turn will significantly reduce the future likelihood of people calling out or calling in their colleagues, and so stalls the development required to continue down the path of building an antiracist and high-performance organisation.

Whether we are calling out or calling in as a way of holding people accountable to meeting cultural, behavioural, or performance expectations, or as a way of bringing awareness to racist microaggressions, the key ingredient which ultimately determines the success of the process is psychological safety. Importantly, both calling out and calling in help to strengthen the foundation of a high-performance culture, because they are really about accountability.

Whether we are calling someone out or in on a microaggression or an issue with their performance, we are using the same cultural muscle. Calling out and calling in cultivates a culture of shared accountability that both requires and builds the psychological safety needed for the next time somebody being called out or in is warranted. There is clearly a feedback loop where, when done well, calling out and calling in develop greater levels of psychological safety, and greater psychological safety enables subsequent microaggressions to be addressed in a more effective, timely, and safe manner.

While a central outcome of an antiracist organisation is to create a culture of shared accountability in how it addresses microaggressions, where everybody believes the cultural buck stops at them, initially it is leaders who need to set the tone. This might require them to model a new cultural competency or create a 'cultural template' for how microaggressions are addressed. This is so people feel educated and empowered with the right tools, as well as affirming that they have the permission to call colleagues and teammates in and/or out, depending on what is required.

The inherent challenges of the calling out/calling in process, means that leaders need access to the context-appropriate vulnerability needed to establish trust, empathy, and connection so that the process feels as safe and as non-judgemental as possible. But, at the same time, they also need access to the authority to make clear boundaries and be non-negotiable with regards to certain behaviours. This requires leaders to firstly ascertain the position on their power continuum which maximises their effectiveness. And then, once again, to have resolved (at least partially) those LSMs which keep them trapped in power states which lack the fluidity needed to calibrate their power to these levels.

Finally, whilst calling out and calling in primarily focus on individual behaviour, to foster psychologically safe and culturally safe environments we must also take into consideration the dynamics and impacts of structural discrimination. This requires us to understand how structural discrimination itself influences the cultural context. By the way – this is why I spent most of part one on this subject. If a central feature of structural discrimination is the effectiveness at which it normalises itself, then we need the capability to ascertain where elements of the cultural context have been built upon, and subsequently been normalised, by structural discrimination.

While structural racism, is one manifestation of structural discrimination, if our goal is to create psychologically and culturally safe environments, and then addressing racism, but not paying equal attention to sexism, gender diversity, homophobia, anti-Semitism, Islamophobia, transphobia, classism, ableism etc., will be counter-productive to our goal of building organisations that are culturally safe for all people.

Reflection #13A:

Tracking psychological safety

1. As a team, decide on the most appropriate/useful situation to deepen your understanding of psychological safety, for example, a team meeting, or a session where you are working on culture.

2. Allocate some time after the meeting to discuss the following questions:

   - Did the levels of psychological safety shift during the meeting? Keep in mind, this will be a subjective assessment, and may be different for different people.

   - What made people feel like there was a shift in the levels of psychological safety during the course of the meeting?

   - What were the behaviours that preceded those moments where there was a change in psychological safety? In other words, what behaviours contributed to an increase in psychological safety, and what behaviours diminished it?

   - How have these same behaviours been normalised in the culture, and therefore become part of the cultural context?

   - For those behaviours that were helpful in increasing psychological safety, what development needs to occur for them to become more part of the cultural norm?

- For those behaviours that diminished psychological safety, what can you do to resist those behaviours so that, over time, they are no longer normalised?

- During the meeting, did you get triggered, even slightly, or have an LSM activated? If so, refer to reflection #12B, and then imagine what you might have done differently after doing this reflection.

Reflection #13B:

Leading and shaping an antiracist culture

From the perspective of your leadership role, formal or informal:

1. Reflect on the levels of psychological safety in the organisation or team you lead. Remembering that it exists along a continuum and is continually recalibrating, how would you assess the typical levels of psychological safety?

2. What are the behaviours and/or dynamics that you have noticed that change the levels of psychological safety? What increases it? What decreases it?

3. As a leader, what is your personal experience of psychological safety? How safe do you feel admitting to mistakes? Asking for help? Demonstrating context-appropriate vulnerability? Revealing certain aspects of your thinking, personality, or culture? Exercising the power and authority you have by virtue of your role?

4. How are the areas where you feel less psychologically safe reflective of similar dynamics in your organisation or team?

5. What are your psychological barriers to low-power states?

6. What are your psychological barriers to high-power states?

7. How do these undermine your ability to lead for psychological safety?

8. Spend some time reflecting and connecting one of these psychological barriers to an unresolved latent survival mechanism (LSM).

9. Use reflection #12B to start to address and resolve this LSM.

10. Does this now change your experience of the psychological barrier to that low-power or high-power state? If not, you may want to repeat the reflection a couple of times.

11. With this barrier now removed (or reduced), does this improve your ability, even slightly, to lead and shape an antiracist culture? If so, how?

Reflection #13C:

Calling out and calling in

1. What are some of the microaggressions you have noticed that occur in your team or organisation?

2. What are the ways the current culture subtly makes sense of racism (or another form of structural discrimination) by not actively resisting these microaggressions?

3. What are some of the cultural barriers to calling out and calling in?

4. How are these barriers linked to structural racism?

5. Are the levels of psychological safety sufficient so that calling out and calling in can happen without people feel belittled or ashamed? If not, what are some steps you can take to increase psychological safety?

6. As a leader, how are your own unresolved LSMs affecting your ability to call people out or call people in? What can you do and what support might you need to address and resolve these LSMs? (See reflection #12B for more assistance with this)

Chapter Fourteen:

Bringing it all together

Every organisation's journey towards antiracism will be different. Many factors will influence the pathway taken. These factors include, but are not limited to, the purpose and vision of the organisation; the current context (macro and micro) in which it is required to operate; the maturity of the organisation; and the urgency and the timeframe of the organisation's need to create an inclusive and high-performance culture.

Therefore, the suggested approach designed around the following ten steps is generic. Obviously, it is impossible to consider the individual needs and contexts which will be most applicable to your particular organisation. For some organisations who are well down the pathway towards antiracism, they may have already built significant capability, and the following recommendations provide validation they are on the right track, or the opportunity for minor refinements to what has already been accomplished. For other organisations, who are in the initial stages of their journey, they may well need to start from step one, and follow the process in a more regimented manner. Much like cooking with a new recipe, I recommend adhering to the suggested plan more closely at the start. And as you become more accustomed to what is needed, and the fundamental capabilities get built, there will be greater freedom to modify and adapt the approach based on your distinctive needs and developmental outcomes.

For most of these steps, I will not elaborate a great deal in terms of their rationale or implementation, as these have been explored throughout the body of this work. However, in the case of step nine (promote inclusive hiring practices), which has not been discussed up till now, I will provide some detail about its rationale and practical applications.

While I have presented these ten steps in a discrete and sequential manner, in reality, their implementation is far more circuitous. As you will see, there are significant areas of interdependence and overlap between the steps. So, while some steps can be completed as one-off initiatives, others represent the need for ongoing work and development, and require integration with other critical steps along the way. However, each one of these steps represents a component that is essential in solving the complex puzzle of building inclusive and high-performance cultures.

Step One: Review part one: Unpacking the dynamics and impacts of structural racism

Review part one, ensuring you have a basic knowledge of the dynamics and impacts of structural racism. In particular, focus on deepening your understanding of the following definitions and concepts:

- Antiracism and an antiracist organisation.

- Racism and how it gets manifested primarily through inequity.

- Structural racism.

- How structural racism enforces systemic racism.

- The three strategies systems of oppression utilise to perpetuate themselves.

- The terms 'diversity', 'equity', and 'inclusion'.

- Cultural load and how it impacts the well-being of BIPOC.

- Privilege and how unacknowledged privilege reinforces racial stereotypes.

- Internalised oppression and internalised superiority and their impact on development and performance.

- The four developmental sticking points we will almost invariably encounter on the journey towards antiracism (see reflection #4A).

You might want to form small discussion groups so that you can share your understanding of these principles and concepts. As part of that discussion, you and your colleagues can support and challenge each other in applying these principles and making them relevant and practical to your organisation, context, and role.

Step Two: Align the purpose of antiracism to the purpose of the organisation

If a compelling and emotionally engaging purpose has not already been discovered and then socialised, use reflection #6A or #6B, or a combination of both, to unearth the purpose of your organisation. Remember that the purpose is the 'deepest why' of the organisation and is intrinsically woven into its history and identity.

Then use reflection #7 to clarify the purpose of building an antiracist culture within your organisation.

Ensure there is alignment between the organisational purpose and the purpose of an antiracism initiative. If you are unable to find alignment, it will be worthwhile re-evaluating if now is the most appropriate time for such an initiative.

Once there is alignment, internal communications from leadership must clarify the purpose and intention of the antiracism initiative. Ideally, part of this communication should include those aspects of structural racism the organisation is no longer willing to tolerate. Additionally, purpose fosters an emotional connection, so it is helpful if leadership is explicit about the intended outcomes and benefits of such a program – that is, an emotive 'why' of the program. For example, team members, regardless of their race, will feel like they and the work they do matters, as well as ensuring that people have a deeper sense of inclusion, belonging, and connection.

Step Three: Clarify the organisational vision and evaluate the commercial benefits of antiracism in delivering that vision

If a clear and explicit vision has not already been agreed upon, use reflection #8 to construct and/or clarify the vision for your organisation. It is preferable that this vision is based on one key metric which correlates to the overall success of the organisation.

Use the first part of reflection #9 (questions 1–4) to evaluate the commercial benefits of creating an antiracist organisation. This evaluation will need to take into consideration the macro and micro context of the organisation.

And then assess from a commercial standpoint if these benefits justify the investment of time and money that the organisation will be required to make as it moves towards an antiracist culture. Sometimes this evaluation also needs to be explored from the perspective of risk mitigation. In other words, those organisations already facing discrimination lawsuits and/or wanting to avoid allegations of unsafe workplaces will need to consider, 'From the perspective of risk mitigation and potential reputational damage, can we afford not to embark on the journey towards antiracism, and greater diversity and inclusion in general?'

If leaders are unable to justify this investment in terms of the commercial benefits and/or risk mitigation, consider pausing any antiracism initiatives, at least until such point where the benefits justify the investment.

Step Four: Plan and conduct antiracism forums

Look for and pay attention to subtle signs and behaviours that may be attributable to BIPOC's resistance to emotional buy-in and full engagement with the vision. Ensure that this resistance is framed as a natural reaction to racial capitalism, as opposed to a deficit in the motivation, work ethic, or capability of the individual.

Use the latter part of reflection #9 (question 5) to begin to construct the strategy for antiracism forums. Consider what is the most appropriate format for these forums, given the maturity of your organisation and its ability to have safe and constructive conversations about racism and people's experience of racism.

Remember, ideally, these forums need to address two critical outcomes. Firstly, to ensure that people feel heard, witnessed, and validated in their experiences of workplace racism. This is particularly important for those at senior levels of leadership who do not identify as BIPOC, or do not have a lived experience of racism, so they start to develop an understanding and an ability to walk in the shoes of these experiences.

Secondly, is to collect data about people's experiences of organisational racism in order to understand and then address processes, policies, and aspects of the culture, that may perpetuate racial capitalism. The data about the ramifications of racial capitalism, needs to be integrated into the strategy (see step six). Leadership therefore needs to contemplate, 'Are there subtle dynamics or remnants of racial capitalism ingrained in our processes, policies, and culture, that need to be addressed in how we construct and execute our strategic plan?'

Step Five: Keep building the capability to have productive conversations about people's experience of racism

Having safe and constructive conversations about people's experience of racism, as well as other forms of discrimination, should not be thought of as belonging only to antiracism forums, but also seeing this as a cultural capability, and working to embed this as part of the day-to-day cultural norms. Antiracism forums, or a version thereof, should also be regarded as a *people engagement* strategy. This is because, until BIPOC feel sufficiently heard and enough of the historical and current injustice caused by racial capitalism has been acknowledged, it is unlikely that BIPOC will be able to fully buy-in to a vision that is based largely on a capitalist pursuit.

As the cultural capability to have conversations about racism gets built, what might begin as antiracism forums may evolve into team discussions or one-on-one check-ins. Ongoing work in this area, where challenges are viewed as opportunities for further development, will keep strengthening those aspects of the culture that build psychological safety, which in turn supports conversations that are more constructive (see step eight).

Step Six: Explicitly detail how and where antiracism initiatives are positioned within the strategic plan

Specify, in some part of the strategic plan, how the organisation intends to create an antiracist culture. Included in the plan needs to be how the organisation is going to develop the capability so that people can effectively take up the cultural component of their respective roles (see reflection #11A). This need to be incorporated as part of 'What does success look like?', and then integrated as an actionable item somewhere within the strategy.

Additionally, as part of the strategic plan, propose how the organisation is going prioritise the ongoing professional development that is essential to create an antiracist culture. This could include team members addressing their tendency to form stereotypes and have unconscious biases (see reflection #11B); better understanding their privilege (see reflection #4B); or educating themselves about historical events pertaining to structural racism within their geographical region and context (see reflection #12A).

Finally, in the way the antiracism component of the strategic plan is constructed, delivered, and socialised, it is essential that it is clearly framed as being everyone's responsibility. This minimises the tendency for BIPOC to get othered, or for the organisation's developmental sticking points or cultural challenges to be seen as 'their' problem, 'their' responsibility, and therefore 'their' fault.

Step Seven: Start to create an antiracist culture

Determine the kind of leadership, including the essential capabilities, that is needed to move your organisation towards an antiracist one. This is because leaders are the key to shaping positive cultures.

Next, ensure that leaders have the necessary support to develop these capabilities, and that these support mechanisms are linked to people's professional development, and embedded in the strategic plan (see step six). These areas of development also need to be clearly linked to the cultural component of a leader's role (see reflection #11A).

Leaders, therefore, might need support in one or more of the following areas:

- To resolve the LSMs and the accompanying narratives which create barriers to context-appropriate vulnerability (see reflection #12B).

- Being able to access to both their high-power and low-power leadership states (see reflection #13B). And being able to discern, in terms of their power state, what is required of them from the perspective of context and role.

- Deepening their understanding of the dynamics of privilege, including working on their own privilege (see reflection #4B). This minimises the propensity for privilege to remain unacknowledged.

- Getting comfortable with calling out or calling in as a way of providing constructive feedback for attitudes and behaviours which promote and/or perpetuate structural racism and racial inequity (see reflection #13C). The ultimate goal for leadership is to model and foster a culture where calling out and calling in get embedded as cultural norms, as opposed to cultural outliers.

These capabilities individually and collectively enable leadership to model and therefore create the kind of culture where people can have constructive conversations about their experiences of racism, as well as other forms of discrimination. This has an enormous positive effect on psychological safety, and reduces the cultural load experienced by BIPOC and other people with marginalised social identities.

These kinds of behaviours hardly ever occur organically in organisations. But when there is a strategic prioritisation (as per the strategic plan – see step six), and ongoing professional development is structured around these capabilities, the cultural infrastructure is in place for the creation of an antiracist organisation.

Step Eight: Have a dedicated focus on increasing psychological safety within teams

Teams are the functional components of organisations. Therefore, in terms of creating inclusive and high-performance cultures, teams are the greatest beneficiaries from a dedicated focus on increasing psychological safety.

Increasing psychological safety starts with appreciating that this work is primarily psychological – deep, slow, introspective, and sometimes confronting psychological work. This is because culture is primarily determined by our behaviours, and behaviours are so deeply rooted in our psychology.

Increasing psychological safety is far from a straightforward process, primarily because there are so many factors which either increase it or undermine it, but also because its subjective nature makes it difficult to quantify. However, as part of a dedicated focus on increasing psychological safety, and with the overarching objective of building an antiracist organisation, teams exploring the following will be immensely beneficial:

- Get better at tracking and understanding the subtle dynamics that create barely perceptible shifts in the psychological safety within the team (see reflection #13A).

- Work on acknowledging privilege and identifying the signs of stereotyping when it remains unacknowledged (see reflection #4B).

- Share and appreciate fellow team members' experience of internalised oppression and internalised superiority, preferably across a range of structural discrimination experiences.

- Work on recognising signs of unconscious bias and stereotyping, and making them more conscious so they can be addressed directly (see reflection #11B).

- Discuss, share, and unpack the personal and cultural barriers to context-appropriate vulnerability.

- Regularly check in to evaluate how the team is tracking with continually deepening levels of trust, empathy, and connection.

In terms of teams working on these elements of the culture, not only is the content of the discussion essential, but growing the capability to have such challenging and, dare I say it, intimate conversations is transformative. Developing the cultural muscles that enable meaningful discourse about such complicated and personal matters is a potent driver of psychological safety.

The power of greater psychological safety is that not only does it establish the cultural infrastructure required for an antiracist organisation, but it is also conducive to fostering more inclusion, engagement, and belonging in general. Additionally, it is a potent driver of performance because so many of the essential drivers of a high-performance culture require psychological safety to fully unleash their potential.

Step Nine: Promote inclusive hiring practices

An essential aspect of creating diverse workforces is adopting inclusive recruitment practices that actively seek candidates from varied backgrounds. The goal of encouraging fair and equitable hiring processes is to eliminate discrimination and bias in the recruitment process.

Organisations can foster inclusive hiring practices by adopting intentional strategies that prioritise diversity and equity throughout the recruitment process. Firstly, it's essential to establish a commitment to inclusivity at all levels of the organisation, starting from leadership. Leaders should communicate a clear stance on diversity and set the tone for an inclusive workplace culture. This needs to be aligned with the purpose (see step two), the vision (see step three), and the strategy (see step six) of the organisation.

To attract a diverse pool of candidates, organisations can review and revise job descriptions to eliminate biased language and ensure they accurately reflect the skills and qualifications necessary for the role. Additionally, they should explore diverse recruitment channels and partnerships to reach underrepresented talent pools.

During the hiring process, implementing blind recruitment techniques can help minimise unconscious bias. Removing personally identifiable information from resumes and standardising interview questions can ensure that candidates are evaluated solely based on their skills and experience. Training recruitment managers and interviewers on DEI principles and strategies can further enhance their awareness of potential biases.

Establishing diverse interview panels is crucial to providing multiple perspectives during the evaluation process. This not only promotes fairness, but also signals the organisation's commitment to diversity. Moreover, organisations should actively seek feedback from candidates about their recruitment experience to identify areas for improvement.

Continuous monitoring and assessment of hiring metrics related to diversity and inclusion are essential. Regularly reviewing these metrics allows organisations to track progress, identify challenges, and adjust strategies accordingly. Moreover, fostering a culture of inclusivity extends beyond recruitment; organisations should prioritise ongoing diversity and inclusion training, employee resource groups, mentorship programs, and inclusive policies to create an environment where all employees feel valued and supported. This should be seen as an ongoing process of education and professional development (see step seven and step eight).

Creating inclusive hiring practices involves a holistic approach, from crafting inclusive job descriptions to fostering a psychologically safe culture. It requires commitment, ongoing effort, and a willingness to adapt practices to promote diversity and equity in the workforce. Remember, while representation alone will not dismantle structural racism, it is certainly something to aim for and a significant milestone along the journey towards antiracism.

Step Ten: Celebrate successes, large and small

While I have included this as the final step, in actuality, this step needs to be woven through every other stage of building an antiracist organisation. It is important to remember that what we are endeavouring to do is far from straightforward. There is no ideal strategy, no guaranteed formula for success. Our undertaking requires a commitment to genuine transformation, as well as the agility, adaptability, and resilience to continually reassess our progress, and see both our successes and our failures as opportunities for development.

Being mindful that what we are doing, in many ways, is forging new territory, carving a path through the unknown as we are walking it, it is crucial that organisations and teams, acknowledge and also celebrate small victories as well as breakthrough successes. In addition, the dedication and courage it takes to undertake such an arduous challenge should not be underestimated and, therefore, these also need to be acknowledged and commended.

When we do not take the necessary time to intentionally stop and celebrate successes, it can breed hopelessness and burnout because people only identify with the challenges yet to be conquered, as opposed to what has already been achieved. The hope and the sense of forward progress that gets highlighted because of celebrating success is a vital ingredient to fuel the next steps on the journey towards antiracism.

Conclusion

I can't help but feel we are living in perilous times. Across the global landscape, we are still grappling with the challenges of addressing racial injustice, not to mention other forms of structural discrimination and oppression. Looking around, one could be forgiven for feeling like we are making very little progress in our approach to diversity and inclusion, but also simply how we get along with those we perceive to be different from ourselves. In what feels like a blink of an eye, the divides we once had along lines of race, sexuality, gender identification, class, political ideologies, and religion, have now become gaping chasms.

And at the risk of being melodramatic, something about this situation feels a bit like life-and-death; there is something existentially unsustainable about it. Maybe it is because for some of us, perhaps even for many of us, living in a world or working in an organisation where the wholeness of our humanity is not seen, welcomed, and celebrated, has progressively become too much to bear.

Therefore, in the journey towards creating antiracist organisations, the culmination of insights, strategies, and transformative actions *must* converge into a single, powerful call for lasting change.

This journey begins with acknowledging the existence of structural racism within our organisations and recognising the biases and unacknowledged privilege embedded in policies, practices, and interpersonal dynamics. This introspection, while uncomfortable, is also necessary, because it serves as a catalyst for building the capability needed for genuine transformation.

Throughout these chapters, we have explored the critical role of leadership in steering organisations towards antiracism. Organisations and their leaders are tasked with the almost impossible mission of having to focus on those critical elements of performance that drive core business, and at the same time being required to succeed in an environment where creating antiracist organisations is no longer a choice but a necessity. As leaders, how do we attend to the urgent need to go beyond traditional diversity initiatives and actively engage in more inclusive practices? We have addressed this by delving into the depths and intricacies of how structural racism manifests within organisational systems, and then offered an unconventional roadmap for delivering greater performance via fostering a culture of inclusivity, connection, and belonging.

Leaders are therefore required to embrace (context-appropriate) vulnerability, engage in uncomfortable conversations, and confront the origins of their own biases. They will need to lead by example, setting the standards for accountability, continuous learning, and professional development. In how they actively dismantle structural racism and foster an environment where every voice is heard and valued, there is the need for leadership to be both visionary and empathetic; resolute in their conviction, yet nimble in navigating an undertaking with so many unknowns.

Furthermore, the significance of education and ongoing training in antiracism cannot be overstated. Our discussions have highlighted the need for continuous learning, encouraging organisations to invest in comprehensive programs that develop cultural capabilities and personal awareness. This educational journey extends beyond the workplace, reaching into communities and influencing societal norms.

What I had hoped to do in the preceding pages is not just write a book, but to also construct a fervent call to action. My hope is that by providing a roadmap for leaders and organisations to navigate the complex and controversial terrain of antiracism, this book has the potential to facilitate positive change in workplaces worldwide. At a time when the need for inclusive and equitable organisations has never been more critical, my wish is that these pages feel like a beacon of guidance and inspiration for those committed to creating a future where everyone feels seen, heard, and valued.

This hope has not only been constructed upon my professional role and ambition; it is also deeply personal to me.

There have been so many times — too many to count, in fact — where my own experiences of racism made me feel like I did not belong, and that I was not welcome. This has been true, to some extent, my whole life, but particularly during those latter years in primary school and early years of high school where I was the only, or one of a handful of, brown-skinned kids. For much of that time, and sometimes even now, I feel there is no place for me.

So, fast forward the best part of four decades. It is perhaps unsurprising that so much of my work involves supporting organisations and teams to create cultures where people feel welcomed, like they belong, and that their experience matters to someone else. For many of us, what shapes our direction in life is an attempt to create the kind of world that we, ourselves, needed as kids. This is certainly true for me. Growing up, I yearned for a world where I felt like I belonged, where I was included, and where my inherent humanity counted for something. As a result, my hope for the potential of this book resides at the intersection of my personal purpose and where I see my own pain reflected in the world around me.

The path to creating antiracist organisations is not a linear one; it requires agility, adaptability, and resilience. The book underscores the importance of perseverance in the face of challenges, as well as the need to celebrate small victories along the way. Building antiracist organisations is a marathon, not a sprint, and so our commitment to change must be unwavering.

In contemplating the future, this book envisions a landscape where antiracist principles are intertwined with the DNA of organisations. It dreams of workplaces where diversIty is not a checkbox, but a lived experience; where inclusion is not a buzzword, but a daily practice; and where equity and justice are embedded in the very fabric of an organisation's culture. Somewhere, this dream belongs to us all and to our shared humanity. So, the responsibility lies with each individual, with each leader, and with every organisation, to heed the call, to confront the uncomfortable, and collectively build a future where connection and belonging are fundamental tenets. This book, therefore, serves as a guide, an ally, and hopefully a source of inspiration for those committed to the arduous yet rewarding journey of creating workplaces that reflect the principles of antiracism.

The vision of this work is for organisations to actively contribute to a broader societal shift towards justice and equity. So, in the final analysis, *The Antiracist Organisation* is not just a book; it is a roadmap for a profound societal shift. It is a rallying cry for organisations to recognise their role in either perpetuating or dismantling structural racism, and to take decisive steps towards the latter. As you close the book, you are armed not only with knowledge, but hopefully, with a renewed sense of purpose – a commitment to building workplaces that stand as beacons of antiracism amidst the turbulence of our times.

Acknowledgements

Firstly, to all the organisations, teams, leaders, and individuals that I have had the pleasure, and the honour of working with in some capacity: thank you for everything you have taught me. I cannot begin to express the gratitude I feel that I get to work with such quality people, doing work that is always interesting, frequently challenging, but most importantly, meaningful.

To all those people who shared their stories with me, some of which have been included in this book: thank you for your courage, and for trusting me with such painful and personal experiences. Many of you shared your stories in the hope that they would make a difference in how we start to have conversations about racism. *My* hope is that, by having this conversation, I have done justice to your stories.

To Arlene Audergon, PhD; Jean-Claude Audergon; and Anup Karia: thank you for being my teachers and collaborators as I have struggled to understand the complexity of structural discrimination and come to terms with my own experiences of racism. I deeply appreciate the opportunities we get to work together, because I continue to learn so much from you all.

To my dear friend Pippa Grange, PhD, who also happens to be the founder of Bluestone Edge: thank you for teaching me so much about culture. No doubt, you will see a host of Pippa-isms scattered throughout this book. In my opinion, nobody understands culture and can explain the complexities of culture in such poetic and eloquent ways. I feel blessed that our paths crossed, and that

I continue to have the good fortune to bask in your genius and wisdom.

To my friends and colleagues who at various crucial stages of this endeavour have provided me with constructive feedback, editorial assistance, and, perhaps most importantly, encouragement and emotional support: I am deeply grateful. Lane Arye, PhD; Simon Benjamin; Padraig Cotter, PhD; Jessica Genauer, PhD; Rosie King; Stephanie Mendis; Dawn Menken, PhD; Marnie Nichols; Joy Warmington, CEO of BRAP; and Julia Wolfson, PhD.

To Kev and Les and the team at Busybird Publishing: thank you for your support and care as you have guided me through the publishing process. Working with you has been an effortless pleasure, which I very much appreciate.

To Max Schupbach, PhD, and co-founder of the Deep Democracy Institute: all those years ago, you inspired me with the magic and the power of your facilitation and set me on a course to discover my own magic. Thank you for igniting the fire that allows me to find so much joy and meaning in my work.

About the author

Errol Amerasekera is the owner of Bluestone Edge Pty Ltd where he supports organisations and leaders to create inclusive and high-performance cultures. He has worked with organisations, schools, NGOs, as well as in international war zones such as Sri Lanka. He applies his business management experience in Australia and overseas by facilitating organisations to manage the complex and  competing demands of building successful enterprises. He is passionate about creating a safer and more equitable world for all by mediating conflict, coaching ethical leadership, and facilitating transformation in individuals, communities, and organisations.

Errol uses a person-centric, trauma-informed approach to optimising culture, leadership, and performance. He holds a master's degree in Conflict Facilitation and Organisational Change and is a qualified psychotherapist.

Printed in the USA
CPSIA information can be obtained
at www.ICGtesting.com
LVHW060544240524
780939LV00013B/235